ADVANCE ACCLAIM

"No better primer on globalization exists than Six Billion Minds. Mark Minevich, Frank-Jürgen Richter and Faisal Hoque have drawn from some of the best thinkers on globalization and its consequences from all around the world to stimulate our minds and help us to think more clearly and deeply about the issues. This is a book that everyone affected by globalization should read and, more importantly, learn from."

—Dr. Irving Wladawsky-Berger,
   Vice President, Technical Strategy and Innovation, IBM
   and Fellow of the American Academy of Arts and Sciences

....

"This is quite a piece of work. In my opinion this book is not only about globalization and outsourcing but also represents an anthology of thoughts and reflections on the dramatic shifts in geopolitical, economic and social dynamics which we are seeing and experiencing today. Globalization means taking down artificial barriers erected since the beginning of mankind. Outsourcing is a rational workflow that takes processes to places and people across the traditional barriers. This book will provide future political and business leaders with acumen to address the challenges and opportunities of tomorrow's societies and corporations. We can no longer afford to be driven by greed, incompetence and narrow mindedness. The young, new generation of managers who will take us forward into this century will be intellectually stimulated by the opinions, dialogues and visions throughout this book."

—Alex Sozonoff,
   Vice Chair, Peter Ustinov Foundation
   and former World Wide Chief Customer Officer, HP

....

ADVANCE ACCLAIM

Minevich   Richter   Hoque

SIX BILLION MINDS

BTM Institute

Published by Aspatore Inc.

For corrections, company/title updates, comments, or any other inquiries, please e-mail store@aspatore.com.

First Printing, 2006
10 9 8 7 6 5 4 3 2 1

ISBN 1-59622-427-4
Library of Congress Control Number: 2006921287

Minevich   Richter   Hoque

SIX BILLION
MINDS

BTM Institute

Dedication

To those who continue to push globalization to advance the human potential in this ever-connected globe, I dedicate this book. For those who continue, with unyielding faith, to push beyond the horizon, full of never-ending hope and enduring performance to change the world and bring us closer together, we have an obligation to do better.

—Mark Minevich

To those who seek the means to make an important intellectual and practical contribution to addressing one of the most dramatic business trends in current history—global outsourcing in the knowledge economy—as we attempt to enact visions for a sustainable future.

—Frank-Jürgen Richter

To those endeavoring to provide the next generation of leaders with the multi-disciplinary skills they will need to excel in our global knowledge economy, in which the convergence of business and technology management holds the key to sustainable innovation.

—Faisal Hoque

Acknowledgements

We would like to personally thank our Chief Editor, Terry Kirkpatrick, for his tremendous help and contribution to this massive project, as well as bringing this book to the highest level in the industry. In addition, I would like to thank Michelle Zelsman and Loretta Prencipe, our senior staff editors, who worked very hard and gave their best effort in a short period of time to help us pull this amazing book together, as well as helping us with the manuscript and interviews. My warm thanks goes out to Lorenzo Ottaviani for his creativity, amazing design and really global artwork. I would like to personally acknowledge and thank my friend, Diana Manashirov, who contributed her personal time and dedication to work on various important aspects of this book. Many thanks to our colleagues who offered their talent and support throughout the process: Diana Mirakaj, Michael Fillios, James Lebinski, Joel Plaut, Alex Sozonoff, Tsvi Gal, Thierry Laurent, Zvi Raviv, Ami Eyal, Orry Kalev, Susan Dorfman, Jason Silver, Vadim Pevzner, James Wolowicz, Mila Manashirov, Yury Vayman, Ellen Pearlman and Mike Cormier.

I owe an enormous debt to the many contributors and colleagues whose great ideas fill this book, and to everyone who has taken the time to teach me about globalization and outsourcing over the years.

I am blessed and thankful for my dear parents who gave me a unique opportunity and passion to live an American Dream. Thanks to my in-laws who constantly inspire me and stimulate discussions on different subjects, and who encourage creativity. Thanks to my brother, Roman, and my brother-in law, Eugene, for pointing out that I am "Global Mark and Innovation Champion," and my dear friends around the United States and the world for reaching out to me, and for being part of my extended global family.

Most of all, a special eternal thanks to my wife, Susanna, for continuously inspiring and pushing me beyond boundaries. She makes every day a joy as she encourages my out-of-the-box ideas, tolerating my ups and downs throughout the last five years as I have pursued my global dreams.

I believe the future belongs to those without limits on what they believe can be accomplished. This book is an important and timely brain trust of global knowledge, representing business leaders, thought leaders and visionaries from all over the world. It will serve as a catalyst for discovering and targeting dynamic emerging opportunities for identifying the next wave of the knowledge economy, even before the trends and problems can emerge. Global outsourcing will be the key element of transformation as we move deeper into the knowledge economy. I am convinced that global outsourcing will create the next generation of entrepreneurs, knowledge workers, and business leaders.

—Mark Minevich

This book is the product of a profoundly creative and dynamic collaboration with many esteemed friends and colleagues. Researching and writing Six Billion Minds proved to be a complex journey into an incredibly vast subject, and their insights were the compass that continuously helped us find our course amid a constantly changing landscape.

I gratefully acknowledge the support of the members and friends of Horasis: The Global Visions Community, who helped me to think through the concepts that follow. To them go my thanks and best wishes.

I would like to thank our contributors, who provided terrific insights based on their rich experience and accomplishments in the sphere of economics and outsourcing. I am also grateful to the numerous government officials, from large countries like China and the United States, to small countries like Singapore and Switzerland, from prime ministers and heads of states to ministers of various duties, who willingly shared their time to discuss with me their visions for their countries. I was also able to meet large numbers of senior business executives who gave their time as they described the challenges of coping with globalization.

My hope is that this book will be of use to the widest possible audience concerned with globalization.

—Frank-Jürgen Richter

Over the past year I have had the privilege of traveling the globe and meeting an extraordinary array of leaders of multinational corporations, non-profit organizations and social enterprises whose work and thinking are shaping our globalized knowledge economy. Their insights and advice have helped me appreciate the tremendous promise of globalization and the absolute necessity for innovative approaches to the world's problems.

With a massive collaborative project such as Six Billion Minds, in which coordination must span the globe, it is easy to forget the people behind the scenes who sometimes matter the most. I am indebted to the talented team who edited the book, Terry Kirkpatrick; designed it, Lorenzo Ottaviani; created its website, Cyrus Clemensen and Alex Zinder; and managed the marketing, public relations and legal issues, Diana Mirakaj and Edward Burke.

The Co-Chairs of the BTM Institute's Research Council, Professors V. Sambamurthy and Professor Robert Zmud, have been instrumental in shaping our thinking about how organizations can navigate the ever shifting currents of the 21st Century through innovative business models and the strategic application of technology. The members of the Institute's Research and Leadership Councils, as well, have made valuable contributions to the Institute's understanding of the strategic role of technology.

—Faisal Hoque

Contents

List of Expert Voices

Authors

Mark Minevich

Frank-Jürgen Richter

Faisal Hoque

Contributing Authors

Carlos Alvarez
Vice Minister of Economy and CIO
Government of Chile
Santiago, Chile

Simon Bell
Director
A.T. Kearney
Alexandria, Virginia

Marjan Bolmeijer
CEO
Change Leaders, Inc.
New York, New York

Augustine Chin
Consultant
A.T. Kearney
Alexandria, Virginia

Eugene Goland
President
DataArt
New York, New York

Anupam Govil
CEO
Global Equations LLC
Austin, Texas

Stefan Inzelstein
President
Indiggo Associates, Inc.
Aventura, Florida

Ram Iyer
President and CEO
Argea
Princeton, New Jersey

Dr. Michael Jackson
Founding Member and Chairman
Shaping Tomorrow
Sussex, United Kingdom

Dr. Bruno Lanvin
Senior Advisor, E-Strategies
The World Bank
Geneva, Switzerland

Dr. David Hee-Don Lee
Vice Chairman
World Trade Centers Association
Washington, D.C.

Phyllis Michaelides
President
C-Level Associates LLC
Providence, Rhode Island

Janet Pau
Consultant
A.T. Kearney
Alexandria, Virginia

Umesh Ramakrishnan
Vice Chairman
Christian & Timbers
New York, New York

Atefeh Riazi
Worldwide CIO & Senior Partner
Ogilvy & Mather Worldwide
New York, New York

Randy Terbush
Vice President and CTO
ADP Employer Service
Roseland, New Jersey

V.N. "Tiger" Tyagarajan
Executive Vice President
Genpact
New York, New York

Huib Wursten
Managing Partner
ITIM International
Amsterdam, The Netherlands

Expert Voices

Dr. Jagdish Bhagwati
University Professor
Columbia University
Senior Fellow
Council on Foreign Relations
New York, New York

Osvald Bjelland
Chairman
Xynteo LTD and the Performance Theater
Foundation
Oslo, Norway

Robert B. Carter
Executive Vice President and CIO
FedEx Corporation
Memphis, Tennessee

Dr. Vinton G. Cerf
Vice President and
Chief Internet Evangelist
Google
Ashburn, Virginia

Jim Clifton
Chairman and CEO
Gallup Organization
Washington, D.C.

Dr. Soumitra Dutta
Dean of Executive Education
INSEAD
Paris, France

John Furth
Executive Vice President
Discovery Communications
Washington, D.C.

Alan Ganek
Chief Technology Officer
Tivoli Software, IBM
Somers, New York

Dr. Hubertus Hoffmann
Co-Founder
General Capital Group
Munich, Germany

Rustam Lalkaka
President
Business and Technology Development
Strategies
New York, New York

Mitchel Lenson
Former Group CIO and
Managing Director
Deutsche Bank
London, England

Harald Ludwig
Founding Partner and Chairman
Macluan Capital Corporation
Vancouver, Canada

Valerie Orsoni-Vauthey
CEO and Founder
MyPrivateCoach
San Carlos, California

Ramalinga Raju
Founder and Chairman
Satyam Computer Services Limited
Secunderabad, India

Dato' Dr. Jannie Tay
Vice Chairman
The Hour Glass Limited
Singapore

Dr. Shashi Tharoor
Under-Secretary-General
United Nations
New York, New York

Martin Wolf
Associate Editor and Chief Economics
Commentator
Financial Times
London, England

Ratings Contributors

Judy Arteche-Carr
Executive Director
Unisys
New York, New York

Oebele Bruinsma
Founding Partner
Synmind
The Netherlands

Konstantin Caploon, Esq
Intellectual Property Attorney
Montclair, New Jersey

Steven Carlson
Organizer
First Tuesday
Budapest, Hungary

Lionel Carrasco
Managing Director and CTO
NEORIS
Miami, Florida

Cyrill Eltschinger
CEO
IT UNITED
Beijing, China

Dr. Ami Eyal
CEO
Bio Light
Tel Aviv, Israel

Tsvi Gal
CTO
Asset Management.
Deutsche Bank
New York, New York

Anand Govindaluri
Director
Temasek Group
Singapore

Thierry Laurent
Founder and CEO
Stream2Peers, Inc.
Dallas, Texas

Serhiy Loboyko
President
TECHINVEST
Kiev, Ukraine

Ajoy Malik
Vice President
TATA Consulting Services
Mumbai, India

Dr. Joseph O. Okpaku, Sr.
President and CEO
Telecom Africa International Corporation
New York, New York

Ellen Pearlman
Editor-in-Chief
CIO Insight
New York, New York

Pichappan Pethachi
Associate Partner
IBM Consulting Services
White Plains, New York

Joel Plaut
Vice President
SendWordNow
New York, New York

Tatiana Raguzina
Vice President
American Chamber of Commerce
Moscow, Russia

Karl Robb
Executive Vice President
EPAM Sysems
Budapest, Hungary

William Sanford
Principal
Columbia Strategy
New York, New York

Dr. Gurinder S. Shahi
Director,
Global BioBusiness Initiative
University of Southern California
Los Angeles, California

Alex Sozonoff
Vice Chairman
Peter Ustinoff Foundation
Geneva, Switzerland

Andre Spatz
CIO
UNICEF
New York, New York

Derek Stephens
Managing Director
IBM Corporation
White Plains, New York

Alistair Stobie
Managing Director
DFJ Nexus
Russia, Ukraine

Dr. Ruben Vardapetion
Executive Director
EuroTex
Brussels, Belgium

Globalize or Die?

The reality of a connected world is that the next idea that can make or break your company might come from anywhere, originating in one of the nearly six billion minds on this planet. The game today is knowledge, and the only winning strategy is finding innovative ideas and employing them before your competitors do. The organizations that succeed in this game put no national or geographic limits on their quest for knowledge. They go where the people are. As the title of this book suggests, they have an awesome opportunity, and an incredible challenge, as they learn to manage in a global, knowledge economy.

Just a few years ago, the press warned multinationals to innovate or die. Today, their headlines have a different spin—globalize or die. The world may be flat but it's not deep. Flat is surface. The human experience is more. Are we outsourcing the personal human scale experience for the sake of multinational corporations' expansion? Whether the world has flattened or continues to create centers of excellence, it is quite clear that countries, developed or developing, must become competitive in tapping into the world's six billion minds if they want to be a part of the knowledge economy.

Globalization is leaving a lasting impression. While not perfect, globalization has been extremely successful. It has created millions of jobs, raised millions out of poverty and improved the quality of life in countries that once were considered incapable of contributing to the world economy.

Indeed, the benefits of globalization and global outsourcing are far reaching. With shared interests in building robust markets, generating greater profits for all and building stronger relationships, East and West are more interdependent upon one another than ever before.

While the United States continues to hold its position of power in the world, booming economies in China, India, Russia and Brazil are very real. A threat? No one is using that language. Not yet. But it is clear that America and Europe, which traditionally set the standards for business, could be in a position to lose that coveted world status symbol—power.

The relative importance of the emerging economies as an engine of new demand growth and spending power may shift more dramatically and quickly than expected. Emerging economies have enhanced the world's infrastructure to deliver services in any geography based on a concept of real value-based virtual organizations. Capital flows might move further in favor of emerging economies prompting major currency realignments. As today's advanced economies become a shrinking part of the world economy, the accompanying shifts in spending could provide significant opportunities for global companies.

Outsourcing—a product of globalization—has become a supercharged issue thanks to fears of job loss. But as *New York Times* foreign affairs columnist Thomas Friedman points out, people need to be aware of the consequences of a flat world. There is no such thing as an American job. And we have to get over that. As we all know, the human experience is constantly repeated throughout time. America is going through dramatic change. We are exporting much of our manufacturing, design, engineering and innovation, which further decreases the costs of goods we import. Friedman says, "When the world is flat, you can innovate without having to emigrate." What Friedman means by "flat" is connected. In other words, the lowering of trade and political barriers along with the exponential technical advances of the digital revolution has made it possible to do business, or almost anything else, instantaneously with billions of other people across the planet. Friedman states, "It is now possible for more people than ever to collaborate and compete in real time with more people on more different kinds of work from more different corners of the planet and on a more equal footing than at any previous time in the history of the world."

Despite the concerns in the United States that outsourcing is taking away jobs from Americans, the reality is it's not the abyss it's made out to be at the water cooler. In fact, a study released in November 2005, *The Impact of Offshore Software and IT Services Outsourcing on the US Economy and the IT Industry*, conducted by Global Insight, an economic analysis forecasting and financial information company, found that "world-wide sourcing of computer software and services continues to increase the number of U.S. jobs, improve real wages for American workers, and has many other economic benefits as a result of pushing the U.S. economy to perform at higher levels." Outsourcing IT services generated an additional 257,043 net new jobs in the United States during 2005. It is expected that 337,625 net new jobs will be created by 2010, according to the study. The U.S. GDP increased $68.7 billion in 2005 and is expected to reach $147.4 billion by 2010, the study reported.

It used to be that information was power. Not anymore. Information is becoming a commodity. The real power in a globalized world is knowledge. It turns out that a good deal of creative work—software development, accounting, legal work, engineering—can be outsourced to India or China. The solution to becoming powerful is to focus on innovation and to design new core corporate competencies.

America may be at risk of losing its distinctive innovation as a result of "irresponsible optimism" during the so-called boom years. Perhaps Americans are too easily drawn to their dreams to be responsible all the time. A gradual decline in American innovation and its inventive spirit could affect our global leadership. The erosion did not begin with the widespread introduction of the Internet—it began when U.S. corporations outsourced manufacturing. Today, many U.S. companies are little more than brand names selling goods made in Asia. Many computer, electrical and electronics engineers—most of whom were well paid just a few years ago—now cannot find work. Some would say that a country that does not manufacture doesn't need as many engineers, because much of the work is being outsourced. And yet, through this erosion, it is not a stretch to say America may be transitioning into a third world economy. Falling pay and rising prices of foreign goods will squeeze U.S. living standards faster than most Americans may realize.

For more than half a century, the United States has led the world in scientific discovery and innovation. It has been a beacon, drawing the best scientists to its educational institutions, industries and laboratories from around the globe. However, in today's rapidly evolving competitive world, the United States can no longer take its supremacy for granted. Nations from Eastern Europe to Eastern Asia are on a fast track to pass the United States in scientific excellence and technological innovation. We must create products and services that satisfy needs consumers don't even know they have yet. Mastering new innovation is the key to corporate success, if not survival. Smart companies now have a senior level executive charged with driving innovation or sparking creativity.

Another major change is that we now live a virtual world. When it comes to work, geography does not matter anymore. Even in small companies, a growing number of people now operate in teams spread across the world. They use the latest hardware, laptops, e-mail addresses, mobile phones and intranet access to collaborate and share information. It is irrelevant whether you are in Wayne, N.J., Geneva, Switzerland, or Tel Aviv, Israel. Globalization makes it possible for workers to collaborate with their team members around the world. The result is a 24-hour endless day. And while we are much closer to each other now, the need for a global community never goes away.

The Knowledge Economy is upon us. More than 60 percent of U.S. workers are in a knowledge business, but we still live in the data world. In most companies knowledge-sharing rarely occurs. Only in 25 percent of companies is knowledge reused. Only 10 percent of companies have access to lessons learned and best practices. And every year, companies waste more than $12 billion by duplicating work.

Those numbers make clear that many companies haven't learned to manage business and technology together, to design business models and processes and their enabling technology at the same time so that they can see—and not just guess—where in the world they must go to acquire the knowledge and resources they need.

Today China graduates four times more engineers and computer scientists than the United States. America is facing serious problems with both its education system and its immigration laws, and it wonders how to attract more students to science, improve education and open its borders. It is vital that tomorrow's leaders have a multi-disciplinary education—training in both business and technology with a global perspective—so that we can eliminate the disconnect that exists in too many organizations today. The future is leaders who understand how business and technology have converged and who know to manage both in a global, knowledge economy.

Today, more than 70 percent of the products we buy in Wal-Mart are made in China, but still there is no equal distribution of wealth. The United States, with six percent of the population, has 50 percent of the wealth. Meanwhile, 47 percent of Chinese and 86 percent of Indians make less than $2 per day. How does this impact the growth of the global economy and how will this change? It always has been a global economy. Many wars have stemmed from trade disagreements.

A large proportion of college students in the United States today have the mistaken view that the degree is more important than the education it is supposed to represent; so they look for the easiest possible route to a degree. What they don't know is that there are students in India, China and elsewhere who are out-studying them, out-learning them, and in a few years will be out-competing them in the global job market. The K-12 school system also is falling behind in the United States. These things must change if the United States is to retain its envied position as the country with the highest standard of living in the world. We can no longer take for granted that the United States will continue to be No. 1. We have to work hard to keep it that way.

Yet, the current world is seeing some incredible success stories in global outsourcing due to the selection of quality vendors, the degree of trust and openness, acceptance of virtual organizations, collaborative teamwork, and a values-driven success and motivation. Outsourcing is set to dramatically lower cost and increase profitability for American businesses.

Three-quarters of U.S. companies outsourced some—or all—of their information technology activities in 2004 and that percentage is likely to increase in the coming years. While a smaller percentage of companies are outsourcing those activities offshore (32 percent), half of that 32 percent have cut full-time jobs as a result. But companies need to be able to assess the risks and benefits of each country they're considering as an outsourcing destination.

By 2005 standards, India is the most competitive and popular technology outsourcing destination in the world. However, by 2015, China will surpass the Indians to become the locomotive for growth as it did in manufacturing—only this time it will be in IT-related services—boosting world economic output and productivity. The world economy will certainly benefit from China's lead function, but what will happen with all those workers, IT engineers, and managers losing their jobs in the United States and in Europe? Places like Singapore and Israel will continue to specialize in research and development outsourcing. Russia eventually will evolve as a major R&D outsourcing giant. The political and economic dimension is still not entirely clear, as policy makers around the world have not thoroughly thought through that maze. But one thing is obvious—we are witnessing a sea change of what the future division of labor will look like. The old working class in the West is disappearing as developed nations provide capital and opportunities for the developing nations of the East. And the former underdogs may have a sustainable solution as more of their people have access to higher education.

Globalization is a reality. Global outsourcing is fast becoming one of the greatest organizational and industrial shifts in modern history. Instead of debating its merits, we could better spend our time learning how to thrive in it, rather than letting ourselves get trampled by it. That is the intent of this book. We believe that Global Outsourcing = Knowledge Economy. Global outsourcing allows companies to break complex tasks into many small parts, outsource each part to whoever can do it most efficiently, and then combine all of the completed parts into the final product.

This book tackles the subject with great insights and blunt realities from the business leaders pioneering and setting the pace of global outsourcing as the next generation of the knowledge economy. Our book centers on the knowledge economy in which human intelligence, creativity and insight are the key resources. Innovation. Intellectual capital. Creativity. Culture. Foreign policy. International governance. Technology. Social responsibility. All these topics are examined throughout this text to make it easier for newcomers to make their way through the nuances and complexities of this trend.

It is our objective throughout this book to offer examples of new collaborations that are emerging in global outsourcing—each of which has its own expertise or strength—to form unique solutions that serve global customers and individual needs more effectively than ever before.

We have covered the open-sourcing movement, which is opening new ways for grass-roots voluntary collaboration among programmers that humbled giants like Microsoft and IBM. We are spotting new business models and trends like homeshoring and multisourcing. We have uncovered this new way for America to lead the knowledge economy. Homeshoring is a way to revive U.S. and Western economies.

Homesourcing and rural outsourcing are catching up in the United States to complement, if not compete, and slow, if not stem, the politically volatile outsourcing and offshoring tide. Its proponents predict that many advantages—infrastructural expenses of offices and related amenities, lower travel costs, fewer cultural and management differences, higher employee retention rates and minimal overhead costs—will be competitive alternatives to off shoring.

Gartner predicts that 10 percent of all U.S. call center activity may develop some homeshoring component. Many homeshoring aficionados feel that software development and support work in low-wage U.S. areas, like Arkansas or rural North Carolina, can compete with Asian destinations. DC, a market intelligence company, estimated that in 2004 there were more than 100,000 home-shoring jobs in the United States.

Rural Sourcing, a North Carolina-based IT services company, claims to provide information technology services at 30 to 50 percent below most U.S. consulting firms by tapping into the increasing number of IT professionals in rural America, where overhead and wages are lower than in metropolitan areas. The company claims 20 clients, including Mattel and Cardinal Health, and averages $1 million in revenue and 50 full-time employees at five IT centers in Arkansas, North Carolina and Missouri. The company is charging $35 to $50 per hour for IT expertise, which may cost around $100 in New York City. While the cost is no match for outsourcing rates in India, the company propagates that their clients benefit from local accents and similar time zones.

The homeshoring movement is aimed at moving call center jobs or jobs requiring basic IT skills to home-based U.S. workers and software programming jobs to low-cost U.S. metros or rural areas instead of to India, China, Brazil, Taiwan or other countries. Homesourcing is taking off, and teams of home-based professionals can be trained to replace outsourcing as the preferred approach by enterprises looking to deliver quality work at lower cost.

We did not write this work as a textbook or academic treatise. From the outset, we believed that the book should have as much relevance for managers and consultants in practice as students and professors in the classroom. So we set out to write an easily accessible explanation of the fascinating field of outsourcing and globalization. Our intention was not to be encyclopedic or to present a universal solution to the challenges of globalization. Rather, our intention was to identify the most universal success factors to advance corporate globalization to ensure corporate survival.

By **Faisal Hoque**

Chairman and CEO
Enamics, Inc.

Founder and Chair
BTM Institute

"Knowledge-based innovation is the "super-star" of entrepreneurship. And like most "super-stars," knowledge-based innovation is temperamental, capricious, and hard to manage. Not to mention it has the longest lead time off all innovations. One other key characteristic of knowledge-based innovations - and a truly unique one - is that they are almost never based on one factor but on the convergence of different kinds of knowledge, not all of them scientific and technological"

—*Peter F. Drucker,* Innovation and Entrepreneurship, *1985*

Sustainable Innovation

Look what innovative business approaches can do, when technology is used strategically:

- In the parking lot of a Wal-Mart in hurricane-ravaged Chalmette, La., just outside New Orleans, Dr. Enoch Choi examines a newly homeless woman who can remember only that she takes "blue pills." He pulls a microcomputer from his belt and wirelessly connects to a network created in just days by 150 corporations, nonprofits and government agencies. From it, Dr. Choi retrieves her prescription records and safely restores her medication. In this hot parking lot, hundreds of Katrina refugees begin to see some order replacing the chaos of their lives.

- A man on a bright red motorcycle roars through the stilted houses of rural O Siengle, Cambodia, and slows as he passes the elementary school. At this moment, a WiFi chip in a box strapped to the cycle shoots email wirelessly to a solar-powered computer in the school, and receives outgoing email in return. Later, the driver and four others rendezvous at another school with a satellite uplink to send the email on its way. The 800 villagers of O Siengle, who have no electric or telephone lines, are connected to the globe.

- In Cincinnati, Ohio, the consumer packaged goods giant Procter & Gamble needs new ideas quicker than ever to keep its 300 brands ahead of the competition. Despite a stellar in-house research team, the company has started reaching out via the

Internet to "knowledge clusters" with ideas and solutions to problems. One is a company that has assembled scientists from 170 countries to respond to challenges from P&G and other corporations. "If I've got a problem I've got to solve," one executive says, "I can be in touch with someone somewhere around the globe within 24 to 48 hours who has the answer or idea that I need."

This is the face of business innovation in the 21st Century. "Innovate or die" may be a cliché, but the world solves its problems and moves ahead today on the back of innovation.

And more often than not, information technology is at the heart of it. That is because technology has so permeated our organizations as to be indispensable. At many companies, it accounts for more than half of capital spending. Simply put, business and technology have converged. Effective management of business technology can not only create more profits for mega corporations but can also forever alter social enterprises that serve the "bottom of the pyramid"—the underdeveloped and the underprivileged.

Innovation for its own sake, however, is meaningless, or worse. The dot.com mania proved that if you jump in the sandbox and start playing with new toys without a serious plan, you just get sand in your eyes. But that hasn't been the end of it. Today fully half of all information technology projects undertaken by corporations fail. The results have been productivity shortfalls, imposed workforce reductions, damaged corporate reputations and downward market valuations.

Corporations and the investment community have wasted billions on ill-conceived technology investments. And there's a huge opportunity cost. It's not just the $170 million the FBI wrote off on a failed system, to take just one example, it's the agency's weakened ability to fight terror. What appears to be the fault of the technologist ("Can't you make this stuff work?") is really a failure to unify business and technology decision-making.

Unfortunately, our ability to manage business technology has not kept pace with our creation of it. In many organizations we still have two camps—technophiles and technophobes—and if they aren't at war, they are wary of each other. In too many organizations the "business side" comes up with a plan and throws it over the wall to the "technology side" to implement. Because technology is so embedded in the way things work today, they should have been sitting and planning together from the very beginning.

But for the first 50 years of the computer age we had no standardized way of doing this. We depended on creative but ad hoc decisions about business technology. Technology executives would create a plan, and if it worked, fine; if it didn't they moved on.

But innovation isn't haphazard. Its core is a creative idea, of course, but it only becomes effective when part of a process: a leader recognizes a need, assembles an organization and designs processes to meet it, and then applies business technology to make it work. It is not the invention of a new technology that matters so much as it is its application—understanding its role when developing a strategy or designing an organization or its processes. That is why I call it "business technology," to underscore the fact that information technology is of value only when it advances the organization's "business."

To create an environment where technology helps shape (rather than simply enable) strategic choices, leading enterprises are working to synchronize (rather than simply align) their business and technology decision-making. And in the best-managed modern enterprises, technology will converge with the business as completely as, say, sound financial management.

Increasingly, this will be the source of all competitive successes. That's why we do not call this business and technology or the business of IT, but rather Business Technology Management (BTM). It is a cross-disciplinary management science that allows professionals to innovate sustainable business models.

Sustainable innovation requires a seamless, structured management approach that begins with board and CEO-level issues and connects all the way through technology investment and implementation. BTM offers this, and it has the potential to forever change how corporations, governments, education, NGOs, and social enterprises think of technology's strategic use for socioeconomic development, which will in turn have a profound effect on the human condition.

I have seen sustainable innovation first-hand. In my native Bangladesh, 97 percent of homes and virtually all rural villages lack a telephone, making the country one of the least wired in the world. This has contributed to underdevelopment and the impoverishment of individual Bangladeshis.

To address this, Grameen (the Bengali word for "village") Bank, a micro-finance institution founded by world-renowned Professor Muhammad Yunus, formed two entities: Grameen Telecommunications, a nonprofit organization to provide phone services in rural areas, and Grameen Phone Ltd., a joint venture of Grameen Telecommunications and Norway's Telenor. It has become the country's dominant mobile carrier. Grameen helps local entrepreneurs set up village phones, selling services to residents. The company and the entrepreneurs profit, and the villagers get affordable connectivity.

My father grew up in the village of Khorshuti, which did not have electricity until six years ago. He went to engineering school and became one of the national government's most senior civil engineers, dealing with water resource management. Retired now, he visits Khoruti often, and when he's there I can talk to him, wherever I am in the world, thanks to the innovations of Telenor and Grameen.

Telenor is the majority owner of Grameen Phone. I had the privilege of meeting its CEO and president, Jon Fredrik Baksaas, in Oslo last October just before the 2005 Nobel Peace Prize announcement. He shared that, despite Grameen's altruistic aims, Bangladesh is one of his company's fastest growing markets and has one of its highest gross profit margins. This is the meaning of "global knowledge economy"—technology innovation in Norway and business innovation in Bangladesh.

To navigate in this kind of world, where knowledge can appear anywhere and be applied anywhere else, where organizations of all stripes mix and match their efforts, leaders need a holistic management framework to determine their strategy, decide on the business capabilities that will support the strategy, and deploy the technologies that will enable these capabilities.

In New Orleans, it was not the technology Dr. Enoch Choi used so much, but how he managed it that mattered. He was sponsored by a Presbyterian church in California, worked under a tent erected by the National Guard, hooked into a prescription database through a wireless cell connection set up by Verizon, used five microcomputers he borrowed from OQO Inc., a new California company pioneering tiny computers, and treated up to 50 patients a day.

As he looked around, however, he saw no other such innovation. "FEMA," he said, "was using paper and pen."

In 2003, we launched the **BTM Institute** (www.btminstitute.org) - the Michael Nobel Harriet Fulbright Institute of Business Technology Management (BTM), the first international nonprofit organization of its kind that brings together a select group from the academic, corporate, government and thought leadership communities as a think tank to address the long-standing need to manage business and technology together. Today, it is the world's largest and most influential community solely focused on business technology management.

The goal of BTM is to lead the industry in 'Making Business and Technology One.' The BTM Institute is a knowledge network that allows the next generation of leaders to learn from each other. The Institute has attracted a global who's who, established an aggressive research agenda, produced major publications, and has begun a much needed and first-ever cross collaboration among multi-disciplinary experts and academics.

In 2004, the Institute published the definition of a management standard based on the core processes of business technology decision-making and began to expand its research agenda. The initial outputs of the Institute include a series of management papers for each of the BTM capabilities. The BTM standard put forth by the BTM Institute provides a structured approach to decision-making that allows enterprises to align, synchronize and even converge IT and business management, thus ensuring better execution, risk control and profitability.

Following its research agenda, The BTM Institute's first major publication, *Winning The 3-Legged Race: When Business and Technology Run Together* (Prentice Hall, November 8, 2005), shows that it is possible to subject business technology to a comprehensive set of management standards. Furthermore, this book shows that this is not just a technology issue. It is, instead, a business issue, and it will not see resolution until enterprises have a fundamentally better way to manage technology's contribution to

the value chain. The book comprehensively addresses the critical concepts for Business Technology Management (BTM), and offers concrete executive agendas.

By collaborating with the most accomplished global leaders in *Six Billion Minds: Managing Business and Technology in the Global Knowledge Economy*, we look into the management challenges and innovation opportunities in light of the profound impact of globalization and the emergence of the knowledge economy.

What exactly is the "global knowledge economy," and what does it mean for innovation? First, it is people who innovate and develop new knowledge, and to tap into it, you have to connect to them or be where they are. Innovation is so important to Procter & Gamble that it casts a global net. It connects its worldwide employees with collaboration tools. It employs 7,500 scientists throughout 22 research centers in 12 countries. On its website, the company invites anyone, anywhere, to submit ideas.

Cisco Systems thinks along the same lines. When it opened an R&D facility in China to build voice over IP (VOIP) technology, CEO John Chambers cited China's good universities and pool of talent as a key reason for moving there.

Here is a glimpse at this global talent pool: India graduates 3.1 million from college every year, China graduates 2.8 million and the U.S. only 1.3 million. Young people are more at ease with technology and more willing to experiment. In India 53 percent of the population is below 25 years of age, 41 percent in China, only 35 percent in the U.S.

What are these young, educated people doing? They're not just taking on humdrum, outsourced tasks from the U.S. In China they are innovating new business models—dozens if not hundreds of firms networked to design various components and subsystems of digital cameras, computers, motorcycles and other products. It is incremental, bottom-up innovation in ever-changing modular organizations. "I worry that there is actually a lot of management innovation going on around the design process in China that we frankly don't understand and have not begun to even develop the skills around and are going to be critical to success," the author and strategist John Hagel said at the Fortune Innovation Summit.

This activity is organizing itself into "knowledge clusters." Shanghai is emerging as a center of semi-conductor design;

Shinzan is a center of networking equipment design. Think of global networks of specialized knowledge centers. The shirt you're wearing may have been designed by a team in Italy; dyed, printed and manufactured in China, Indonesia or Mexico; shipped by a U.S.-based company, and all of this activity was coordinated in the U.K.

What knowledge does your organization need, and where is it?

To answer those questions, to navigate in this kind of world, leaders need a cross-disciplinary management framework to determine their strategy, decide on the business capabilities that will support the strategy, and deploy the technologies that will enable these capabilities. This is a holistic approach to management, which can factor in the knowledge and partnerships necessary to be innovative.

Innovation enabled by business technology will keep our corporations vibrant. It will also invigorate non-profits, social enterprises, and governments—that is, of course, if we get the management of business technology right.

The email project in Cambodia, for example, was the work of two former MIT Media Lab students who created a company called First Mile Solutions to provide asynchronous Internet connections in remote areas. The company's DakNet (from the Hindi word for "postal") has also been deployed in rural India.

A company called Drishtee ("vision" in Hindi) contracts with a state government to provide services to remote Indian villages—land records, driver's licenses, and complaints about government services. WiFi-enabled buses pass village kiosks and communications between government and villagers are asynchronously exchanged. Local entrepreneurs run the kiosks, taking 80 percent of the profits. The cost to the villagers is far lower than if they had to give up a day or more to travel to the state offices.

The real innovation is not technological. It is in the business model, a partnership of government, Dishtree and local kiosk operators. Moreover, their innovation was the insight that real time connectivity was too expensive for the villagers and not even necessary to meet their needs. These people don't even need telephones. "Who would I call?" one asked. No one he knew had a phone.

Superimposing a massive telecommunications infrastructure on these rural areas—a "If we build it, you will use it" strategy—would have been folly. The potential customers could not have afforded it. I think of this when I see companies spend hundreds of millions on computer systems that give end users far more than they need, or that are far too complicated for them to adapt to, or that do not let them do what they need to do.

Or when I see companies spending multi-millions on systems because other companies are. This has been called the "cocktail party" solution—someone heard about a cool new thing the night before. I call it the "teenage peer pressure" solution—"But, Mom, everyone else is doing it!" It indicates an absence of strategic thinking.

The DakNet story illustrates two other things important to innovation. One is that it could only happen when WiFi technology had matured sufficiently. When business and technology are intimately aligned, the organization knows how to appropriately take advantage of new technologies. Sometimes the technology takes the strategic lead. We call companies that have achieved this level of integration "synchronized."

The second is that the idea of DakNet was hatched in the United States, but implemented in Cambodia and India. Innovation today requires finding the knowledge that seeds it, wherever it is. The "global knowledge economy" is not a buzzword.

Indeed, while it has provoked anxiety in some quarters, this global economy has connected forgotten millions to the rest of the world, offering them a way out of poverty and promising sustainable development in their remote areas. Forming new partnerships for the sourcing of manufacturing and services, once suspicious nations are becoming increasingly dependent on one another—and when people are business partners, there is less chance for ill will.

And for companies, global sourcing allows them to find the best and most effective partners for the component parts of their businesses, and then to knit these disparate efforts together into a final product. Increasingly, it is hard to put a national stamp on a car or a shirt or a piece of software.

That is the link between global sourcing and the knowledge economy. Innovation springs from the minds of people everywhere in the world today, and the challenge is to discover what they know and to connect to them. It is a heady time for those at the helm to find the specialized knowledge they need wherever it is and to put it to work in their interest. More often than not, the innovation will be in new business models and processes, enabled by technology. New management skills will be required, particularly the ability to manage business and technology as one.

If you look at this next generation definition of management, one of the fundamental things is that in a knowledge economy information equals success. And technology retrieves, manages and disseminates this information. Time becomes the critical factor, because time to market, time to please a customer, time to remake a business strategy or process all spell success or failure. Technology, at the end of the day, mitigates this time constraint. And that's why technology is relevant. At the end of the day, technology facilitates time management, and time management equals information retrieval, and information retrieval equals knowledge, and knowledge drives the economy.

This latest publication of the BTM Institute is a wake-up call to global leaders. We, the society at large, have a once in a lifetime opportunity to build excellence by leveraging the vast global knowledge pool of the "six billion minds" that make up the emerging knowledge economy. And it is undoubtedly driven by the convergence of business and technology.

Dr. Vinton G. Cerf
Vice President and Chief Internet Evangelist
Google
Ashburn, Virginia

Unexpected Digital Surprises

Question: *How does the Internet impact globalization and global outsourcing?*

Cerf: Computer networking has been vastly enabling. The most obvious example is the Indian town of Bangalore, which made a very determined effort to focus on information technology, taking advantage of a high number of engineers graduating from the Indian Institutes of Technology. As more and more communications capability is involved in the world of business, we will see more opportunities for outsourcing of services that go far beyond the ones we have seen so far. The Internet is the backbone of globalization. And globalization is conducive to building a better tomorrow.

Question: *How will information technologies impact our daily work and life?*

Cerf: We are facing a very interesting digital future and I think there are probably going to be many unexpected positive surprises. In fact, we have already seen some. The ease with which new applications can be mounted on the Internet without having to get permission from the underlying service provider has lead to fairly dramatic increases in innovation. Also, technology can help to improve the economic conditions of people in Africa and South Asia as the digital divided narrows down.

Question: *Is there a downside as well?*

Cerf: Of course, IT also produces a variety of side effects. Concerns over intellectual property protection being one of them, security another. We are going to need more legal standards that might have to be international in scope in order to assure that business transactions can be properly protected. Globalization would make arbitration an increasingly important and popular alternative to litigation as a dispute resolution mechanism. However, IT in general and the Internet in particular should not become politicized. That would be a recipe for a serious risk in terms of keeping the system running.

Question: *What does outsourcing mean to the developed economies in Western Europe and North America? How do they sustain themselves and how do they continue to become significant players in this age of globalization?*

Cerf: It is an important challenge for the developed world to cope with the shift towards the developing world in dimensions that historically have not been present. The only counter to off-shoring is to work harder, think harder and come up with better ideas. Our need here in the United States and other developed parts of the world is to figure out how to integrate lower cost capabilities into a more comprehensive business model. If we don't figure out how to do that, we deserve what we might get—a creeping erosion of our living standards.

Question: What does the business model of the future look like?

Cerf: Outsourcing has become popular because of potential cost benefits and the possibility of 24-hour operations. But I have seen an increasing amount of outsourcing being brokered or offered by firms in the United States with experience managing the outsourced components. Multinational corporations are turning to system integrators who will supply them with outsourcing capability. However, the multinationals want to stay in control. In some cases they want to even acquire providers of outsourcing services. One thing is clear: the business model of the future is closely linked to the outsourcing paradigm. Companies keep the brand and the intellectual property—the rest, IT services, manufacturing, sales and even R&D, can be outsourced.

Question: The 17th century philosopher Thomas Hobbes said that humankind has to surrender individual power to the authority of an absolute sovereign. How did the Internet change this worldview? What do you think is the underlying philosophy of the future?

Cerf: I believe in an open world. Censorship and control are almost never the right answer to dealing with information quality. The Internet is a symbol of human creativity and freedom. Instead of restricting civil liberties we should create and safeguard more information that counters the extreme opinions that some people might have. I am persuaded that we are going to see the empowerment of the individual. But critical thinking is increasingly important—to distinguish what is good and what is bad. I clearly prefer Jean-Jacques Rousseau to Thomas Hobbes. Generally, humans adapt very quickly to convenient information sources and take advantage of them.

Question: How does the world in 2050 look?

Cerf: There is no doubt that nanotechnology will have matured substantially in that period of time. Its application to medical matters will be dramatic. Our ability to repair neural damage using electronics will be standard practice. Nanotechnology will also be heavily used for automatic assembly in manufacturing, and bacterial engineering will become an important component in using genetic methods to get special effects from biological production. It would not surprise me if we can literally grow personal computers on trees.

Question: Any changes in terms of our macroeconomic and geopolitical reality?

Cerf: National boundaries will erode and multinational corporations will become powerful, quasi-geopolitical entities. There might be possibilities for more regional aggregations similar to the European Union, for example in Africa and Asia. I am fascinated to imagine that we might someday see larger political entities emerging out of the national patchwork, including virtual aggregations. New geopolitical entities emerge virtually even though the aggregated countries do not share land borders. The new entities will be sustained by virtue of communication and telecommunication systems that will be available by the middle of the 21st century.

Question: *And outsourcing is here to stay?*

Cerf: Definitively—outsourcing will be an integral part of our daily life. We started by talking about outsourcing to other populations and it occurs to me that at some point, maybe by the mid-21st century, outsourcing may go not to people but to computers and robots. Technology may get to the point where we could outsource a lot of our customary human activities to these artificial devices. This sounds like an utopian scenario, but it is one I would not discard out of hand, because in fifty years time one could imagine very capable computing systems and robotic systems to which one might be able to outsource a great many normal human activities. And even though we might be far away from any likelihood of outsourcing processes to the Moon or Mars, it is tempting to imagine that assembling things that require a vacuum environment might be pretty interesting on the moon because there is no atmosphere there. The future is wide open.

Part 1

The Changing Face of Globalization

India is the leader in outsourcing. Its workforce is well educated, it has a strong IT ability, and its people not only speak English but also understand the Anglo-Saxon legal system. Some leaders believe it is difficult to challenge India's position in the global marketplace at this point. And yet China is the current media darling. With China on the rise as its businesses sign agreements on a range of services from manufacturing to R&D, African treaties and oil deals in South America and Eastern Europe, its clear China's presence in the global outsourcing playing field is as significant as India's.

What gives these countries the leg-up? To answer that question, you must understand what the contenders bring to the marketplace beyond the obvious cost efficiencies. In the next 10-20 years, as these countries continue to invest significantly in the development of world-class technology outsourcing centers with international sites, which country will become the world's largest in purchasing power parity? While many believe it will be China, questions remain for the immediate and intermediate term. Not only are multinational corporations sending work to India and China, but they are also targeting these countries as growth economies and seeking to capture market share.

This section looks at emerging trends shaping the global outsourcing landscape and impacting outsourcing users as well as vendors. It offers analysis of several factors and drivers moving these trends—including the rising resistance against offshoring in the United States and Europe, technology developments that enable certain modes of outsourcing, changing customer expectations and maturing outsourcing models. Security is a concern in rising superstar China, as well as other parts of the world. Brazil has great potential, according to experts, but the risk of its internal security issues may disturb normal conduct as well as its local disdain for the United States.

Shaping future outsourcing is the convergence of ITO and BPO. Established IT outsourcing vendors, seeing a slowdown in IT growth, foresee that additional revenue streams can be garnered from existing clients by offering BPO services that are tightly integrated with their IT offerings.

This section reviews China as a destination for IT and business processes. A vast and growing country, China beckons and businesses listen, wondering how they will capitalize on the combination of growth, investment, developing capitalism and fresh technology that is changing that country's face. A chapter discusses China's strengths and weaknesses, and dispels some long-held misconceptions. It offers perspective on China's efforts to become a preferred ITO and BPO destination, as well as its potential as a competitive location in the future.

This section reviews the major structural challenges to global ventures and looks at sustainable ways to address them by adopting a values-based approach. And finally, it reviews globalization as a mega-force drawing products, services, companies, civic institutions and even the fates of nations into its wake.

1.1

By **Anupam Govil**
Founder and CEO
Global Equations LLC
Austin, Texas

Nearshoring, Homeshoring and Other Emerging Trends

Offshore outsourcing has been described as a megatrend, an irreversible phenomenon, a paradigm shift, a strategic imperative and many other adjectives of varying hue. It may be many things to many people, but it is certainly an inescapable reality that has captured the minds of the public from the highest executives to the freshest recruit just out of college.

Even though outsourcing has been around as a business practice for several decades, it has only caught the mainstream's attention in the past five years. The rise of offshoring was actually precipitated by the economic recession the United States went through in the years 2000 through 2002. The years prior to 2000 were the foundation-laying phase for overseas providers who were able to enter into timely relationships with major corporations to solve the critical Y2K problem.

Due to an acute shortage of local talent that was busy migrating to Internet-related ventures and riding the Internet wave, India-based labor served as the stopgap filler to address the most mundane of problems that no one else wanted to touch. Large corporations riding an economic high were really in no mood to cut costs and hence business process outsourcing was not yet a significant phenomenon. Strategic IT development initiatives were handed out largely to U.S.-based specialized e-business players who could charge an arm and a leg for Web-based programming.

The offshore providers could nibble at some of this work but usually had to use an American firm to interface with the customers. The term "offshoring," which had been in use since the mid-1990s, was considered a very isolated activity and definitely not a threat to the work force or the U.S. economy.

This scenario drastically changed in 1998-99 when a large number of overseas IT resources became idle after coming off of Y2K work and forced the offshore providers to aggressively market themselves to their customer base. The shift in business dynamics forced companies to consider offshoring as a more strategic tool than they had done hitherto. The boom in IT outsourcing that began in the late 1990s due to labor constraints actually gained self-sustaining momentum when the dot-com crash and subsequent recession created the perfect conditions for a foreign foray.

Simultaneously, the availability of limitless international data and voice bandwidth provided an economic model that made the labor arbitrage between the developed and the developing nations an attainable reality. Corporations that had grown large, bottom-heavy operations found that this new phase of the new economy required an agile enterprise that could evolve with business conditions and an economic strategy that required flexibility in cost models and a global outlook. Business process outsourcing, which had been gathering momentum during the 1990s, suddenly became a buzzword in the boardrooms and a necessary lever in the COO/CFO toolbox.

Initially, the rising popularity of the offshoring service delivery model caught the incumbent outsourcing providers unprepared. They had been comfortably ensconced in their relationships with major corporations, and the threat from offshore providers had largely been downplayed. Offshoring was linked to cheap, unreliable, and low-end work and the overseas-centric providers were considered as annoying minor players engaging in bottom feeding.

This perception was swiftly eroded as cost pressures and a mature process and service delivery culture, along with an eagerness to provide customer-friendly offerings, gave offshore companies an entrée into the upper echelons of corporate management, which would naturally convert into larger and more strategic deals. The reality sank in as the public markets accorded the overseas providers a valuation far superior to the heretofore outsourcing leaders.

At one point Infosys, the leading Indian outsourcing firm, which barely made the global top twenty in terms of revenue, had a market cap greater than six of the top ten outsourcing firms, excluding Accenture. Majors like EDS and Cap Gemini had always maintained relationships with the offshore providers for farming out overflow and lower-margin work. However, the change in customer attitude (why not work directly with the offshore experts?) and pricing pressures would soon force them to rethink their overall strategy. Interestingly, these dynamics worked both ways. While the onshore providers looked for ways to embed offshoring into their service offerings without cannibalizing their own high-margin services, the foreign-based stalwarts also realized the value of having a robust and meaningful front-end presence in the home territory of their customers. We saw the emergence of a profusion of terms ranging from "best shoring" to "right shoring" to "blended shoring."

No matter which way the cookie crumbled, the resulting impact was the rise of a global delivery model that would permanently reshape the landscape of the outsourcing sector.

Throughout this period of rapid evolution of the outsourcing model there has been a dichotomy between the decision makers and the stakeholders. As the scope and impact of outsourcing climbed from fringe and tactical work to high value and strategically important initiatives, the organizational dynamics have been in a flux, resulting in mixed and confusing messages to internal and external stakeholders. Is outsourcing about focusing on core competency or is it about reducing headcount? Does outsourcing promote efficiencies and economies of scale or does it increase dependencies on third parties for non-core functions? Does outsourcing make companies leaner and more agile or does it strip them of their DNA? These are profound questions with no simple answers.

In the absence of academic or scientific rigor, the perception of outsourcing and specifically offshoring has hinged upon the viewer's own interests. Rather than being the rallying force for companies seeking greater agility and competitiveness in a tight market, outsourcing has actually become an internal flash point. It is indeed surprising that few universities have offered curricula around organizational change management and decision-making focused on outsourcing. Outsourcing in its truest form is a disaggregation of a monolithic organization into the core, contextual and non-critical divisions, which are then evaluated for their outsourcing potential. Be it in the avatar of a shared services center or a joint-sourcing/co-sourcing deal, this signals a fundamental shift in the way corporations manage their operations, optimize their capital needs, and streamline their balance sheets.

Rising public sentiment and politicization of the outsourcing debate has forced companies into pushing outsourcing behind closed doors. Though outsourcing is the magic word in boardrooms, analyst meetings and earnings calls, most firms have shied away from publicly embracing it as one of their key strategies. Is it any coincidence today that two of the most profitable companies in the world, General Electric and Citicorp, are both pioneers and active proponents of the global outsourcing model?

Taking advantage of this heightened sensitivity, some overseas-based firms have developed variants of the offshoring model that blend convenience of onshore locations with lower costs. "Home-based sourcing" and "rural sourcing" are recent trends that are using cost arbitrage within the domestic region to counter the benefits of offshoring. Rural sourcing is the practice of operating call centers, data processing facilities, as well as software development outfits, in rural and semi-urban areas that offer lower cost of infrastructure and labor. A decade ago, cost and resource pressures had precipitated a shift of call centers and back office processing units to smaller towns. These tended to be based around small university communities where the supply of skilled personnel was not an issue, and the job market was relatively flat. In fact, due to high turnover rates in call centers, it was preferred to base them in areas with concentrated student populations who tend to take up these jobs to augment their income.

Rural sourcing currently represents a small sliver of the overall outsourcing market within the United States. Some specific segments of the industry like HR outsourcing find a better fit in rural sourcing since these functions require sensitive, personal contact that can be difficult to handle from international locations. The biggest challenge facing rural sourcing is the lack of sufficient talent, which impedes rapid scaling up efforts. At best, rural sourcing can absorb a fraction of the overall market demand for outsourcing, and therefore this is not considered a threat to offshore destinations.

Home-based sourcing is another trend that started as a trickle in the late 1990s as a low-cost alternative to call centers. These virtual call centers became an alternative to offshoring, providing closer to home services at rates typically 20 percent cheaper than domestic call centers. In recent years this has become very popular, with IDC estimates of more than 100,000 agents fielding customer service calls from home. Gartner has also predicted that over the next two years, 10 percent of U.S.-based call centers would likely shift to at least partially to home-based agents. Some companies such as JetBlue airlines have proudly proclaimed use of home-based reservation and customer service agents as one of their unique attributes—touting the benefits of protecting U.S. jobs while providing more personal service. Home-based agents are typically used to handle overflow and seasonal work to avoid extra investment in facilities that may only be used periodically. Home-based sourcing can save up to 30 percent or more on overhead costs such real estate, support staff and transport. However, lack of a controlled environment brings in new challenges such as monitoring agent productivity, data privacy and security, which are critical factors preventing this trend from becoming a full-fledged alternative to offshoring.

Rise of global sourcing or "rightshoring"

One of the significant trends that have emerged in the last few years is that of global sourcing or "right shoring." This approach combines onsite, offsite, nearshore, and offshore delivery to provide a risk-and-reward balanced delivery model to corporations. Typically, the decision-making tree splits functions between onsite and offsite. Subsequently, the offsite activities are evaluated for their offshore-ability, and if they do not fall into that category, then they are retained at an onshore or nearshore location.

Functions performed onsite would include program management, requirements definition, prototyping, high-level design, usability testing, acceptance testing, user training and implementation/cutover. Potential activities for nearshore might include quick-turnaround development, emergency fixes, interactive development, prime time support, iterative testing, risk diversification, and an alternative to onsite work for high-level design. Functions typically performed offshore include detailed design, coding, unit testing, documentation, ongoing maintenance, and project management of offshore staff. This provides companies a way to optimize use of global resources to balance their needs of risk mitigation, high productivity and cost efficiency. This trend has heralded the rise of several favorable nearshore destinations serving the U.S. and European markets. Canada, the Caribbean, and Central America in the Americas along with Ireland and Poland in Europe are prime examples of this.

As offshoring has matured, having a balanced outsourcing strategy has become an imperative. There is a need to have an enterprise-wide outsourcing roadmap, which diversifies delivery and exogenous risks by having a multi-vendor and multi-nodal strategy. By applying portfolio management principles to outsourcing planning and management, enterprise buyers can work with service providers that offer a range of global sourcing alternatives, including onsite, domestic, nearshore and offshore capabilities. External service providers (ESPs) worldwide are responding to this demand by providing high-touch and higher value services closer to home, while moving the bulk of their transaction and more labor-intensive functions to lower-cost markets, such as India and nearshore hubs like Canada and Ireland.

The concomitant rise in nearshoring and offshoring was the subject of a study conducted by Gartner in 2003. Based on an analysis of trends, and discussions with enterprise buyers and IT service providers, Gartner declared its "80/80/80 Discuss, Analyze, Act" prediction for the growth of global delivery models—both nearshore and offshore: "Through 2004, despite the potential human resource backlash, 80 percent of U.S. executive boardrooms will have discussed global delivery options (nearshore and offshore); of those, 80 percent will pursue an analysis of global delivery options (nearshore and offshore) and 80 percent of those enterprises using global delivery models will act by increasing their level of people resources (nearshore and offshore) by as much as 30 percent (0.8 probability)." As corporations balance between the need to cut costs and keep outsourced functions closer to home, nearshore destinations will continue to find favor.

A key factor to address is the role of labor cost arbitrage between the origination and destination regions in sustaining a nearshoring trend. How large should the cost differential be to spur companies to consider nearshore versus an offshore destination (given that the processes could be outsourced anywhere just as effectively)? One example that can be looked at is that of Nova Scotia, Canada. Through a sustained effort to develop this region as a hub for IT outsourcing and R&D, Nova Scotia has emerged as one of the top nearshore destinations for North American companies. In its 2004 competitive alternatives report, KPMG rated Halifax, Nova Scotia, as one of the most cost-competitive locations for business in North America and Europe, with an almost 20 percent cost advantage over the United States and 30 percent over Western Europe. KPMG also compared cities on the east coast of Canada and the United States. Halifax came out on top, being roughly 30 percent less expensive to run a business there than in Boston. This illustrates that a net cost differential of 20 to 30 percent with the target market is sufficient to generate significant nearshoring opportunities.

Changing organizational dynamics drive new outsourcing disciplines

As the scope of processes, functions and activities outsourced offshore expands, it is having a ripple effect across the firmament of the corporate world. Roles are being redefined, business models are shifting, organizational structures are evolving, and the economic feasibility of various business functions is being re-evaluated. This signifies a gradual shift from bottom-line cost justification to top-line business drivers as the primary rationale for outsourcing. ROI calculators are being re-tooled to accommodate the long-term capital and process value benefits of outsourcing and offshoring. There is an inexorable drive to redraw the boundaries of the organization to eke maximum business value while achieving optimum process efficiencies. From one perspective, organizations are shedding assets and devolving ownership and authority to their outsourcing partners. Yet from another vantage point, these same organizations could be perceived as expanding outwards to include the ecosystem of the third party outsourcing vendors.

Whatever the viewpoint, organizational change is the only constant. We are seeing the impact of outsourcing reaching out from the back office (transaction processing, IT maintenance) to the middle office (analytics, patent research, software development) to the front office (customer interaction, marketing, telediagnostics). Analyzing the trend in a different plane, the scope and breadth of processes being offshored is expanding from labor intensive and workflow based activities to more skills based processes to decision-making and high-value knowledge based functions. And these trends cut across various industries such as financial services (data analytics, equity research, analyst support, risk modeling), insurance (claims adjudication, actuarial), mortgage (data mining, fraud and credit analysis), healthcare (remote diagnostics, revenue-cycle optimization), pharma and life sciences (data mining, drug discovery optimization, gene sequence analysis), manufacturing (market research, buying pattern analysis, sales channel optimization) and legal (patent research, paralegal support). Interestingly, the drivers for outsourcing higher value and more knowledge intensive functions are significantly different than the ones for lower end transaction processing or voice services. The non-core and more contextual back-office functions are very price sensitive and will incessantly migrate towards regions that can offer the best costing model for reasonable quality. Labor-cost arbitrage will continue to be the key decision lever for these tiers of services. But prominently, companies seeking to outsource more elite white-collar positions will do so for other reasons, such as access to a highly skilled talent base, ease of scalability, access to global markets, developing an intellectual property asset base and expediting the delivery window by leveraging time zone or demographic differences.

Looking at the IT outsourcing market, similar explosive growth is projected across different segments. One of the areas poised for such growth is outsourced research and development. Worldwide spending on R&D and engineering offshore will increase by a whopping 860 percent, from $1.25 billion in 2004 to as much as $12 billion in 2010. Overseas spending on infrastructure outsourcing will grow from between $100 million and $250 million to between $3 billion and $4 billion over the same period. Offshore spending on application development services is expected to more than double from $23 billion to as much as $50 billion. With growth of this magnitude, there will be tremendous opportunities ahead for offshore and nearshore outsourcing destinations.

As large corporations internalize offshore outsourcing as business-as-usual, technology and product development companies are beginning to embrace this as a way to weather fickle business cycles and competitive cost pressures. Product companies realize that their success relies not just on core technology but on their market responsiveness, time-to-market development path, and competitive pricing. Setting up offshore development teams either with outsourcing partners or as a captive unit gives product managers the flexibility to slice markets and define product architecture, while letting their virtual development teams do their part.

Innovation and not cost reduction will be the main reason for companies to outsource their IT requirements over the next decade. With the maturing of the outsourcing model, corporations seeking to gain higher value will consider offshoring not just for cost savings, but also to tap into new talent and to open up new markets for their services and products. With all levels of IT jobs going to foreign places, business executives will need to innovate and create new classes of corporate divisions, services, and

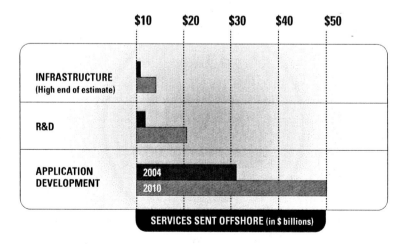

Figure 1   Offshore Growth

Projected growth in some of the fastest evolving segments of global outsourcing. Source: Gartner.

jobs. This will lead to businesses moving away from a model where they protect their intellectual property and instead adopt "global innovation networks" based on collaboration, partnerships and outsourcing.

For companies thinking in terms of global innovation or global sourcing networks, the major conundrum is not about what processes to offshore but which offshoring model to adopt. There are several schools of thought that advocate different strategies ranging between a fully outsourced model to hybrid setups to fully captive options. The right answer lies in an organization's own ability to identify its key business drivers, risk appetite, priorities, and readiness. Following the example of a competitor or making decisions based on industry trends is a recipe for disaster.

The typical strategy involves a phased approach, which allows the company to develop confidence and knowledge in its offshore initiative. For a company that has never gone overseas, outsourcing to an experienced third-party service provider is the preferred option. Whether it is in the form of a single vendor or a multi-vendor relationship, outsourcing does provide the company the fastest route to achieving its desired results. Companies that have offshored for years and have gained experience may consider taking greater ownership in their overseas operation. Various options, including a joint-sourcing relationship with a vendor or a fully independent captive operation, can be considered. Some firms prefer to build their offshore operation through a joint venture or a build, operate, transfer (BOT) route. Whichever way the company performs it, managing an offshore delivery facility reduces operational and business flexibility. This can be addressed by employing a judicious mix of offshore "captives" and outsourcing vendors that can satisfy the business and operational requirements. As companies become comfortable using overseas resources, they will move towards a hybrid global sourcing model, where critical IT projects or BPO services are sourced from multiple offshore firms located in different regions of the world and managed through sophisticated service management systems.

Evolution of global outsourcing vendors

As automation, collaboration and communication technologies become more sophisticated, business process transformation will diminish the significance of the human component in routine back office functions. This will put China and Vietnam on the same quality plane as India, the current outsourcing leader. Outsourcing decision-makers will increasingly focus on the lowest cost destination for routine and non-core back-office functions. Indian vendors have realized that this shift is happening and since their own costs are rising, staying competitive would be difficult at the lower end of the outsourcing spectrum. As part of a conscious strategy, many of the leading Indian companies have been diversifying geographically and functionally. By developing end-to-end process capabilities in key verticals and by leveraging a lower cost base in second or third tier cities within India, some of them have been positioning themselves as Business Service Providers (BSPs). By specializing with deep domain expertise and adopting a business outcome and process ownership approach, their intent is to become the single sourcing solution for outsourcing buyers.

These outsourcing companies have to demonstrate both breadth and depth in services as well as the ability to scale up and diversify their global footprint. The successful players in this category will make intensive capital investments for expanding facilities, acquiring local firms and establishing a presence in other locations. For providing a nearshore advantage, Mexico and Eastern Europe will be the favored destinations, while for tapping a cheaper labor pool, China, Vietnam and the Philippines will be the preferred offshore locations. Eventually these firms will be perceived as global players rather than offshore players with multi-site/multi-country operations.

On the other hand we are seeing the emergence of smaller niche service providers focusing on certain segments of knowledge services. These firms are in many ways a cross between consulting and BPO companies, defining a new category called Knowledge Process Outsourcing, or KPO. Counter to the popular practice of outsourcing only the non-core and non-critical functions, functions falling under KPO are actually often very core to the companies. This places a tremendous burden on the vendors to deliver results with minimal margin for error and ensure a labor pool that is highly skilled and stable. Another differentiator between BPO and KPO is that of length and nature of contracts. KPO contracts tend to be of shorter duration and non-transactional in nature and their billing models are usually T&M or fixed-price based. Even though the KPO market is growing at a healthy rate of 46 percent per annum, the service providers will find it more difficult to scale up because of the complexity and specialized requirements of functions performed and the difference in the sales and account management approach.

Another trend that is shaping the outsourcing sector is the convergence between ITO and BPO. Established IT outsourcing vendors, seeing a slowdown in IT growth, foresee that additional revenue streams can be garnered from existing clients by offering BPO services that are tightly integrated with their IT offerings. The premise is that clients are more comfortable working with their IT outsourcing partners and will trust them with their back office outsourcing needs as well. There is also the belief that working with the company's IT systems gives the vendor a better understanding of their business processes and service needs. Today, clients are sourcing out technology maintenance to Company A and the business process riding on that technology to Company B, which leads to a great deal of pain in the process. The evolution will lean towards converging both the ITO and BPO to a single entity, which in turn will handle the process in a completely different manner.

Once the convergence is in place, pricing in the industry will change. An increasing number of outsourcing projects are executed on a fixed cost basis, with defined cost/timelines for development projects and agreed-upon service levels for maintenance engagements. But with the convergence of ITO and BPO, service providers will now be required to truly partner with the client in their business, and the outsourcing will be reviewed on a "per transaction" or "result delivered" basis. This dramatic shift will transform the previous fixed cost into a variable cost, as the service provider will now play a role in the business revenues of the client company. Business services will move from just "services" to "services-on-demand," where the service offer will be tied in to the client's own profitability.

For example, in an insurance claim, one company runs the infrastructure that opens a window for the claim to be entered, another runs the processing and finally a third party applies business rules and domain knowledge to make adjudication on the claim. Convergence will collapse these numerous partners into one entity, generate one SLA and one cost-per-transaction, where the insurance company pays the service provider a fixed fee for every transaction successfully executed. Now, how profitable the service provider can be depends on how nimble it is in executing this transaction and engendering more orders from the client. This puts a different flavor to the relatively simpler price-per-seat or price-per-hour model, but it also allows both the clients and the vendors to create a win-win business scenario for eking better process efficiencies and higher value from the deal.

Jannie Tay
Vice Chairman
The Hour Glass
Singapore

The Asian Impact on Globalization

Question: *What do globalization and outsourcing mean to Singapore today?*

Tay: Singapore is mainly a services and financial center. It is no longer a manufacturing center. But there's something very interesting taking place here; because Singapore has signed a lot of Free Trade Agreements (FTA), a lot of companies outsource their final packaging to Singapore so the product can then be distributed to all these FTA countries without having to pay tariffs. For instance, one of my products is manufactured in Malaysia, but we're now looking to outsource to Singapore to do the final packaging so we can capitalize on the countries that have an FTA with Singapore.

Question: *So Singapore is almost becoming an integrated hub, where a lot of the details, negotiations and legal agreements are taking place for convenience, privacy and other fiduciary advantages because it's become a safety zone?*

Tay: Not only that, but we follow British law. In fact, a lot of the companies, even if they have dealings with China, prefer to use a Singapore company because they can trust the law and banking system in Singapore. European and U.S. companies state very clearly that they want the banking and the contracts to be executed in Singapore, even though the customer is from China. So it's another form of outsourcing.

Question: *What does China's rise mean to the developed economies? Is this a natural cycle?*

Tay: I would like to think that everything moves in the natural cycle. If you look at what Wal-Mart has done in retail, they were the first to outsource their products to China. They helped develop the capability, the design, the manufacturing, and the products for Wal-Mart from China. And if you use cost benefit and cost-efficiency as a marketing tool, Wal-Mart has been way ahead of everyone.

China is beginning to use its own technology and they understand they have to be competitive, even though it is one of the major importers from the rest of the world. If you look back at Japan 30 years ago, no one wanted Japanese goods. The same is true of Korean goods. But look at today's Samsung. Because China is more cost-effective, and they are using Western designs, they will create a brand of their own, which will be of similar quality but at lower price. At the end of day, that is what the consumer wants, and that will launch China as a major net exporter.

So I think in the globalization context, we have to know where our strength is, and we have to try to integrate this with partners in China so that we do not become competitors, but complementary to each other. In the end the globalization process will become more about sharing knowledge, markets, and profits. That would be the ideal market.

Question: *What does it take to be an entrepreneur in countries such as Malaysia, Thailand or India, and now starting up your own global outsourcing firm? To be a company such as InfoSys or Satyam, what must you do to maintain competitive advantage?*

Tay: India is unique. India has people who are very well educated, and they are very good in IT. I don't believe anyone can challenge India at this point. In Malaysia, unfortunately, English is not the first language, and that creates a setback. And in IT, you MUST have English as the first language. As for costs, no one can compete with India in outsourcing IT. Satyam and the others are trying to establish bases in Singapore, and from Singapore they can become the outsource center to the regions around here because it's closer to the customers. But there is no way we can ever beat what India has. They've got a greater head start, they've got a lot more PhDs who are very good in math, and their cost is very low. As for China, because the basic language in IT is English, they have a long way to go.

1.2

By **Mark Minevich**
Chief Strategy Officer,
Enamics, Inc.
Co-Chair, BTM Institute
Stamford, Connecticut

Dr. Frank-Jürgen Richter
President, Horasis
Former Director,
World Economic Forum, Asian Affairs
Member, BTM Institute
Geneva, Switzerland

Where the Action Is: Today and the Future

To understand globalization, it's important to understand the countries playing signifi-cant roles in the outsourcing marketplace. What follows are brief highlights of the countries and their positions.

India

India is the clear market leader, having the largest global out-sourcing volume at present. Its position is bolstered by specific government policies and a 20-year head start in the outsourcing industry. India will continue to provide software technology excel-lence with its "India Software Advantage," as the first mover advantage in software development offshoring, English-speaking personnel, lower costs, quality assurance, high-speed datacom links, and a 24-hour workday cycle.

Indian technology clusters are moving from software to systems design and on to a complete on-demand solution. If political processes and economic reform can be managed successfully, India's "middle class" of more than 200 million people—larger than the middle classes in either the United States or the European Union—presents an enormous market opportunity. India has good intellectual property protection and a strong engi-neering base. But its competitive advantage may be changing rapidly.

Local salaries in India are rising at 20 percent annually. It appears that outsourcing to India will be reduced dramatically within the next ten years as other countries mature and prepare to enter the global economy.

China

China will be India's major challenger. So far, China has focused on hardware development and manufacturing, but this is changing. The government, clients and suppliers are currently discovering and developing China as the next outsourcing heaven. According to Cyrill Eltschinger, CEO, I.T. United, "China's rates can undercut India's rates by 30 percent on average, and in many cases even higher. Most Asian-Pacific headquarters across industries are currently relocating to China from places like Singapore, Hong Kong, and Australia."

This will further spark the Chinese outsourcing industry. China already has started focusing on providing outsourcing services to markets in Asia and the Pacific—especially Japan. Chinese firms will create major new market opportunities in the next few years by strategically acquiring business outsourcing companies. In the next 10 to 20 years, China will continue to invest significantly in the development of world-class technology outsourcing centers with international satellite offices in Singapore, Russia and the United States. If political transition matches economic performance, then China's economy is poised to become the world's largest in purchasing power parity.

And yet, China is not without challenges. Major questions remain for the immediate and intermediate term. Intellectual property rights, a potential increase in the exchange rate, the inability to manage large projects in Western-management style, language skills and poor infrastructure will hamper China in the intermediate term. Time zone differences and travel distance will remain a challenge, as well as the cost of doing business there. William Sanford, Principal, Columbia Strategy Group, a New York-based secondary market advisory firm, explains, "China may soon experience a sharp withdrawal of outsourced product/service development and may merely be utilized as a market for the sale of foreign products. Political issues are quickly drawing China as a security concern, and the country has been steadily 'proprietizing' and developing internal substitute technologies."

Sanford adds, "China is currently undergoing massive growth and development, but such a quick transition will undoubtedly yield much corruption along the way, and perhaps growth will fail to compensate for the enormous debt incurred, resulting in a depression that may create many negative issues for U.S. companies."

Brazil

Brazil has huge potential due to its large population, the creativity of its engineers, and government programs supporting the IT outsourcing industry. Brazil already operates world-class innovation centers. In years to come, Brazil will continue to invest in innovation and research institutes to allow for the commercialization of technology and value-added outsourcing in IT and biotech. On the downside, like China, Brazil has serious risks such as major internal security issues that may disturb normal conduct. Furthermore, a "populist" movement has arisen against the United States, and may result in a backlash if outsourcing gets out of the closed innovation centers and into the main cities.

Eastern Europe

Other countries are getting closer as well—mainly from Eastern Europe—led by Russia, Hungary, and the Czech Republic. Armenia, Romania, and Ukraine will be among the future champions. Central and Eastern Europe will become an increasingly important offshoring destination for the E.U. and Nordic countries.

Russia and Eastern Europe will become more focused on high-end niche services. Juha Christensen, a former vice president of Microsoft and a key player in Psion, Symbian, and Macromedia, founded Sonopia in 2005. He says, "When we first looked at Ukraine, despite initial doubts, Ukraine is probably the best kept secret in the software development world. Their approach is very different from other contenders in that they have a proven track record in R&D, as well as exceptional software development skills."

In Russia and Ukraine, skilled programmers and advanced scientific institutions will provide the basis for a high-tech/IT industry sector for the rest of the world. In fact, the 20th century Cold War confrontation between the United States and the Soviet Union was a strong impetus for culture change, pushing Russia to be innovative with IT outsourcing. The offshoring capability will be visible through:

- High-level research in fundamental science.
- Rigorous science and math education.
- Managerial experience with complex projects.
- Innovative problem-solving spirit developed in response to the Soviet Union, its nuclear and space R&D during the Cold War.
- Descendants of Soviet military R&D facilities carrying on cutting edge, world-class science.

Russia's challenges include intellectual property, rule of law, corruption, and lower level processes. Within the next 10 to 20 years, intellectual property will become the important revenue generator for Russia and stimulate idea creation for exports to the rest of the globe.

A promising future in Russia and Ukraine is possible only if Russia is able to adopt a favorable market economy, attract more investments and experienced business management, and develop a rigorous approach to fight corruption.

Fundamental shifts must occur in the laws, courts, policing, and enforcement of IP rights and assets in countries such as Russia to reduce the legal risk of IP, and for those countries to become important revenue generators and stimulate ideas for the rest of the globe.

Africa

As noted by Dr. Joseph Okpaku, president and CEO, Telecom Africa Corporation, Africa, especially South Africa, Ghana, and French-speaking Senegal, are likely to emerge as outsourcing centers serving E.U. countries. In places like Tamarindo, for example, American companies like ReMax and Century 21 are buying land to build golf courses and resorts, while Delta and American Airlines have increased their flights to Liberia by a factor of five during the last twelve months. Because the risk of terrorism is at a minimum in this region, these destinations will become a staple of the American traveler.

North America/ Homeshoring/ Nearshoring

Customers are adding near-shore locations only a few hours away by air and usually in proximate time zones. For U.S. outsourcers, that's Latin America, where back-office operations are blossoming from Argentina to Costa Rica. European companies turn to Central and Eastern Europe.

William Sanford noted, "Many large U.S. companies pulled outsourcing of customer relations jobs from India and moved them back to the U.S. or Canada, because of language and accent barriers. Many customers have been very upset with their inability to communicate well with customer support representatives with strong accents, let alone the discomfort of speaking with someone who is not located in the same country. This prompted the large move of such operations back to local soil and Canada."

Andre Spatz, CIO of UNICEF, has noted that in the future, there will be a strong potential for the United States to become a major player in "homeshoring," "smart sourcing" and "nearsourcing" for higher value-added services, since this will be done in the U.S./Americas geographic region with its close proximity to customers, knowledge-based economy, and deep experience of managers and skilled professionals. It is further noted that the U.S. government and U.S. corporations must address the innovation policy and high cost of doing business to become a hotbed of high value-added innovative outsourcing in the future.

Transformational Outsourcing

Many executives are discovering that global outsourcing is really about corporate growth, making better use of skilled U.S. staff, and even job creation in the United States, not just cheap wages abroad. Labor savings from global outsourcing could accrue. However, bigger benefits could be gained in efficiency, productivity, quality and revenues in fully leveraging the global outsourcing talent pool. Work processes in practically every big department can now be outsourced and managed to some degree offshore. Once the transformation is complete, companies can deliver products faster at lower costs, and be better able to compete against anyone in the world. The future is a totally "disaggregated corporation" wherein every function not regarded as crucial is stripped away.

Regional Analysis

The following observations regarding geopolitical considerations are based on Dr. Okpaku's analysis of the future domination of the offshore outsourcing in the two blocs, Eastern Europe and Asia. According to Dr. Okpaku, "developing countries continue to sharpen their already reliable high-end programming capacity."

Eastern Countries

(Czech Republic, Ukraine, Slovakia, Latvia, Hungary, Armenia, Romania, Belarus, Russia, Poland)

The market size of Central and Eastern Europe is $3.3 billion. The former Soviet bloc influence tends to move faster to Western habits, culture and economy. Perestroika is definitively accepted, despite the wish of Russia to continue to "affiliate" them with the Ukraine-Ushchenko crisis. The people of these countries found the way to their economic independence by fully integrating a European-American system. They have huge technical potential because of their level of Western world comprehension as well as their educational system. The potential for innovation is definitively here. These people are hard, smart workers. Even Russia will make a slower move to the Western system to keep a role in the world economy and compete for integration and try to be as attractive as India or China. A problem for these countries is the price of technologies. In ten years, these countries will be absolutely ideal for high-core competency outsourcing and outstanding software innovation. The stimulation is definitively here.

Asian Countries

(Malaysia, Philippines, Singapore, India, Thailand, China, Vietnam, Sri Lanka, Indonesia)

The market size is $3.1 billion. China and India remain in the top spots in the future. Given the rapidly aging Chinese population, they will look for greener pastures such as Singapore. India, with a much younger population, will embrace as much outsourcing as possible within its own borders to sustain economic growth. India and China will definitively run the show in the next decade. It would be a trade-off between cost-effective ways to run their business and strategic control over sensitive technologies and price control over time.

Political instability and IP protection can be great concerns, but at the same time there is a significant opportunity to open wide, new markets and export products by increasing the buying capacity of these countries. After being colonized and revolutionized, these countries have the capacity to emerge and are showing economic strength.

Hispanic Countries
(Brazil, Mexico, Costa Rica, Chile, Argentina)

The market size is $2.9 billion. These nations still have educational and infrastructure problems. They can be attractive for specific types of jobs, such as customer services and support, but there are language limitations and an unmotivated workforce. Countries like Costa Rica tend to develop tourism as a greater source of revenue. Another important factor attracting American companies is that the Costa Rican tax system is very friendly to foreign investors.

Western European Countries
(Ireland, Scotland, France)

These countries are marginal players in the offshore outsourcing arena. Despite their high level of education and cultural integration, which brings talented people to the table, the cost of labor and labor favoring legislatures are limiting outsourcing here. In fact, these talented populations tend to move away from their own countries—France, for example, has 10 percent of its population living in Canada and the United States. They are also starting outsourcing processes for the same reasons that make them unattractive. Plus, conditions are leading to a European brain drain as other countries offer better wages. Currently large numbers of French and German workers are moving away from their own countries to immigrate to U.K., Canada, and the United States.

High-cost/high-quality outsourcing centers like Ireland, Canada and Singapore are increasingly focusing on high-end services like complex programming and R&D innovative initiatives. Their long-term competitiveness, however, is shrinking as the cost of doing outsourcing business becomes unattractive. Singapore and Chile are useful for companies looking for low-risk and maximum return. They also are facing competition from Eastern Europe.

Middle East/Africa

We would note the complete absence of Middle Eastern countries, except Israel. World disparities on that level are creating major clashes of cultures. But Egypt, Jordan, United Arab Emirates, Ghana, Tunisia, South Africa, Turkey, Morocco are up and comers in the global outsourcing game.

Ramalinga Raju
Founder and Chairman
Satyam Computer Services, Ltd.
Secunderabad, India

Issues Impacting High-Tech Companies in India

Question: *What was your inspiration when you started your business?*

Raju: In the late '80s when we looked at the opportunity of IT outsourcing, we entered the industry without a clear recognition of what commercial opportunities this may bring to the table, but this industry appeared to be a very exciting industry to be in. We believed it was exciting because it had something to do with knowledge, it had something to do with technology, and that it was something that addressed the creative aspects of operation. Therefore we entered the industry more as a hobby rather than recognizing this to be a growing business and to be what it is today.

Question: *How do the outsourcing providers of the future look like?*

Raju: Companies like IBM or Accenture may have stepped up their operations in India and other low-cost and high-quality human resource countries. While this is the case, the talent they are accessing in these low-cost countries is still a small percentage of overall company size and in most cases it is less than 10 percent.

The challenge for a company like Satyam is to be able to do it fast and to do it well. Our view of things going forward strategically is to offer to global customers services that in every respect far exceed in terms of innovation the services we provide and the value we create now.

Question: *How do you view the relationship between a company such as Satyam and global customers?*

Raju: In the last five years or so, we had to move towards establishing relationships with the customers as opposed to executing projects for them as a large system integrator servicing fairly large sizable companies. For example, most of our revenue comes from the Fortune 500 companies; therefore, the companies we service are large, and the needs that they have are wide ranging. And, therefore, from a customer perspective they are giving much greater importance to a relationship, and they are willing to invest in relationships. They want to work with fewer companies, but they also want to work with companies much more intimately, so that the service provider is able to understand their needs better, and understand their customers better to more efficiently service them. Therefore, in a way things have moved from a project mode to a relationship mode to almost operating at a strategic level as though the relationship is a partnership. These are the trends we have seen. The larger companies are not looking to going to ten different niche players. From what we have observed, regardless of the nature of the company, its customers are looking to build relationships with fewer companies and have stronger relationships with those fewer companies.

Question: What is your feeling today when you travel to the U.S.? Do you feel any kind of "India-bashing," people saying that India is stealing American jobs?

Raju: Much of what we do is service global customers. Less than 3 percent of our revenue comes from services we provide today within India. In fact, India is not being serviced as a market from India, but from Singaporea—the headquarters for our Asia-Pacific region—and India is part of that region. Therefore the customer base is global, not Indian. Even from that perspective, Satyam is not an Indian company. The fact that a company like Satyam does well means that an investor in the United States does well and an investor in the United States is unwilling to compromise on his returns so that his compromised position would help to create a few more jobs within the United States, because he is looking for efficient companies to provide better returns. It is not about one country versus another. In my opinion it is about investor and customer versus an employee.

Question: What is the economic model of the future?

Raju: The commoditization process in the service economy has been operative to a much greater extent than the commoditization we witnessed in the manufacturing world. The cycle times are significantly reduced, and they are having a major impact on value creation. We are finding that the compression in the cycle times, and the gap between the birth of an idea and the time leading not only to products emerging out of it, but them getting produced, is very quick. That is a trend that we can expect to continue.

One thing I have personally been able to recognize is the fact that the importance of ideas is growing, the importance of intellectual capital is growing, and therefore the importance of innovation is growing. Just to give you some examples, as much as existing products and services are getting commoditized much faster, we also are finding that the birth of newer services is taking place much more rapidly, and the birth of new services, new ideas is driven naturally by innovative ways of looking at things, and that is becoming paramount to survival of any organization. But if they are not introducing sufficiently newer, workable ideas, they are likely to lose out in a marketplace, because as organizations they may not be sufficiently supported by the products and services they are dealing with in a commoditized space, because the commoditized space is a limited margin opportunity.

1.3

By **Simon Bell**
Director
A.T. Kearney Global Business Policy Council
Alexandria, Virginia

Janet Pau
Consultant
A.T. Kearney Global Business Policy Council
Alexandria, Virginia

Augustine Chin
Consultant
A.T. Kearney
Alexandria, Virginia

China as an Offshore Destination

China has long been the world's factory and is already the top producer of various IT-related products. In recent years, demand in related services such as IT offshoring (ITO) and business process offshoring (BPO) has been growing, as companies consider China a viable candidate for their global offshore strategies. This chapter takes a deeper look at China, assessing its attractiveness as a destination for ITO and BPO services, highlighting findings from a recent study by the global management consulting firm, A.T. Kearney, based on interviews with approximately 50 corporate executives and government leaders, supplemented with secondary research. The findings indicate that China is most popular as an ITO and BPO offshore destination for companies serving their Asia Pacific markets, and Chinese providers are building capabilities to capture multinationals' offshoring business. This chapter also offers perspective on how China is doing in its efforts to become a competitive offshore destination for ITO and BPO services, identifying three key areas for improvement: intellectual property protection, education and language proficiency, and management skills.

Introduction to China

A vast and growing country, China beckons and businesses listen, wondering how they will manage to capitalize on the combination of growth, investment, developing capitalism and fresh technology that is changing the country's face.

China is an appealing target. The seventh-largest economy in the world with a 2004 GDP of US$1.6 trillion, its real gross domestic product has expanded at an average of 9 percent a year for the past 25 years. And every week, more than US$1 billion of foreign direct investment flows into the country. Long known as the world's factory, China is now becoming an attractive offshore location for ITO and BPO. These markets are expected to grow as the Chinese government continues to entice foreign multinationals with tax and tariff incentives, subsidies, and administrative convenience.

Increasingly China is becoming part of multinationals' offshore strategies, as firms consider the country an option from which to serve the region as well as China's growing domestic market. Similarly, Chinese-based ITO and BPO providers are working to improve their capabilities with an eye toward the West. The goal is to move beyond providing services to companies in the Asia Pacific and begin capturing business from multinationals in the United States and Europe.

Fast emerging challenger

China-based ITO and BPO providers are strongest in the Asia Pacific market due to geographic proximity and China's language and cultural affinity to nearby nations. For example, due to a large concentration of people in northeastern China who speak Japanese, offshore clients are predominantly from Japan. In fact, more than 60 percent of China's offshore software development revenue is from companies based in Japan. Dell Computer and CSK Corp are opening Japanese-language call centers in the northeastern city of Dalian. And according to Dalian Hi-Think, one of China's largest software exporters, more than 70 percent of revenues are from Japanese clients.

"The Japanese feel comfortable dealing with the Chinese," explains an executive with a leading Chinese ITO company. "It's easy for us to gain consensus and build trust with our Japanese clients."

In 2004, China's ITO market was roughly US$0.6 billion, with almost all activities centered around lower-end services, such as IT activities that involve modular programming (developing a smaller component of a larger application), and testing. Most of the offshoring work performed in China today is for the financial services and high-tech industries. Within the next four years, China's ITO business is expected to grow between 40 to 50 percent annually, potentially becoming a US$3 billion industry by 2008.

The number of BPO service providers establishing a presence in China is also on the rise. Most current BPO activities in China are in back-office processes, such as customer support (call centers), finance and accounting, payables, and some research and development. In 2004, China's BPO market was about US$0.2 to US$0.3 billion. Over the next five years, industry insiders expect China to increase its BPO market by 20 to 30 percent annually.

China is becoming a world-class player

Reasons for sending IT and business processes offshore remain the same whether the destination is China, India or anywhere else. Offshoring can result in significant savings in operational and labor costs. For example, an entry level IT programmer with English-speaking skills based in Beijing or Shanghai makes roughly US$7,000 per year—comparable to that of an entry-level programmer in a major city in India but significantly less than the average salary of US$48,000 earned by an entry level programmer in the United States.

In addition, a major factor contributing to the attractiveness of India and China—and to a lesser extent Russia, Brazil and the Philippines—is the sheer breadth and depth of the skill base in terms of education levels. In recent years, the Chinese government has moved aggressively to improve technical education, both to serve the booming economy and to make the country less reliant on foreigners. The move has paid off. In 2004, China's universities cranked out 2.8 million graduates, 300,000 of whom are engineers—almost ten times the number in Germany. India, by comparison, graduates some 3.1 million students from its colleges every year; the United States turns out 1.3 million college graduates a year.

China's large domestic market and potential for economic growth also make it a strategic offshore location for multinational corporations (MNCs) planning to serve new markets in the future. This is a different focus than that of India, whose market is dominated by export demand. Companies with offshore centers in

China plan to use these centers later as a foothold for serving the regional and domestic outsourcing industry. In fact, when Genpact (formerly GE Capital International Services) initially entered China, its main goal was to support customers in its Japanese and Korean markets. Genpact's China unit, based in Dalian, is a remote processing operation that handles back-office functions for 20 different GE businesses. Because the China market was growing so fast, Genpact now supports Greater China's domestic outsourcing market as well. "China is unique in that China itself could become a big business process outsourcing market," explains Pavan Dhamija, business development and transitions leader, Genpact. "We hope to use the BPO facilities in China to support not only Japan and Korea, but also China itself, and eventually other Asia Pacific regions."

China's entry into the World Trade Organization is spurring further investment. Western companies have established more than 130 R&D facilities in China, and the government has established five special economic zones (SEZs) and fifteen national software industrial parks to facilitate more investment in the country. Cisco Systems announced an expansion plan that is largely aimed at serving China's booming economy. In a news conference, John Chambers, Cisco's chief executive, told reporters that China was well on the way to becoming the world's technology hub as he revealed plans for building his company's first research center in the country. Chambers said that over the next decade, half of Cisco's top twelve business partners and half of its main competitors would come from China. "China will become the IT center of the world," he said.

China's role is expanding among other companies' global business strategies. For example, aircraft maker Airbus is setting up an engineering facility in China to strengthen its R&D strategy. France Télécom opened its first wholly owned R&D facility in China to pave the way to future expansion in the world's biggest telecom market. "This allows us to become one of the first foreign telecom operators to set up an R&D center in China," said Pascal Viginier, executive vice president of France Télécom Group, in an interview with *China Daily*.

India and China

In a country-to-country comparison of factors driving ITO and BPO location decisions, India retains a commanding lead over China largely due to experience, scale, and quality perceptions. China offers similar cost advantages and workforce availability, but still lacks India's depth and breadth of experience in offshore services and hence a strong cadre of firms with global scale and quality certifications.

Still, the rapid growth of the services offshoring sector in India has led to tough competition for qualified professionals and wage inflation in cities such as Bangalore and New Delhi. China is not so much a substitute for India as it is a complement. China's market potential, growing services sector, and increasing workforce expertise are prompting even Indian outsourcers to consider China a prime offshore destination. Tata Consultancy Services (TCS), an Indian software solutions firm, unveiled its China operations in mid-2002, citing, among several reasons, the ability to focus on providing disaster recovery, risk mitigation and offshore services for its clients in Japan. More recently in 2005, TCS formed a strategic alliance with the Sino-India Cooperative Office (SICO) and Microsoft in China to support both the global and Chinese IT outsourcing markets. The joint venture, which will be located in Beijing's Zhongguancun Software Park, was to begin its operations in early 2006.

In August 2005 another Indian IT giant, Infosys, announced its plans to establish centers in Shanghai and Hangzhou for training, research and delivery, as well as expand its Chinese staff from 250 to 6,000 employees within five years. TCS and Infosys are also among the growing number of companies, such as Accenture and BearingPoint, that plan to leverage China for domestic growth opportunities and to meet the growing IT needs of global companies in China and other countries in Asia Pacific. As Indian firms expand their global footprint and compete with MNCs, China is becoming an integral part of their growth strategies.

At the end of the day, the most successful global companies are those that adopt multi-country strategies, moving operations to multiple locations as a way to diversify risks and tap into the broadest possible pool of global talent.

Government role

The historical role the Chinese government played in growing China's software and IT services sector could not be more different than that of India. India's initial success in the sector prior to the 1990s was not the result of deliberate policy, but rather circumstantial factors. The government originally invested in elite education centers such as the famed Indian Institutes of Technology to drive domestic development, but limited local opportunities and growing demand in the United States led many talented young Indians to seek opportunities there, thus establishing India's reputation and nurturing the first Indian IT firms. The government and NASSCOM have only in recent years played a more prominent role in the continued development of the sector.

In contrast, China's central government has supported the development of the software and IT services sector since the early 1980s, when the Ministry of Electronics defined software development as an industry. By the early 1990s, China's economy had opened up with widespread use of personal computers and local government offices established to support and foster software development. These offices were soon followed by the development of software parks in the late 1990s that host both foreign and domestic firms.

China's central and municipal governments offer preferential treatment (e.g., tax incentives and quality certification subsidies) to qualified software companies. In 2000, China's State Council issued Document Number 18, which provides tax incentives and export promotion assistance for software companies and encourages development of software clusters.

In addition, foreign direct investment has poured into China, especially in the hardware sector, and has flourished in the wake of China's WTO entry in 2002. The Chinese ITO market is currently fragmented and focuses mostly on lower-end software development and IT services. But with the liberalization of the services sector under the WTO, and increasing partnerships between multinationals and homegrown companies, more sophisticated services capabilities in domestic and export markets will likely develop.

Shattering Western mantras

Although China's growing attractiveness as an offshore destination is evidenced by improvements in factory conditions and industry demand, the country is still working to change negative perceptions of skeptics. China-based providers are working with the government to change these misconceptions, beginning with pointing out how the country has stepped up its infrastructure and technology improvements.

Compared to India, China's infrastructure is far stronger than people think. Because manufacturers have established production facilities in China for the past twenty or so years, the government has made significant investments in roads and rail systems. Highway and rail construction are being accelerated under the current five-year plan to adequately support the growing merchandise shipments being sent to second- and third-tier cities. Next on the agenda is connecting inland second- and third- tier cities to coastal areas and ports.

By the same token, China's software parks guarantee an uninterrupted power supply, with most equipped with backup power generators. Also, these parks and high-tech corridors provide a single point of contact, which cuts down on red tape, bureaucracy and approval time, and encourages an industrial cluster effect. "Shanghai (Pudong) is hands down better than India," asserts one survey participant.

China's telecommunications system is improving as well. For example, the bandwidth of China's international Internet broadband connection is expanding. It is now 83 gigabits per second (Gbps)—more than 235 times the bandwidth China had just five years ago, with international connection points in Beijing, Shanghai and Shenzhen.

Making the China connection

While China and its leading companies continue their work to shake off the perception of weakness in the areas of infrastructure and telecommunications, there are three areas that deserve further attention and improvement:

1. Protecting intellectual property—is it really an issue?
The question of IP piracy is an important one for many Western companies. However, for companies pursuing lower-level IT off-

shoring initiatives in China, IP piracy should not be a major factor. IP piracy is always a risk, but it can be managed.

"It's known to everyone in the industry that incidents of IP problems with a client would cause significant damage to a vendor's reputation and future business," one executive explains. "Therefore, most vendors implement internal systems to ensure IP protection."

Protecting intellectual property is high on the Chinese government's agenda. With lost sales from counterfeiting, the government is moving quickly to ensure that property rights are respected. For example, China's IP legislative framework conforms with TRIPS (Trade Related aspects of Intellectual Property Rights), which is the WTO's standard for IP laws. China's constitution provides guiding principles for IP legislation. Civil law specifically states that IP is a major civil rights issue, and infringement on trademarks, patents, and copyrights is a criminal offense.

The Chinese government and local industries realize the importance of IP protection to continued economic growth, and there are indications that China is cracking down on the counterfeiters. In September 2004, China vowed strong official action against intellectual property rights violations, including a targeted crackdown and tougher anti-piracy penalties. The crackdown, which began in September 2004, targeted trademark, copyright and patent-law violations in fifteen provinces and municipalities including Beijing and Shanghai.

For companies considering operations in China, tackling the piracy problem will hinge on selecting the right business strategy. For IP-sensitive activities, companies tend to adopt a "captive" business model (setting up their own facilities in the offshore location) for IP sensitive activities and perform regular internal IP audits. Companies also build high-tech firewalls between their China operations and other facilities that house data-sensitive materials. Companies that establish joint venture operations in China, or outsource to a local provider, typically conduct rigorous due diligence on the providers' internal IP protection policies and systems, and define strict guidelines for the selected vendor.

2. Improving language proficiency and education
The single biggest challenge for China is to increase English language proficiency. Although numerous English-language profi-

cient students graduate from China universities, most have solid writing and reading skills but are still not fluent English speakers. The reason, according to interviewees in the A.T. Kearney study, is there are not enough opportunities to talk with native speakers. "How can we increase our language proficiency if we fail to practice," laments one executive.

Interestingly, China's lack of European language abilities does not emerge as a major concern for employers. What counts most to employers are the same qualities and experience that matter in any supply market—workers with value-added functional skills, a track record of achievement, and an ability to execute the job successfully. And among local professionals, these qualities are becoming increasingly common.

As the Chinese improve their English language capabilities, more U.S. and European companies will likely consider China as an attractive offshore locale. Already, the country is increasing its emphasis on English training in schools, and has more than 100,000 English teachers in its IT colleges. In Shanghai, some elementary school students are receiving math and science instruction in English.

Education in China is by no means limited to improving language proficiency. China is rapidly increasing its number of college graduates, which provides a huge potential pool of professional talent. There are currently about 700,000 IT professionals in the IT services industry. About 80,000 new IT professionals entered the industry in 2003, representing 60 percent more than 2002, when 50,000 graduated.

"Like other successful IT houses, we build into our China-based growth strategy various cooperative programs with leading universities and technology institutes," explains Cyrill Eltschinger, CEO of I.T. United. "This effectively shortens the time required to bring up to speed a fresh college graduate into an independent programmer from about one year to several months."

After many years of government efforts, China is experiencing an excess of university graduates. In 2004, 2.8 million college graduates hit the job market, an increase of 680,000 over the same period a year earlier. In 2005 it grew to a record of 3.4 million. The unemployment rate among university graduates was 25 percent in 2005, meaning that at least 850,000 graduates joined the ranks of the unemployed upon leaving school. "There are simply not enough jobs to absorb the huge number of people with bachelor's and master's degrees," explains an executive with *Foreign Policy* magazine. "Needless to say, this is a huge pool of talent that offshore service providers can tap into."

Indeed, when explaining Cisco's US$32 million investment in establishing an R&D facility to build voice over Internet protocol (VoIP) technology in China, CEO John Chambers cited China's good university system and the pool of talent from which to recruit researchers as a key reason for moving into China. He also noted the government's business-friendly policies.

In recent years, the Chinese government has been accelerating its efforts to create a first-class high-tech labor force. China is providing coding training to workers, and cities are helping local firms cover the costs of acquiring the Carnegie Mellon Capability Maturity Model (CMM) certification. Multinationals such as IBM and Indian firms are also providing training in partnership with the government.

There is still room for improvement, however. For instance, only two providers in China, Lenovo (formerly Legend) and Shanghai Wicresoft, have adopted COPC (Customer Operations Performance Center) standards. COPC, an emerging standard in assessing contact-center performance, has become the performance standard in more than 30 countries and has certified some 300 business locations around the world.

3. Improving management skills

With education levels on the rise, China-based ITO and BPO providers are now in a race to improve the business management skills of key employees and to increase the pool of high-caliber project managers. More than 80 percent of executives interviewed listed project management skills as a key success factor for operations in China.

Today, the challenge for China-based providers is to update the skills within their middle-management ranks. Managers who have been accustomed to more bureaucratic and hierarchical organizations need help to adapt to modern business management principles. Unfortunately, many are overwhelmed by the fast-changing environment and the realities of a market economy. Many

Chinese managers grew up expecting never to change jobs and only know how to do one thing.

Multinationals in China have invested heavily in management training programs to address these issues. IBM and Motorola are both experienced in such programs. Motorola has a China Accelerated Management Program (CAMP) where managers are trained in global business concepts. In addition, firms are focusing on training "softer" skills such as accountability, initiative, curiosity, business perspective, effective communications, team building, and appropriate business conduct.

Also, more multinationals are interested in hiring Chinese "homegrown" professionals. They are motivated by a growing market of local talent that is better able to handle such roles, and by the bottom-line implications. "Although companies always tell us they are looking for the most suitable person for a position, the cost factor inevitably has a major impact in many final hiring decisions," explains Kevin Wang, an executive with Wang & Li, a China-based human resources firm, on the company's Web site.

Local management talent is becoming far more commonplace in China, thanks to the multinationals and their extensive training programs. Motorola and IBM alone have almost 10,000 employees in China, including hundreds of people who have been trained to handle middle management roles and responsibilities.

However, local managers with a global perspective are still relatively scarce. China has long counted on managerial talent from Hong Kong and other parts of Asia, who have brought know-how on how to handle regional customers. But to satisfy a broadening client base including domestic and foreign customers, a new breed of Chinese managers is required. They need to be able to advance into managerial roles with responsibilities for overseeing a multinational's global operations—from China.

For now, returnees to mainland China are becoming popular new hires within more senior management ranks. Nearly 64 percent of companies in a recent study by Hewitt Associates are currently employing returnees. And, according to Wang & Li, about 50 percent of director level positions and above are filled by expatriates who return home with both high-caliber business skills and international exposure.

"Chinese returnees with extensive experience in studying and living in other countries are particularly helpful to our business dealings with western companies," explains an interviewee.

According to interviewees in A.T. Kearney's study, many firms that hire returnees count on them to share their management skills and experience with their Chinese colleagues. Also, more firms are introducing mentoring programs to help younger workers move into the executive ranks. Workers are matched with experienced expatriates or former employees of multinational firms. As more workers retire, and younger workers move into management positions, workers with western-style business skills will become increasingly valuable. These skills are particularly relevant to companies that are in the business of providing BPO and ITO services to global customers.

The regions of China

After choosing China as an offshore destination, the next question is where to locate within China. Companies often make this decision based on insights learned from the pioneers—firms that have both experience and success in certain cities. Not surprisingly, the majority of firms head for the major, or so-called tier-one cities.

For example, about 90 percent of China's offshore software development revenue is derived from Beijing, Shanghai, Liaoning province, and Guangdong province. Beijing and Shanghai are the preferred location for BPO captive units, with HP and HSBC supporting their clients in Japan and Korea from these cities, and Cisco setting up its new R&D center in Shanghai. Both cities are attractive because they have an ample supply of young college graduates who speak a variety of languages. In addition, tier-one cities boast solid infrastructures. In fact, when Cisco CEO John Chambers was asked "Why Shanghai?" he was quick to note the "excellent infrastructure."

In recent years, several other tier-one cities have become attractive destinations within China. For example, Dalian is a top destination for BPO service providers serving the Asia Pacific region. The city boasts many workers who speak Asian languages, and it offers strong local government support. "Dalian is only three hours to Japan, two hours to Seoul and one hour to Beijing," says an interviewee. "The location itself is very advantageous."

Similarly, Guangzhou and Shenzhen are becoming home to most call centers serving Hong Kong customers. Shenzhen has stronger local government support and better infrastructure than Guangzhou, but both cities boast an abundance of Cantonese and Mandarin speakers.

China presents a unique opportunity for MNCs to support their Asia Pacific operations or increase their China presence. The country has the necessary cultural similarities, Asian language speakers, and a geographic advantage. Over the next few years, the ITO and BPO sectors are expected to experience rapid growth, especially as Chinese providers pursue and gain more MNC clients. Providers in China will also grow through partnerships with multinational companies that are interested in supporting the Chinese domestic market.

Will China overtake India? Not in the short to medium term. As mentioned earlier, India currently has a commanding lead over China in terms of skill sets and experience in ITO and BPO. India's exports of ITO and BPO services are more than 20 times greater than China's. Based on historical trajectories, the China ITO sector lags India's by about six to 10 years, while the BPO sector is about 10 to 14 years behind India's.

However, China may be able to accelerate its learning curve and close the gap by learning from the India experience. Some Chinese providers are already doing so by building strategic alliances with Indian companies. For example, Broaden Gate, one of China's top service providers, has a joint venture with Zensar, a leading Indian ITO provider, to support the Chinese market. In the joint venture, Zensar provides expertise in areas where China lags, such as in project management.

In the longer term, China is expected to emerge as an offshore powerhouse as it continues to improve its competitiveness, dispelling misconceptions and addressing weaknesses in IP protection, English language proficiency, and management skills. As the globalization trend continues, the question will no longer be whether a multinational corporation should offshore processes to

India or China, but how it can incorporate both countries into its global business strategy to achieve the optimal mix of savings, service quality, and scale.

References

1   Statistics from World Bank, China Statistics Bureau and US-China Business Council, respectively

2   "The China Reality Check," *NeoIT*, June 2005.

3   *The Wall Street Journal*, July 15, 2004.

4   National Center for Education Statistics.

5   "Cisco Sees China as Center of World Tech Market," Reuters, via *News.com*, November 2, 2004.

6   China Internet Network Information Center.

7   *The Wall Street Journal*, September 7, 2004.

8   "China emerging as a threat to India BPO," *GlobalSourcing*, June 2004

9   China Software Industry Association.

10 "Chinese university graduates squeezed by job, love as commencement nears," *People's Daily*, June 21, 2005.

Osvald Bjelland
Chairman
Xyntéo, LTD and
the Performance Theater Foundation
Oslo, Norway

The Nordic Evolution

Question: *How have Nordic countries approached outsourcing?*

Bjelland: Norway was the second poorest country in Europe after the Second World War. Today, it is one of the most affluent and has a tremendous standard of living, but it is also very expensive to live there. Today, major Nordic industries and companies have outsourced production, with many turning to lower-cost Eastern European countries.

The Norwegian offshore oil and gas industry has evolved from nothing. To build cost-competitive vessels for the Norwegian continental shelf and for the offshore business, the supply industry started building modules. For example, to build an oil rig, part of the rig is built in Spain or even Poland or Yugoslavia, and then the modules are brought together to be assembled and a very efficient vessel is produced. This method has been known in the oil and offshore sector for some time and has evolved. In recent years, when it has come to manufacturing a luxury yacht, a growth sector with increasing demand for these products in many European countries, some companies

and executives are investing in small shipyards in China where they build the yachts and then export them to Europe. A large Nordic shipbuilder has created joint ventures and built partnerships in Korea. As a result, this company has actually emerged from being a shipping company to becoming a logistics company.

Question: *What has been the response in Nordic countries to the adoption of outsourcing?*

Bjelland: People are concerned about how to maintain the same or even better quality by outsourcing, as well as how to create the same team spirit in the staff when you don't own the company. How do you stimulate internal competition between your own staff and people you outsource to? There is this famous example from one German company: they outsourced to their own business in Poland. The German engineers were so upset about the lost jobs in Germany that they burned the drawings. It's a lesson for any executive. Even outsourcing work within your own company will produce competition between your original staff and your new staff—whether you own them or they are outsourced. The executive must also ask whether the partner you outsource to is able to recruit the right people with the right motivation.

Question: *Are large multinational companies, whether they are based in Sweden, Norway or the United States, creating their own outsourcing zones?*

Bjelland: Creating your own outsourcing zone is one way to avoid many risks. But outsourcing is not a one-way street. We see outsourcing from Nordics or U.K. to India; that is one way. But we also see outsourcing from Eriksson to IBM and from Telenor to IBM. Distances are less relevant than they used to be. What is needed is a new generation of expertise and competencies, both in due diligence in preparing for outsourcing and for follow through and execution on a strategy.

The huge challenge, whether you are a small or large company, is philosophical: are you genuinely there to serve customers? I know several companies where they haven't made that commitment yet. There are many service companies today mostly surviving by manipulating assets rather than genuinely adding short or medium term value to customers.

1.4

*By **Atefeh Riazi***
Worldwide CIO and Senior Partner
Ogilvy and Mather Worldwide
New York, New York

Selecting Sourcing Destinations

Outsourcing IT functions by non-IT firms has failed 70 percent of the time it has been tried, because too often it is undertaken for the wrong reasons.

It could be that there is not a good fit between the IT staff or the IT department with the end users, a competitor has recently outsourced the IT function (a copy-cat approach), or that outsourcing seems like a painless way to cut costs—the shareholders believe replacing IT staff with outside services, where presumably the cost can be easier to shed if business worsens, will be the right approach. Or maybe it's just that the outsourcer itself sells a good story.

I have been in many situations in which outsourcing of all kinds was necessary or took place. Some I would rather not talk about. But after 20 years of being in this business, I have reached a point where I see that "selective" sourcing is what works. In terms of the IT function in general businesses, where IT is not the firm's core competency, this means keeping critical IT functions, such as security and some other critical applications, in-house, while looking open-mindedly at everything else. It is essential to determine if there is any task that would be better performed by an outside firm specializing in that function, and so able to offer a cheaper and/or higher quality service.

When selective sourcing does uncover a possible role for an outsourcer, there are seven rules to follow for success:

Rule 1

Diagnose the problems before making a decision. Sounds simple, if not simple-minded, but a decision to outsource precedes analysis with surprising frequency in American business. There are no no-brainers here; every situation requires careful thought. Review and diagnose all aspects of the problem—not only the technical and economic issues, but also the social, cultural and personal dimensions.

Rule 2

Apply chemistry. Chemistry has been crucial in my hiring decisions and partner selection. Some may call it intuition; some may call it cultural alignment. We are ultimately emotional beings pretending to be analytical decision-makers, justifying emotional decisions with logic. So, what makes a partnership truly work is the chemistry between the two partners.

Rule 3

Focus on value, not cost. Some global companies have visions of techies in the less-developed world working for a pittance, with the main reason for much of IT outsourcing being cost reduction. But cost is only one element of value, and with the salaries in these countries rising, retaining skilled individuals is becoming more difficult every day. We must balance this search for greater cost efficiency with values such as quality, time, responsiveness, and other variables we normally take into account for high-end services we've always procured in the marketplace.

Rule 4

Negotiate and continuously engage in dialogue. If you are thinking of throwing your requirements over the wall and waiting for the completed service to be eventually tossed back over, think again. You have to be in constant touch with your outsourcer.

Rule 5

Build a true partnership by practicing reciprocity. Many of the current outsourcing deals are nothing more than purchaser-provider relationships. True partnerships are those where both the client and the vendor are focused on common business objectives and accept outcome-based compensation. Are we after a certain number of help desk calls resolved, or are we after happy and productive end-users? I much prefer to pay for the latter. And to get this, we must treat our partner as we wish to be treated.

Rule 6

Shrink the distance. All else equal, some companies are much more comfortable outsourcing to a local vendor, less comfortable with a vendor a few hundred miles away who speaks the same language and operates within a similar culture, and even less inclined to go with a vendor a few thousand miles away who speaks a different language and comes from a completely different culture. We like familiarity and closeness, and often shy away from distant relationships. It is human nature, but not necessarily good business decision-making. Virtual relationships need to be consummated face-to-face in order to work. Hop a plane and go meet your partners.

Rule 7

Ensure security. Due diligence, of course, requires an extensive examination of the outsourcer's ability to maintain security. This remains a major consideration even for non-critical functions. It is one question I ask of every client of a candidate outsourcer: were there any breaches when the outsourcer performed that function with you? Even a hint of something having happened is enough to rule out the candidate.

Alan Ganek
Chief Technology Officer, Tivoli Software
Vice President, Autonomic Computing
IBM
Somers, New York

Outsourcing and Automation

Question: *How should companies best manage their global IT systems?*

Ganek: Companies need to have much more granular understanding of the processes, as well as the various individuals and technologies, and how they fit together. What we call IT service management, which provides that framework for thinking and executing, is very important. Every company that looks at outsourcing has to decide what they consider commodities they can easily buy, as well as the heart of their competitive edge that they want to make sure they do superior to anyone else. Those things might still be outsourced, but they would not be outsourced to a commodity provider; they have to be outsourced or implemented in-house in a way that allows them to leverage their strength.

Question: *Outsourcing might be conducive to introducing open standards— how do IT companies like IBM embrace open standards?*

Ganek: The culture of openness is the foundation on which we build lasting relationships. Open standards help minimize dependence on software as a service—economic growth excels in the context of interlinked global communities. At IBM, we believe in open standards, support platforms, lead standards activities, and put assets out in the open. We have thousands of business partners and alliances at all levels from huge companies like Cisco to tiny small companies we work with around the world. IBM already outsources many processes to other companies like human resources, insurance and healthcare and other specialist organizations. The belief in and exercise of open standards is outsourcing at is best.

Question: *What is autonomic computing?*

Ganek: The goal of autonomic computing is to help customers build more automated IT infrastructures to reduce costs, improve up-time, and make the most efficient use of increasingly scarce support skills. Autonomic computing is the ability of systems to be more self-managing. The term "autonomic" comes from the autonomic nervous system, which controls many organs and muscles in the human body. Usually, we are unaware of its workings because it functions in an involuntary, reflexive manner.

Question: *Is autonomic computing a sophisticated way to outsource IT services?*

Ganek: Autonomic computing efforts are all about freeing customers to focus more on their business and less on their IT infrastructure. And yes, in a way, this is a very sophisticated variation of IT outsourcing. I think one of the breakthroughs happening now is an understanding of IT as a business: the elements of the business, the roles and responsibilities, and approaching self-managing capability in that context.

Question: *How will autonomic computing impact major offshore outsourcers? For instance, will it impact margins, SLAs, processes that can be outsourced?*

Ganek: Autonomic computing introduces technologies, standards, and IT management processes that make IT solutions more self-managing, reducing the labor-intensive aspects of coping with the complexity while improving availability and time to value. The advent of autonomic capabilities will shift the focus of the IT staff from tedious tasks to higher value functions and ultimately reduce the relative proportion of labor as a percentage of total IT cost. This direction will shift the primary differentiation from labor cost to labor skill. Offshore outsourcers are already increasingly shifting focus from operations and support to development and design, and I expect this trend to continue.

1.5

By *Stefan Inzelstein*
President
Indiggo Associates Inc.
Aventura, Florida

Creating Sustainable Relationships in Global Ventures

It is hard to think of a point in history as loaded with rapid, large-scale fundamental change as the last fifteen to eighteen years. We've seen the crumbling of the Soviet empire, the end of apartheid in South Africa, the emergence of global terrorism, the creation of an enlarged European community, the transformation of China and India, the virtual elimination of trade barriers, the rise to preeminence of the personal computer and, of course, the unprecedented impact of the Internet—a deeply social, much more than technological phenomenon—on virtually every aspect of life. A key difference between this period and previous periods that modified the global landscape—such as the Renaissance and the Industrial Revolution—is speed. The Renaissance and the Industrial Revolution spanned a period of about 150 years. This one is condensed into a time span one order of magnitude shorter.

One major result of this period is the accelerated growth of borderless entities and ventures, ranging from the pure outsourcing of simple manufactured goods or computer code to the design, creation and operation of complex business processes spanning several countries and business entities. This has generated boundless opportunities and correspondingly significant challenges.

While much has been written about the success stories, little has been published about the challenges and failures, except on the subject of job losses in the industrialized countries. And practically nothing has been written about integrated, across the board strategies designed to identify those problems, deal with them in a sustainable manner and, if possible, prevent them.

In our world obsessed by this quarter's results, we often make the classical mistake of not learning from history, even relatively recent history. As a result, we continuously reinvent wheels that were conceived by others long before.

Complexity and degree of risk

Transnational ventures, like all others, are governed by a risk/reward ratio where a high degree of sophistication often acts as an effective barrier to entry by prospective imitators. For simplicity's sake, we will categorize transnational ventures as either transaction-based or process-based.

Examples of transaction-based ventures could be a manufacturing order in China for a batch of plastic shopping bags for a U.S. retailer; the assembly, testing and shipping of TV sets for a Japanese manufacturer; or the one-time outsourcing to an Indian firm for writing the code for a Bluetooth device by a European electronics manufacturer.

Transaction-based ventures can, by and large, succeed in a "business as usual" way. A good performance contract that covers technical and design specifications, materials or methods to be used, price and timing will usually suffice, given sufficient clarity and absence of significant change in the period prior to delivery. When the transaction is repeated, the performance contract can, and ought to be, reviewed and updated.

However, most significant transnational business developments belong in the process-based category. Process-based relationships are those in which two or more parties jointly design, build and run a full process designed to serve them or outside customers. It must, nevertheless, be noted that many outsourced processes, for which the term BPO was coined, do not fall into this category. Activities such as payroll or accounts receivable are sub-processes involving relatively few parties that often can be approached in the same way as transaction-based ventures.

Examples of full process-based relationships include the increasingly customer-driven supply chains in the automobile and PC industries, the design and manufacture of mobile devices and even the design, manufacture and delivery of textile apparel, where fast response to changes in demand volume, style, colors and size distribution makes the difference between success and failure. Though the last example may be viewed as a relatively trivial transaction-based venture, it is not. It may involve a design team based in Italy; textile manufacturing, dyeing and printing entities in China, Indonesia and Mexico; a management team in the U.K.; a global U.S.-based shipper, and retail outlets in a dozen countries. Tight coordination and alignment are essential as demand varies daily and differs from place to place.

Given the multitude of complex, rapidly changing parameters governing the design, construction and operation of these processes, there is no way in which legal contracts or performance documents can adequately govern these business relationships.

Though the benefits of these global ventures can be enormous, the challenges are correspondingly daunting. What are the key differences between transaction-based and process-based ventures that generate such significantly higher degrees of risk? After all, if an agreement is reached on the specifications of the product, the processes that will design, manufacture, deliver and maintain it, the price, timing, the respective responsibilities and degrees of authority of the parties involved and the penalties and bonuses linked to performance, what can go wrong?

The answer is short and simple: the number of parameters and people involved, coupled with the accelerating rate of change, bring about a very high degree of risk. The triggers of change include:

• Customer demand
• Technology
• Politics
• Exchange rate fluctuations
• Faulty processes
• Management and staffing turnover
• Changes in priority, focus or policy by one of the parties

Responses to these challenges typically include one or more of the following:

- Flexible, frequently reviewed contracts
- Frequent issue review meetings face-to-face or Web-based
- The "if it ain't broke don't fix it" approach, i.e., doing nothing until the problems become very severe

These approaches combine the disadvantages of high over-head and focus on the urgent, at the expense of the important, with a consequently high risk of failure. Some more sophisticated partnerships that have recognized some of the pitfalls reduce the risk level with tools such as intensive training in communication and negotiation techniques and team-building exercises. While this approach is a significant step forward, it is not sufficient because it does not address the fundamental cause of project failures and business divorces.

The question of cause demands answers at more than one level of depth.

At the first level, the parties are no longer in alignment, meaning one or more parties have "fallen out of step," causing the process to suffer. This finding is often preceded by unexpressed dissatisfaction because the parties may appear to have breached the contract.

Going one level deeper, the basis for the initial alignment did not cater to changes that occurred. There is absolutely no way to foresee all possible changes, many of which are outside the circle of influence of the parties.

How, then, can alignment be created and sustained in this sea of change? If the foundation on which this venture was built was purely opportunistic, happening to suit the short or medium-term needs of all key parties at the inception of the venture, the chances are that it is too shallow and weak to survive significant change in those needs. Most projects will find as many agendas as people involved. Even if the initial agreements succeeded in aligning the agendas, there is little chance that change will not rock this alignment, pitting people and groups against each other. This may result in more energy being spent on realignment attempts instead of getting the job done.

A strong, sustainable foundation common to the key stakeholders must be created and constantly refreshed. In the same way that any building larger than a shack needs a foundation, a process-based venture needs a foundation to survive and prosper. This very idea may turn off a number of managers bred in a culture where short-term results and a dog-eat-dog philosophy seem to be the norm. They will find all sorts of pretexts to look another way and attend to the urgent rather than the important. The interesting fact is that creating this foundation actually saves time and money and need not be a long drawn out process.

Examples of successful global partnerships based on a common agenda can be found in fields as diverse as retail distribution, engine manufacturing and banking. What these success stories have in common is an emphasis on finding common ground with key stakeholders and the willingness to invest time and money in establishing relationships. However, time, this most precious commodity, is not always available, and many leaders are not willing to spend a lot of money on a prospective venture that may not materialize. A deeper, more structured approach that creates and maintains strong relationships, while saving time and money and allowing a rapid change of course, may be needed.

Learning from history

In 1976, when I created ISM—IBM's first management consulting program and the granddaddy of what became IBM Global Services—we made a relatively small investment, but got a very high return from the realization that there were significant and growing problems for large users of information systems. Large projects were habitually late, well beyond budget and often failed to meet user needs. Operation centers were struggling to find the balance between reliability, coping with change and user responsiveness. I/S planning and business planning were poorly coordinated and communication between I/S, users and management was crisis driven. Teams were picked on the basis of technical skills, with little regard to synergy, motivation and communication. The future started to look dim for IBM, the IT industry and, more importantly, for the large and medium organizations that had become dependent on IT.

In those days, when IBMers didn't know what to do they established a task force to determine the source of the problems. This task force, which was subsequently replicated in a number of countries, came up with some then revolutionary conclusions.

The key finding was that the cause of most problems was not technical, but organizational, psychological and social. The rise of the problems corresponded with the evolution from the use of computers for specific tasks for one department or division, such as accounts receivable, payroll or inventory management, to their use for the management of processes that spanned organizational boundaries, such as customer information systems, production planning or product management. A key underlying problem was that the objectives and measurement systems of the different parts of a single organization were simply not aligned.

In an attempt to do something about this and not leave it as a simple academic exercise, we searched three continents to find insightful people who had encountered these kinds of problems. The core of ISM was created with a small group of such people. One had tackled the task of creating information systems (and processes) from scratch for a newly formed division using fresh thinking. Another had been the chief architect for a huge IBM project called CMIS (Common Manufacturing Information System). The scope of CMIS was to design and implement a single common manufacturing information system for IBM's two-dozen large plants scattered through about 15 countries on three continents. Despite the best brains and tons of money being poured into the project, it was widely considered a huge failure. Most of the plants never succeeded in fitting the single mold and it was conservatively estimated that CMIS resulted in a net loss to IBM of $650 million 1970.

The people who lived through these successes and failures became our initial management consultants. They analyzed their experiences and shared their findings with large customers in several ways: through conversations, seminars and hands-on involvement in projects. This was done entirely free of charge.

The results were nothing short of spectacular for those organizations and for IBM. The knowledge was not transmitted using laboriously constructed methodologies, but by sharing best management practices and helping implement them. Many of the concepts and practices introduced in those best practices conversations became standard in the I/S field in subsequent years.

From a bottom line perspective, almost without exception, client-side companies that took advantage of the free consulting flourished. IBM measured over three years its 20 largest accounts in the country—nine of which received consulting services, and 11 of which did not. The growth of the NIO (net installed and on order hardware and software) in the eleven large accounts that did not benefit from ISM was a respectable average of 10.8 percent annual CGR. But the NIO of the ISM customers grew by an astounding average CGR of 40.8 percent. The figure becomes even more significant when we realize that NIO growth is naturally much slower than the growth of sales.

The single most important factor in this success story is the durable alignment of interests. ISM's mission was simply to do what was in the customers' best interests. Other agendas, such as tying the free consulting to purchase of IBM products, were strictly forbidden. The confidence gained paid off in a spectacular way. Every dollar invested in this small group of consultants is estimated to have generated more than $200 in gross profit.

Other examples exist of measurable results of long-lasting alignment between stakeholders. An excellent one is Toyota's consulting provided free of charge to its suppliers. The win-win spirit results in those suppliers producing higher quality parts in a shorter time and at a cost lower than those of similar parts made for other auto manufacturers. One of the shared goals in this arrangement is for the suppliers to generate sound profits.

About 20 years after the initial work, a group of thinkers—this time outside of IBM, but once again from three different continents—started the task of adapting and expanding those lessons to respond to the needs of inter-company, multi-culture undertakings or ventures. This laid the groundwork for finding the answers to many key challenges facing complex ventures.

Elements of a strong foundation

It is clear that without a strong, shared foundation, the best structured deal between well-intentioned parties will not stand the test of time. Misalignment will occur within a relatively short time span because of inherently different agendas, overall purpose, cultures and value sets.

To create this foundation we must identify some of the key elements of a sustainable process-based relationship, such as:

- Sustained commonality of interest
- Trust
- Authentic communication
- Integrity
- Win-win mentality

These organizational characteristics prove conclusively that values-based organizations outperform their peers by almost an order of magnitude. However, some nagging unspoken questions arise: Is it unrealistic to be values-driven in this cut throat world? Is it not a long-term undertaking to build relationships based on shared values and a shared purpose? The answer to both questions, supported by tons of evidence, is an unequivocal no. A well-known fact is that a dollar invested at the start of a large project is worth $50-$60 eighteen months down the road. Also, a genuine values-driven approach will attract the right people to one's venture—whether they are employees, partners, investors, suppliers or customers. Once again, evidence abounds, ranging from initially small U.S. firms that started doing business with China 20 years ago and prospered—mostly on the basis of dependability and trust—to giants like Toyota, who put the interest of their partners on a par with theirs.

What, then, does an organization, or a venture, need to become values driven?

In this order it is:

- Political will.

- A simple, but comprehensive "holistic" or comprehensive framework that easily permits management to prioritize past, current and future initiatives and relate them to each other and to the overall strategy.

- Good leadership tools for formulating and immediately implementing an integrated values-based strategy and translating it into business as usual.

Political will

Many leaders who would like to clarify and strengthen their organization's core values orientation are inhibited by one or more of these six widespread false dichotomies or irrational fears. These usually unarticulated fears can sap the will of the strongest leaders and should be debunked:

- "I have a choice between doing what is right and achieving financial success."

- "Values-driven orientation is long-term. If I don't give top priority to the short-term, there will be no long term for me."

- "The pie is finite. If I don't grab as much of it as I can, my (internal and external) competitors will."

- "I am the only one in my environment who would like to embrace a deeper and more genuine outlook. If I come out of the closet on this my colleagues, customers and investors will think I am crazy."

- "Implementing this new paradigm demands trust and openness. In the meantime, most of the world operates in the old, fear-driven paradigm. I will become road kill."

- "How can I preach values such as integrity and authenticity? I have not always been authentic or acted out of integrity."

Strategic framework

Clarification of the word "holistic" in this context may be useful. Other adequate terms one could use are integrative, systemic or inclusive. In practical terms, this means:

- Addressing the needs of all key stakeholders; it is clear that without this, no sustainable relationships can flourish.

- Including the three to four key processes of the organization and the major projects.

- Catering to both the long- and short-term.

- Recognizing the multiple facets of people and groups.

The beauty of this architecture is that it enables leaders to easily position each current, past, or future process, project or initiative very clearly; it identifies its level of depth, its output and the specific stakeholder set it addresses, and the level of progress or quality. It can be a powerful tool for planning, resource allocation and other forms of decision-making. It simplifies management's tasks by replacing dozens of weakly connected, separate action items with a single coherent set focused on key stakeholders, major processes and consistent metrics.

It also creates direct links between financial results and the things that bring them about. Finally, it has an important element—the Community Dialogue. The Community Dialogue is a structured set of (mainly Web-based) communications and actions between the stakeholders that create and maintain alignment, generate energies and assure that everyone's interests are safeguarded. While it can be rightly argued that every significant venture has a de facto Community Dialogue, most are inefficient in that more time is often spent on "defend" and "fix" activities than on alignment that prevents friction and breakdowns.

Leadership tools

Success could not be possible without 21st Century leadership tools. Broadly speaking, they fit into three categories:

1. Alignment, communication and motivation.
2. Formulation and communication of a "deep" strategy.
3. Implementation, i.e., translating intentions and strategies into day-to-day business practice.

In the first, a focused set of conversations is launched to elicit personal and shared group values, communicate them, elicit a common purpose and, in some cases, a shared vision. This sets the ground for a win-win culture for the venture and generates productive energies. A number of good tools are available from several sources for these steps.

Once the groundwork is done and a shared purpose elicited, a common strategy is jointly formulated that goes beyond the standard "shallow" strategies dealing with products, markets and distribution models. This "deep" strategy focuses on identity, shared values and a mobilizing common purpose that goes beyond items covered by shallow strategies. This provides the "glue" that binds the partners together in a sustainable way where everyone benefits.

This glue will, nevertheless, rapidly dry if the implementation of this deep strategy does not start immediately; perhaps not across the board, but in pilot schemes. This maintains the energies and alignment and provides the corrective feedback necessary for fuller deployment.

Implementation demands leadership tools that ensure that shared values and common purpose are implemented into every-day business. They include special ways for the structuring and monitoring of major projects, processes and measurement systems. They include unique milestones to ensure that alignment with the core values and the common purpose is maintained and that the interests of the core stakeholders are safeguarded. This not only keeps our aim on the moving targets, but also sees to it that innovation is nurtured and opportunities are recognized and seized. Attention to the needs of groups and individuals at all levels is sustained by the Community Dialogue.

Many, if not most, decisions stem from emotions rather than from pure intellect. This new unfolding 21st Century will be more remembered for the progress it brought in these fields and in relations between people, peoples and cultures than for its remarkable technological breakthroughs.

Robert Carter
Executive Vice President and CIO
FedEx Corporation
Memphis, Tennessee

The CIO Perspective

Question: *What are of the biggest issues surrounding offshore outsourcing for FedEx?*

Carter: Most of the difficulties and complexities focus on the term outsourcing. Outsourcing suggests "work going away" with key positions being replaced with a distant third party. The majority of our work has focused not on outsourcing, but rather on a concept we call "variable capacity." As we work to meet the complex and vast needs of FedEx around the globe, we have found there are never enough people on our team to keep up with the demands of the business. And even though we have a significant team, and make a significant investment in building a core competency in information technology and innovate in that space, we much need the ability to tap into global resources to supplement and to add variable capacity in key strategic areas when the business warrants return on the investment.

Question: *A trend now is moving beyond outsourcing commodity services toward "R&D outsourcing" and into the highest levels of the value chain. How will this affect developed economies?*

Carter: It's incumbent on companies like FedEx that the information product and the information capabilities we offer our customers are a part of the way we work—that we continue to keep a core competency and a level of excellence in our ability to do those kinds of research and development initiatives on our own and with partners, and not to relegate that class of responsibility outside the company.

Question: *What is your view of the growing homeshoring phenomenon?*

Carter: We believe it is a very healthy phenomenon. For multinational companies like ours, we have come to recognize the value of fielding teams that bring out the strength of their homeland and home operating regions—whether it's an IT team or operational team. We count on our team members around the world for global development and support initiatives, for which you might traditionally reach outside of the company. It gives us the opportunity to participate in all the economic, educational and social advantages that exist in those regions of the world.

But at the same time having the global presence allows us to effectively work with other providers in those locations and in those parts of the world where we can have a "variable capacity" capability to reach outside the company's boundaries to provide more expertise and capability in meeting the needs of FedEx.

Question: *Can companies stay focused on homeshoring when China, through acquisitions and growth of its science and technology, potentially has an opportunity to take a lead in five to ten years as the dominant player in the global outsourcing space? How will these trends affect outsourcing?*

Carter: The phenomenon in China is something that must to be seen to be believed. We continue to invest in China. We believe China to be a marvelous opportunity for economic growth and development, not just for their part of the world, but for the entire world. Their education systems are turning out world-class engineers at a pace no other country can match. We will continue to invest in China and put FedEx resources to bear in the China and Asia-Pacific theatres as an important part of our future.

Question: *How do you see governments changing in this age of globalization?*

Carter: We are certainly advocates of global trade, liberalization of trade and treaties that allow businesses and countries to work seamlessly. As Thomas Friedman wrote in his book the world is, in fact, becoming flat. The age of globalization very much levels the playing field and brings a lot of opportunity to all parts of the world. The ability to go online has reached nearly every part of the world now.

Infrastructures are being put in so quickly that they become a great enabler for the third world countries to engage and to be part of the global economy. Marketplaces, being driven by this kind of connectivity, will continue to change everything.

The power of today's network, which allows businesses and consumers to see demand and supply, and match them on a global, instantaneous basis is like nothing we've ever experienced before. We're only 50 years out from the days of crops rotting in the fields 50 kilometers from the starving village. Unfortunately, there are still places in the world where that phenomenon exists. This type of connectivity drives visibility to the need and to the supply. And those things will help drive government and marketplace decisions that reach to the end of the earth.

Question: *What areas are very important to you as a global CIO of a major company?*

Carter: There is an important set of social and risk factors that are well beyond just the basic brute force numbers—well beyond, "Here is how many people are doing this," and "Here are the educational systems that exist." We need a deeper look into the social and cultural factors of successfully integrating and partnering with providers around the world. I have many counterparts who have no interest in handing over intellectual property and their ability to innovate—from a business or IT perspective. But we do have a need to make use of capabilities being created around the world to build core software products and offerings. The question is how best to manage that. What are the best practices in project, process and cultural management that will allow our teams to work effectively together?

IT is fundamentally about people, and their ability to innovate and apply technology to strategic business advantage. It's a people-oriented business. It's not about creating widgets. It's about driving capabilities all the way out to your customers and suppliers and their customers through innovative people. And, if you can do that with partners, then the best practices are around that. But if becomes order taking—"here's the spec, write the code"—chances are you won't be in the world-class innovation space and applying technology to strategic advantage.

1.6

By **Ram Iyer**
Founder and CEO
Argea Inc.
Princeton, New Jersey

Lee Swindall
Vice President, Market Research
Argea Inc.
Princeton, New Jersey

Mid-Market Companies Confront Globalization

Globalization is a mega-force that is drawing products, services, companies, civic institutions and even the fates of nations into its wake. The ubiquity of Internet-enabled connectivity, freer cross-border flows of capital, improved transportation networks and creative workflow processes allow services to be delivered from remote locations never before possible. Capital, people and the competition for markets and resources are breaking national borders, government spheres of influence and former 'exclusion zones' of global commerce. While an idealized global economy is still decades away, the pace of globalization has definitely quickened. In the present day, large multinational corporations are generally regarded as the driving force behind this phase shift from local/regional to global interaction. Until recently, this may have been true, but the landscape is changing. Now, and in the future, mid-market companies will also be markedly impacted by globalization. They must embrace and manage the changes spawned by globalization, and use them to their advantage—or perish.

Historically, the conventional business model in the mid-market described a vertically integrated company. Vertical integration was an appropriate model before the pressures—and promises—of globalization emerged. A different, more flexible business model is required in a global economy. This more adaptive model is known as the "extended enterprise." It allows a company to access resources that provide greatest value to the enterprise and integrate them into the value chain. It requires companies to surrender traditional levels of control and focus upon macro-managing the extended enterprise network—a "best-fit" model to respond to increasing globalization.

One of the shortest paths to begin the building of an extended enterprise, and one with the greatest potential for business returns, is enterprise-wide outsourcing. Outsourcing creates extended global networks of suppliers, resources, skills and advanced capabilities, without the expense of actually building them around the globe. It creates the mechanism for replicating the reach, resources and responsiveness of a true multinational corporation without the cost or scale of becoming one. The effective use of technology is an important enabler for companies to build the extended enterprise.

In this chapter, we will examine the competitive positioning of mid-market companies in the global economy, their future needs as global competitors, and unique considerations when using outsourcing as a first step to creating an extended enterprise.

Mid-market: a working definition

There are numerous definitions of a mid-market company. The traditional definition, based purely on the overall revenues of the corporation, is not appropriate. What is more appropriate is the size of the enterprise for which decisions are made. For example, a $2B company, which has four divisions of $500M each, should be viewed as a $500M enterprise for decision-making. If a company has $600M in revenues and the decisions are made across the entire company, it should be considered as a $600M company for decision-making. Based upon this nuance, mid-market companies could range anywhere between $300M and $2B in total revenues. Joe Vales, of Vales Consulting, and the former director of worldwide marketing for PwC's BPO practice, defines it as companies with revenues between $100M and $1B, and with between 1000 and 5000 employees.

Permanent change in the business landscape

The hottest destinations for outsourcing today are China and India. A mere fifteen years ago, China and India were considered third world countries. Today, China is the manufacturing capital of the world and India is the information technology hub of the global IT marketplace. The BRICs report, issued by Goldman Sachs, predicts that Brazil, Russia, India and China will be among the ten most industrialized nations in the world by 2050. Within three decades, China will overtake the United States to be the world's biggest economy, and India will supplant Germany to be the third-biggest economy in the world. While there are other reasons for their ascendancy, the principal reason is the increased pace of globalization.

The Chinese economy has been growing at a torrid 9.5 percent and India's at 6 percent. China and India, the hottest outsourcing destinations today, will be among the largest markets in the future. Establishing a presence in these markets and learning to do business there will well serve the future of western corporations. Roopa Purushothaman, a co-author of the BRICs report, said:

"Over 80 percent of the value generated by the world's major equity markets will come from earnings delivered more than 10 years away. Developing strategies to position for growth may take several years and require significant planning. The relative importance of the BRICs as an engine of new demand growth and spending power may shift more dramatically and quickly than expected. Higher growth in these economies could offset the impact of graying populations and slower growth in the advanced economies."

The progressive and swift integration of local, national and regional economies into a more integrated global economy is, ultimately, irreversible. In the main, people perceive that large multinational corporations are both ardent supporters and beneficiaries of globalization. Yet, the next wave of globalization will engulf companies of all sizes. Indeed, the universal reach of globalization is already sweeping smaller enterprises into its vortex without partiality for their level of preparation. Companies that merely ponder and delay action will either perish or be acquired. It is those companies that embrace globalization—that become global in their thinking and practices and leverage the benefits of outsourcing to reduce costs, increase innovation and access new markets—that will be the long-term survivors (and winners) in the global economy.

Companies in developing countries like India and China are developing their own business models because they are operating with lower costs and abundant intellect. China and India, together, graduate 500,000 engineering and science graduates, as opposed to the 60,000 in the United States. There are two ramifications. First, the value proposition of these foreign companies will be more compelling to the market, if they can deliver goods and services of quality competitive to Western counterparts (and produced with a much lower cost base). Second, it may not be effective for Western companies using standard business models to compete head-on against foreign companies using indigenous business models. One way to learn how to compete with them is to be engaged with them.

Disproportionate impact: evolve or perish

Globalization is a four-lane superhighway—not a one-way street. Mid-market companies must develop the powers to go global, not just to export goods and services, but to acquire skills, resources and local access in external markets. Mohan Sawhney, McCormick Tribune Professor of Technology at Northwestern University Kellogg School of Management, put it best when he said:

"Getting to global requires companies to think globally, source globally, make globally, sell globally, and learn globally. The Internet has opened up dramatic new possibilities for companies to create competitive advantage by harnessing resources around the world. Even if you only sell your products in Peoria, Illinois, you need to understand that in the networked world of business, the world is your talent pool, your factory, your back-office, your laboratory, your market, and your competitor. The rapid growth of global outsourced manufacturing, offshore business process outsourcing, and offshore R&D are early indications of what the global company of the future might look like."

Globalization is a supremely egalitarian force that favors competitors—not companies. Operating with the same effect as Darwinian natural selection, globalization favors enterprises that can adapt to environmental changes and so evolve. In this way, it confers profit and penalty with equal indifference. The unfortunate ones that cannot adapt are selected for eventual extinction.

Mid-market companies are at special risk in this new economic order and there is ample reason to believe that the next wave of globalization will hit them with violent effect for reasons discussed later in this chapter. Although there are some spectacular success stories of mid-market enterprises that have carved out highly profitable markets abroad, the majority lack the mindset and wherewithal to accomplish the same. If they are to survive and prosper in this epoch of global economic integration, they need to learn the new rules of competition and master them. Some of the changes required for success in the global economy are so drastically different from the past that it may take a new kind of global leadership—enlightened at the top of the company and globally adept in the mid-ranks—to effect change in most of today's organizations.

Unique vulnerabilities

Generally, mid-market companies have particular organizational attributes that make them slower to react to emerging competition, in contrast to both bigger and smaller enterprises. There are several different attributes that, together, create a vulnerability to globalization.

First, mid-market organizations lack the array of business resources that multinational companies command, such as access to working capital, a highly skilled pool of executive or technical talent, and bargaining power. Working with fewer resources (financial, human, and technological) than larger companies, mid-market companies are less able to respond to changing business needs with resource allocations or shifts. Their mindset requires swift, visible and measurable return from spending decisions, and resources will flow only to the projects that meet this test.

Further, as organizations, mid-market companies are generally less agile than either larger or smaller companies. Large multinationals, for example, are globally distributed organizations with a local business presence in domestic and foreign markets. Their competitive intelligence networks are highly developed, as are their local/regional partnerships and alliances. They are endowed with natural capacity to respond quickly to competitive threats and market opportunities. Smaller companies, in contrast, are much leaner entities with more centralized control and local/regional business focus. They operate on intimate terms with their markets and customers and can move quickly to counter moves by competitors and to seize business opportunities. Mid-market companies are usually bound by more risk-averse management cultures because, for them, there is little latitude for making wrong decisions. Larger companies can absorb the financial hit from mistakes in business execution, and small companies can more quickly change course when business decisions are wrong or execution is flawed. Likewise mid-market companies usually have less developed market and partnership networks and so are slower to respond to competitive challenges.

Another reason why mid-market companies will have difficulty embracing the extended enterprise model quickly is because of their closeness to their employees, which makes many of them reluctant to move jobs offshore, or even seek efficiencies driven by technology. Entrepreneurs who grew up with the business and built their success on closeness to their customers frequently lead mid-market companies. Many of these leaders lack the expertise to guide the company to another level and meet the competitive threats of globalization.

Finally, the senior management of many mid-market companies generally lacks the specialized knowledge and preparation for intense and growing global competition. The management in many of these companies was not trained to either anticipate or manage the competitive response that globalization requires. The new skills that globalization demands include macromanagement skills, which require the ceding of some traditional company control, expertise in the creation of global alliances and partnerships, and acquisition of global resources and gaining market access.

Probably nothing illustrates the deficiency better than the rapid ascendancy of Chinese manufacturing prowess and the virtual dominance of the international textile markets by South and Eastern Asia. North American textile manufacturing companies—with many mid-market members among them—have fallen in rank under the weight of these tectonic shifts in market control—with little more than months to respond to the threat. In a globalized economy, business agility is a highly prized corporate asset, as market share can never be viewed as secure and can drop precipitously within a few months.

Surviving globalization: climbing the competitive curve

Large corporations with deep pockets and international presence have become competitive by perfecting the multinational model. They leverage specialized skills, suppliers, and less expensive labor pools to balance quality and cost levels for their business. In contrast, mid-market companies have responded to competitive pressures with extensive cost cutting and selective outsourcing. While multinational behemoths are able to summon the resources of a global organization, middle market companies are forced to make do with less-favorable cost structures and fewer resources.

Consequently, mid-market companies must create a global competitive strategy and cultivate the necessary powers to execute it. This strategy is not limited to crafting plans for increasing market access, market penetration and exports. Instead, it must include a plan to acquire scarce and essential skills, resources and local presence in external markets. Globalization is a bilateral force that moves in two directions simultaneously—delivering vital capabilities to a company, as well as sales opportunities.

Argea has developed a model that can help mid-market enterprises to understand where they place on the Global Competitiveness Curve and how to advance along it. The five stages of the competitive curve basically describe where a company falls in its maturation as a global company. An enterprise becomes more competitive as it becomes freer of local limits and constraints and both buys from and sells to a growing international network of suppliers and customers.

In Figure 1, the 'Y' axis identifies company actions, while the 'X' axis plots the outcome of these actions—what the company becomes. A vertically integrated company—with only local suppliers—is a Stage 1 company. As an onshore/offshore network of partners and suppliers is developed, a company's global competitiveness quotient dramatically improves. Among mid-market companies, many foreign competitors, including those in rapidly developing economies, are already Stage 3-Stage 4 companies. To

Figure 1   **The Global Competitiveness Curve**

How companies mature as global players

Source: Argea 2005

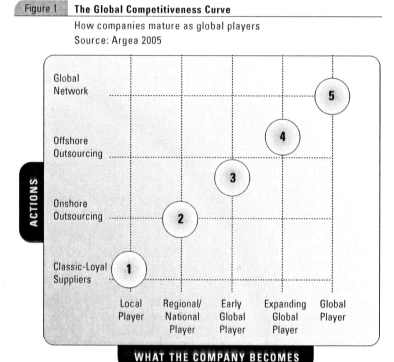

WHAT THE COMPANY BECOMES

compete viably against such companies, a mid-market company would need to outsource functions offshore merely to achieve competitive parity.

To illustrate this point, we might look to Ranbaxy, the Indian pharmaceutical company, as an example. In addition to having a network of Indian suppliers, Ranbaxy has partners in parts of Asia, Europe, Africa and the Americas. When Ranbaxy entered the U.S. market, its global network of partners and suppliers gave them broad, highly flexible capabilities and low costs. Ranbaxy is at least a Stage 3 or Stage 4 global player.

The most competitive international companies, such as Pfizer and GlaxoSmithKline, are Stage 5 companies—fierce competitors with universal market reach, global access to advanced skills, lower labor costs and the ability to rapidly respond to local, regional and global changes in supply and demand. In short, they are super-competitors.

New market realities will compel mid-market companies to adopt a business model that powers business growth through new product innovation, as well as improved operational effectiveness and positioning as capable global competitors. Competitiveness will flow from a deep global network of partners—whether it is to leverage specialized skills, infrastructure, local market presence or cheaper labor costs. The hard truth is that, over time, a Stage 1 or Stage 2 company will be relegated to niche status, perish or be acquired—perhaps by a foreign competitor.

Of course, no company can attain a global reach from ground zero in a single leap. To advance along the competitive curve, mid-market companies need to ascend in sequential stages. One of the shortest paths to becoming a global, Stage 3 player is to adopt enterprise-wide outsourcing and to develop advanced competency in its use.

Enabling the extended enterprise: outsourcing first

Outsourcing is an important first step toward building an extended enterprise and becoming a truly global competitor—one that can match up to both small and medium sized enterprises (SMEs) and multinational behemoths. It is a defensive and offensive weapon, helping to defend against new competitors and diminishing margins, while improving business agility, business control and increasing the top and bottom lines. Outsourcing creates the opportunities to leverage global resources that can increase revenue in new markets with the best efficiency and highest quality business processes.

Outsourcing accomplishes two simple objectives. First, it allows companies to concentrate on core competencies and value creation mechanisms that are critical to their business. Second, it enables companies to minimize risk by using specialists for various functions and processes that are not within the core competencies. By building a network of specialists, companies can achieve 'best in class' competitiveness without the expense of owning the network. Moreover, outsourcing can be highly scalable and expand or contract, as business needs vary according to shifts in supply or demand. In the future, competitiveness will flow from a deep global network of partners—whether it is to leverage specialized skills, infrastructure, local market presence or cheaper labor costs.

When considering candidates for outsourcing, one important criterion is to understand whether the objective is efficiency, optimization or transformation in an outsourcing relationship. If the objective is mere efficiency—for a task that many people can do cheaper, faster and better—the lowest cost provider will be a good choice. If the objective is optimization—which requires higher skills, deep process knowledge and mastery of best practices—a more skilled provider is required. If the objective is to transform a company's business through a relationship with an outsourcing provider, there need to be similar and complementary skill levels and a high level of trust. Many companies choose the wrong type of supplier for specific outsourcing needs.

Current progress

The use of outsourcing as a competitive weapon in the mid-market is quite limited, despite recent gains in acceptance and actual use. Selective outsourcing of functions such as payroll and benefit administration is pervasive in the mid-market. Yet, limited or selective outsourcing yields only limited results and does little to enhance overall positioning as a global competitor. It is only when outsourcing is used as an enterprise tool—applied to myriad processes and functions across the company—that's its full, long-term value is realized. Large multinational companies that use outsourcing as an effective strategic tool include GE, AIG, Citibank, Boeing, Airbus and Lucent.

Recent surveys by Forrester Research suggest that only around one-third of mid-sized companies considered IT outsourcing during 2005 and that mid-market companies still account for only about 10 percent of overall demand for outsourced IT services in the United States. Also, recent data from Gartner indicates that business process outsourcing (BPO) in the mid-market is still largely limited to HR functions, along with some finance and accounting functions. In its recent user survey Gartner reported that 78 percent of respondents of mid-sized businesses that have experience with BPO are outsourcing or plan to outsource one or more of their HR processes. Outside of HR only 16 percent of medium and small-sized businesses are either outsourcing or planning to outsource finance and accounting processes. The limited and highly selective use of outsourcing in these companies belies a tactical focus, in which outsourcing is evaluated at the individual process level, not at the enterprise level. Necessarily, the potential benefits will be limited to the discrete outsourced process, with no chance for greater strategic gain.

Practice makes perfect

To move higher in the global competitiveness curve, mid-market companies will soon need to take the first steps toward achieving Stage 3 capability. Outsourcing is the logical place to begin, but developing advanced proficiency in the outsourcing disciplines, acquired by doing, takes time. Waiting to begin will only favor competitors that are willing to take risks and succeed. It will come as no surprise, then, that companies with limited outsourcing experience enjoy less success than companies with extensive experience, and this disparity is widely documented.

To illustrate, a study in 2004 by Argea and the International Association of Contract and Commercial Managers (IACCM) of over 100 international companies found that companies with little experience in outsourcing are twice as likely to suffer failures and setbacks than those with extensive experience. Hence, the sooner mid-market companies embrace outsourcing, the sooner they gain proficiency to improve business performance.

The future role of outsourcing

In the next 20 years, competition will only intensify with new sellers and buyers entering key markets. Mid-market companies cannot build a physical presence across the globe in the way that multinational companies do. Outsourcing is the best solution for mid-market companies to build and expand a global network of partners and suppliers to remain competitive. In doing so, they will learn to do business in these markets, which can also be important sources of future revenues. Ton Heijmen, senior advisor on outsourcing and offshoring to the Conference Board, said:

"The Conference Board's 2005 CEO Challenge Report points to flexibility and learning in an outsourced/offshored universe as a top priority. In our many interviews with member companies of the Conference Board, global competition is a major issue on the minds of executives and they are unanimous in their agreement that global sourcing is the epitome of flexibility.

"Since many middle-market companies typically do not have ready access to the top-ranked providers of offshored services that can work with their required scale or scope, it is imperative that smaller companies develop new approaches and implement new models for globalization. For example, they could create consortiums to make themselves appealing to the large vendors or contract from industry associations.

"Mid-market companies do not have the luxury of waiting until the appropriate models are developed. In five to ten years, the left-behinds will be those companies that did not take advantage of this route to globalization."

Unique challenges for mid-market companies

The unique challenges to successful outsourcing in the mid-market are not widely understood. Consequently, companies in this sector have been generally underserved or poorly served by the business services market.

Although Argea has identified 10 separate challenges for these companies, there are three major barriers that assume the greatest importance in the context of outsourcing success and global competitiveness. These include a need to retain business control, the lack of experience in global vendor and partner management, and the lack of outsourcing readiness.

(1) Retention of business control: everything is core
There is wide agreement that the preservation of business control is a key value in mid-market companies. Many such companies have achieved success by virtue of tight business control and are loathe to share or transfer it to a third party. Outsourcing, viewed from this perspective, is perceived as ceding control of important business functions to an external provider.

However, successful outsourcing does demand some sharing of power and risks. So, to reap the outsourcing advantage, this natural resistance to changes in control requires some modification in attitude and behavior. Typically, this tight control is reflected throughout the company, from the senior management down through the lines of business. This control bias takes many forms but the most common include those described below.

(2a) Narrow process ownership and control

Among mid-market enterprises, there is a prevailing reluctance to share control of many business processes because they don't readily define certain business functions as non-core. In these cases, any process or function is seen as important in the chain of value creation and delivery. In other cases, the fear of regression in quality is enough to take outsourcing off the table altogether.

Equally, the knowledge of the business process or function is not widely disseminated in the company, and control of it is lodged with a very small set of business-unit staff. In such circumstances, there is great resistance to granting even limited influence or control to other internal or external parties.

Likewise, because people in mid-market companies can wear more than one hat, the control of several business functions or processes may fall in the domain of a single person or small set of people. Such consolidated control is not easily broken apart or shared, and it can make the separation of discrete business processes and their control a daunting task. Nevertheless, this process mapping is exactly what is needed in identifying which process can be outsourced and which cannot.

(2b) Concentrated competence and knowledge lockboxes

It is not unusual to find 90 percent of the aggregate knowledge of policies, procedures, processes and company goals vested in about 10 percent of the company's staff. Often, such knowledge is undocumented. Such "tribal knowledge" is impossible to outsource. Transparent processes can be opened to scrutiny for purposes of process mapping and base lining. Non-transparent processes resist such study and can't be transferred to an external provider.

When such information about competencies is tightly held, it can be problematic to open knowledge "lockboxes" to detailed scrutiny—an imperative first step in core competency definition. Creating transparency in the assessment of core competencies is, in contrast to the opposite view, very beneficial to companies, their cultures and their overall business plans. Safeguarding such data may serve the interests of some, but not the greater good of the organization.

(2c) Improved business control through macromanagement
Although the concept appears non-intuitive, outsourcing can actually improve business control. If a function or process is outsourced to a highly capable third-party provider—whose expertise will often exceed that of the client—it can result in gains in cost, efficiency and quality. Outsourcing can enhance business control by promoting focus on core competencies and integrating the value chain. The extended enterprise model requires companies to give up some of the traditional control they have been used to, and instead focus on macromanaging the enterprise value chain, instead of micromanaging each task that comprises it. In this model, companies concentrate on doing the things they must do, as part of their core competencies. What they care about is how the product/service finally comes together and how it is delivered to the customer, not the details of how each task is done.

The lesson derived from these observations is both simple and revolutionary. To be successful in the new era of hyper-competition, mid-market companies must learn to macromanage instead of micromanage. That can only be accomplished through constructing, managing and optimizing networks, partnerships and external delivery mechanisms that serve company objectives. This is the essence of the extended enterprise.

One of the thought leaders in the extended enterprise model is Jim Karkanias, executive director at Merck & Company. He believes that all companies are information organisms and that all can participate equally in globalization. He said:

"All companies are really information companies, making the task of managing the information and the processes they drive as the principal task. You can take any company and break it into five informational functions—generation/collection of data, validation of data, storage of data, analysis of data and sharing of data. The activities of a supply chain framed with these elements of information are what we call a "business." Progress in data standards, interoperability and the underlying technologies enable the location of discrete parts of this information supply chain in different parts of the world. Globalization is moving the world to an information economy—an intelligent industrialization of business processes across the globe."

(3) Lack of outsourcing readiness

Outsourcing readiness is a comprehensive state of preparedness encompassing all of the 12 key readiness elements. Partial readiness can expose companies to substantial risks that can damage both the outsourcing project and the business of the company. Unfortunately, many companies—both large and small—begin outsourcing without full preparation, and experience disappointing or harmful outcomes.

A 2004 survey conducted by Argea and IACCM found that most companies were learning by doing in outsourcing. In using such risky practices, most were repeating the same mistakes frequently committed by other companies in outsourcing.

The simple truth is that many of these companies, for a variety of reasons, were not ready to begin outsourcing and would have avoided many problems by raising their level of preparedness before launching their outsourcing projects. Outsourcing readiness is an attribute that pays for itself in reduced delays, cost, conflicts, faster time to benefit, and company agility. Basically, if the advantages of outsourcing are worth seeking, they are worth the preparation to secure them.

(4) Limited experience in managing multiple vendor networks

A comprehensive operations review is likely to yield a number of non-core processes that can be outsourced. Multiple outsourced processes will typically require multiple vendors to provide the services. In the main, mid-market organizations outsource limited processes and functions to external providers and have very little experience in the management of multiple vendors, which is a highly specialized discipline. As a result, most mid-market companies lack the readiness for enterprise-wide outsourcing as a step toward building an extended enterprise.

The experience deficit in mid-market companies is multiplied by another factor that increases the challenge of multi-vendor relationships—limited vendor leverage. Because mid-market companies usually do not outsource functions or processes in either the scale or scope of large companies, they lack comparable negotiating power and the dedicated resources of the service provider. Whereas external providers naturally favor greater scale in service delivery, mid-market companies favor provider flexibility, complicating the selection of the right provider.

Many mid-sized companies regard the outsourcing of enterprise processes as a natural fit for large companies but feel that outsourcing of multiple processes to multiple vendors is something that is not compatible with their business model. The limited experience and leverage in mid-market companies tends to have a chilling effect upon their willingness to engage in large-scale outsourcing.

However, outsourcing, per se, is not a business action that mid-sized companies should take to become a big company or even to imitate one. Instead, it is a business tool that can empower them to match the capabilities of larger companies without the cost of acquiring expensive new resources and delaying the time to benefit.

Part 2

The Business Model of the Future

Globalization and its resulting outsourcing trends have put a lot of pressure on leaders to develop additional skills, experiences, personal traits, or know-how. The well-known expression "think globally while acting locally" reflects one of these skills. Although important, it is only the tip of the iceberg. Global leaders need to take a closer look at how and what they need to change about their own leadership to be prepared to succeed in the fast changing world around them.

As you'll conclude from this section, possibly the most important global leadership competency is the ability to affect personal change. "You are who you are," and self awareness is no longer good enough. Ultimately, the will and ability to effect personal leadership changes may very well prove the difference between success and failure at the highest levels of a global business world.

Looking at how innovation is created, we bring together people with different skills or experiences or cultures, and have them work together—sometimes using technology such as the Internet, sometimes by working together in person.

But what about the little things that really affect the way we look at partnerships and how we work together with vendors and partners around the world? This section goes beyond the dictionary description of a partnership to look at the real world practice. This section also examines the important differences between SME and large business outsourcing practices and why those segments are expected to split even further as the market evolves. It explains why SME has more to gain from outsourcing than large enterprises, and why it is bound to evolve faster and with more drastic results.

Finally, this section looks at the characteristics of disaggregated corporations and the future market. Speed, not size, will define winning corporations. It will not be the number of employees but the size of the customer's mind share, the portion of his wallet and the company's position in the marketplace that will define the future corporation.

2.1

By **Phyllis Michaelides**
President
C-Level Associates LLC
Providence, Rhode Island

Coping With Complexity

The business world is morphing. Outsourcing is a single, albeit essential, thread in a whole fabric of expectations, demands and constraints. It is not happening as a single answer or alone in currents of ideas and activities. Most of these movements are happening independently of each other and are seemingly unrelated. But a closer look at the commonality central to each one could signal significant shifts in current business philosophies and structures. It is the confluence of these streams of ideas and directions both known and unknown that will impact the future in profound and perhaps unexpected ways.

The gathering stream of complexity

Information technology has been one important area noticeably affected by outsourcing, and there are some good reasons for this. In the mid-1990s enterprises were faced with several issues that were beginning to be more difficult to handle. The explosion of the Web, ripe with exciting new possibilities and nascent technical structures, only added to an inventory of systems and applications built in different IT generations. Leaders whose careers started when a new COBOL compiler came about once in five years faced a diminution of time intervals between significant changes. New, younger leaders came in to cope with the accelerated pace of change, but the inheritance of legacy systems from the past was their burden. The hoped-for annihilation of dated systems has not been entirely successful. Many of the "ancient" applications still perform meaningful tasks, and often the business case to replace them is weak.

A multi-generational portfolio of systems requires a staff prepared to support it. It is rare to find an IT professional skilled in all technical areas and eras. Expansion of staff to cover critical applications of all ages, the proliferation of smaller but widely circulated applications, many that need integration with others, plus security layers and regulatory compliance, caused budget increases. Concern grew.

More and more businesses set a policy to "buy, not build." This was ostensibly a reasonable route to take. However, eventually staff expertise languished with lack of exercise of their skills and less concentration on building new and greater skills. As an aside: building a skill requires more than simply taking a class or two. It takes practice and insight into the true power of the technology. All of this takes time. Another drain on technology resources has been the large and expensive enterprise applications that are meant to answer more than a few of the issues facing IT needs. Often the implementation of these systems, the integration that might be necessary and the ongoing maintenance require more than most companies can provide. Consultants are called in and add their impact to costs.

All of these systems run on hardware—mainframes, servers, PCs, even hand-held devices—and complicated networks, wired and wireless, connect them. The average user of applications sees only what appears before him/her, not the extensive environment that supports these applications. The layers of hardware, networks, software infrastructure that allow the programs to execute and provide business value add to the vast and growing landscape of administration and the escalation of costs.

The business imperative

Along with this growing complexity of the IT world is the ongoing important business requirement to bring fiscal discipline into all aspects of the business. All departments share in the responsibility to reign in costs and indeed reduce costs where possible. Of course, manufacturing companies have for many years used outsourcing to purchase components of their end products. But outsourcing is now happening or planned in central administrative and service areas of the business.

An analysis of the costs of IT produces some expected conclusions. Resources outside of the enterprise can certainly do some portions of the technical area, and even the entire IT function could be re-sourced. The decision is an important one and is to be approached with caution. The main point of considering different sourcing is, of course, to save money. But there are other potential advantages. Better overall service might be one. Coverage of areas for which there is no in-house resource might be another. The collective thinking in the business world is that outsourcing to a company whose core business is to run and support systems is better than trying to compete with that capability.

An important result of the decision to outsource is that the boundaries of the business become more porous.

Extending horizons

There is a huge demand for low-cost venues equipped to handle the support and maintenance of enterprise systems. Application development, engineering support and some R&D are possible additions to this outsourced environment. Growth has its demands also. Some heavily concentrated offshore technical communities have experienced increasing demands for electricity and provisions for heavier traffic. Some power outages have occurred, and traffic congestion is common. The municipal infrastructure has not always kept up with the growth of the technical needs. This is being addressed but at a price that ultimately affects the cost of doing business. The sequential search for the next inexpensive locale eventually has its limits also.

A current popular location, such as India, mindful of some necessary cost increases to the enterprise customer, will want to establish added value to that client. The support and maintenance model will not suffice forever. Customer loyalty is shallow when increases occur. These suppliers will examine their assets and value to the patrons. They now have a bountiful number of customers, they have a well-educated technical population that is continually fed by new university graduates, and they have intimate knowledge of the applications they are supporting.

With the large enterprise applications such as ERP (Enterprise Resource Planning), CRM (Customer Relationship Management), PDM/PLM (Product Data Management/Product Lifecycle Management), etc., an interesting opportunity will present itself. The outsource vendors know the business functions in these systems, that is, they know what businesses are using now. Perhaps more importantly they know where customers have requested changes or additional functions. There is also knowledge of what simplification customers want and what clients use versus what is actually in the systems. Simply stated, patrons do not always use everything they pay for in an application because they don't need it. It will not be long before these technical support suppliers develop and market their own ERPs, CRMs, PDMs/PLMs systems at a much lower cost then existing ones, and they could continue to support the functions with the new systems. Might this be an incentive for a business to cease looking for a lower-cost venue and stay with them? The outsource vendor would then be aggregating a larger portion of the IT spectrum—support, maintenance AND enterprise applications. SAP, Oracle and other major vendors would, of course, have to answer this threat with product improvements and some cost adjustments. There could be an escalating competition: new functions, processes, lower expenditures. The consequences could be significant.

The impact of open source

What does open source have to do with new business formations and structures? Perhaps more than most once thought. Among the growing number of potential strengths are two salient ones. First, it follows an important new concept of "connected ubiquity," and secondly it is fueled by a curious, but potent drive to innovate, collaborate and create independently of political borders and with little regard for economic benefit. Money can be made from services and support, but that is aside from its core value.

The popular conception of the use of open source software has been that it exists in the computers of techno-geeks and has no place in corporations of any stature. Well, yes and no. There is far more open source in unexpected places than is expected. This is in part because open source tools thus far have been primarily in the application development tool arena. Technically astute professionals have for years experimented with and used open source software: operating systems, application servers, databases, etc. They have even brought these tools to the office, especially in R&D and pilot projects. The U.S. federal government was somewhat surprised a couple of years ago when a study revealed widespread usage within its departments. Some corporations already use and support open source in their IT environments. The two most important reasons for this encroachment into corporate culture are cost savings and ease of use.

Having said this, large and important enterprises are usually cautious to publicly endorse open source. It is with the mid-size companies where a bolder move is being made. It is to their economic advantage to lower costs where large companies might not and, therefore, gain leverage. Gradually business "osmosis" will occur, and the advantages will be felt by all businesses regardless of size.

The transition from an open source inventory of development tools to one of important enterprise business applications is key to reaching critical mass and impact. This evolution has begun. Far from a tsunami, it nonetheless is causing waves that portend future collisions, or at least intersections, with existing main vendor and emerging support vendor applications. Will the future bring an amalgamation, or perhaps a commoditization, of software? Either way the reign of expensive and complex technical environments is under attack.

If there is any one need that transcends all others, it is the requirement to simplify the technical landscape. It is time for a new technical DNA to surface that will reduce the costs, resources and energies necessary to sustain it. It is within the realm of possibility that the open source community could marshal a worldwide army and commitment to spark and propel this movement.

The decentralized, yet global, nature of the open source community is related but different from the more organized outsource vendor world.

Reaching further into the organization

Depending, of course, on the success of initial outsourcing ventures, it is inevitable that eyes will turn to other major functions within the business. Already there are inroads into this space, but it often has a different appellation—"hosted applications." That refers primarily to a situation where a vendor that supplies a certain system also is responsible for executing the software offsite under vendor control. Since most companies still retain major control over the entire process, which entails more than just running the application, it falls short of the more complete coverage of a traditional outsource model. Nonetheless it begins the journey in that direction.

Human resources and financial services might very well be the next opportunities for transfer to vendors specializing in these functions. A pattern develops that forms a strategy to optimize expenditures where the same or better services can be had at less cost. Moreover, these services can be obtained virtually anywhere that linguistic integrity, a stable political climate and proven ability occur. Naturally there are security and privacy issues, but those exist now and can be addressed.

Another area that waits for a better organizational strategy is the supply chain. This is not meant to address the business itself; simply look at the way it is organized. Companies can imagine huge savings and opportunities here, but few have realized these dreams to the full measure. And, again, escaping the walls of the traditional business structure might be a first step.

Looking outside of any traditionally organized enterprise, a different picture presents itself. There is a virtual living and breathing business entity with no overall corporate structure, yet it impacts all of its members. It is the supply chain community that is connected by an existing thread of demand and supply. It can be ephemeral or very long lasting, but at any one point in time it is real. Historically there have been attempts to control this environment but not to the health of all levels. Seeing this in a new light of an inter-connected mesh of entities rather than a hierarchy (first tier supplier, second tier supplier, etc.) presents real possibilities. Perhaps there is an "intra-sourcing" model that could be built to feed the needs of this powerful engine. There could be shared responsibility and reward for various elements of the consortium. Far too much redundancy exists in this sphere. One example is the push for RFID tagged products. Why should each and every member of a supply community pay for R&D, testing and piloting of a new technology that is being mandated? This could be a shared cost and experience. Thinking beyond the boundaries of a company could create this.

In another area of experimentation beyond company boundaries, consider something happening in a few interesting instances. A major industrial outfit has a minor issue or a small idea they want developed. The organization simply posts this on the Internet with a stated amount it is willing to pay for it. Someone, somewhere accepts the challenge, provides the company with the results and receives compensation. It sounds like a common everyday transaction, but not so often within large businesses that usually rely on company employees to do this. Small and inconsequential as this example may seem, the future implications loom much larger. The growing comfort with the reality of worldwide interconnectivity could begin to bring the concept of outsourcing to fine levels of granularity.

The very well defined inner structure of a traditional business and its initiatives are being redefined and expanded.

Taken to what lengths?

If all areas of a business are to be looked at for possible re-sourcing, does high-level management escape scrutiny? Possibly not. It is admittedly the last place one would expect. And yet costs are high even when occasionally results do not support the expense. In many countries outside of the United States, the budget is lower for this function. Can management itself be outsourced?

There are several possible scenarios. Let's look at one. A group of scientists with a breakthrough discovery and products surrounding it want to build a company to market their products. They seek qualified leaders to administer the organization but see this as a function to be outsourced. The scientific foundation of the company is its reason for being and its future. Right or wrong, this could be the view and the direction it will take—treat the management and administration as simply another, albeit highly important, function. If the search is unsuccessful in the United States, they might look to a different venue.

The hierarchy is challenged.

The connections

Are we seeing something more important than outsourcing or even globalization? There is a common thread in the topics offered here. Boundaries and alliances are no longer static but dynamic.

Business and cultural opportunities abound in a new age of connection. It is this power of instant and multi-dimensional connection that is beginning to be felt without even a strong sense of what it really is or what it can mean in the future. There is no current guidebook. But its impact is here and palpable. The convergence of many of the connections into a clearer pattern will affect us all.

This has been called the Age of Information, but it may be more accurately labeled the Age of Connection. Information is certainly a very important component in the mesh of global intelligence, but people and ideas are also included in new and extraordinary ways. The Internet and the World Wide Web continue to exert influences and promise ever increasing profitable gathering points for business and society in general.

The business world may see a fundamental change. Hierarchy which served so well in loosely, or rarely, connected times may not be as successful a model in a world with instant access to information and collaboration with people both inside and outside the enterprise positioned anywhere in the world. Business and other organizational communities stand at the gates of a new frontier. Is it possible that the hierarchical organization model will morph into a more networked model? The energy and time to work up and down multiple internal hierarchies are a drain on the potential achievements of a business. The momentum of the powers of interconnected people, ideas and accomplishments will test the fabric of current structures of organizational models.

This will not happen overnight or even perhaps provide a complete departure from the current model, but the differences are developing. The actual nature of management would need to undergo a metamorphosis. A more networked enterprise needs a different form of governance. Can we imagine what an organization chart would look like? Nothing like the present one and probably more akin to a schematic of the Internet. Inter-related functions wherever they are would have direct connection with one another as, when and if needed. Domain expertise would again have currency within the connected functions.

Can business schools adapt to new models? Instead of spawning more and more young executives to fit into a hierarchy model, could they begin to study and experiment with ways to produce a new breed of leaders that in place of being controllers would be accelerators and enablers of new structures?

Attempts at something like a networked environment have happened in the past, but the intersection of business needs and visions with global connections and instant communication of all kinds heralds a new opportunity of immense power. Hierarchy has been the governance glue that has held organizations together, and the channels in that model provided the information and control that allowed the enterprise to operate. In a networked organization the knowledge is ubiquitous and the glue is replaced by flexibility. Obviously any business, however it is constructed, has issues, difficulties and responsibilities that must be addressed. A networked environment is not necessarily easier to build, but it can be more direct, powerful and productive. An abrupt change is probably as dangerous as staying with an archaic model. New businesses are more apt to try networked environments before established ones, and the hierarchy model will not entirely disappear. But the shift is already happening. Outsourcing and globalization are harbingers of the new order.

Harald Ludwig
Founding Partner and Chairman
Macluan Capital Corporation
Vancouver, BC Canada

U.S. Homeshoring

Question: Why have globalization and outsourcing created this perfect storm for business process outsourcers?

Ludwig: The whole business process outsourcing segment, driven by globalization and the competitive market, is geared towards optimizing financial performance to drive shareholder value by making the corporation more efficient. The trend to offshore outsourcing in this sector is merely a competitive advantage in seeking lower-cost components to an enterprises' success. With globalization and capital mobility, the BPOs themselves are becoming finely tuned organizations with the same inherent characteristics of the well-established domestic corporations. They will enhance their financial performance through diversification, growth and superior financial performance as their specialization becomes optimized through jurisdictional expansion and consolidation. Today's BPOs are tomorrow's leaders and can set themselves apart from existing multinationals by being able to turn on a dime, and avoid disruptive intermediation and technology by staying ahead of the pack through resource reallocation and geographic diversity.

Question: Why the growth in BPOs and what are the challenges for companies using BPOs?

Ludwig: We will see more movement to virtualization of corporations that will outsource processes, except core competencies, to the BPOs and reduce their capital costs where they are not strategically effective in creating value. The BPOs will become larger, more successful. From a corporate standpoint, the risks associated with that will relate to information security and the ability to execute uninterrupted an expedient customer service. What's more, they run the risk of weakening [shareholder] responsibility and social responsibility.

Sarbanes Oxley is a challenge to the U.S. companies. Because of the requirement for management to assess their financial controls, and have it backed up by an auditor, there is exposure to shareholders' lawsuits resulting from outsourcing, particularly as it relates to finance. However, I believe that Sarbanes Oxley accountability will be curtailed, because it is not efficient. Common law will develop along the lines of what's been developing in terms of CFO/CEO responsibility.

Question: *Which political issues in the United States, Europe, United Kingdom and other developed countries are affecting outsourcing and, thus, BPOs?*

Ludwig: First, this is an important question because BPOs are driving trade balances and the reverse brain drain.

There are negative political issues because many feel that companies are basically outsourcing domestic jobs. There is a redeployment of wealth that takes place to the lesser developed countries that have a highly skilled workforce. However, outsourcing does not happen without government support.

The positive is that it there will be an increase in communication and integration globally that will enhance markets as well for companies using BPOs. The BPOs will benefit, too. But in the future they will be faced with more competition. If I were running a BPO today, I would set up in more than one jurisdiction and become the service source whether I am in Costa Rica, India, or Romania.

Going forward from a cost and skills standpoint, there could be political connotations and trade issues that might impact the future—whether it is a renegade country or Western civilization that may overturn those issues they feel are unfair trade practices.

The issues facing BPOs will focus on protectionism versus free trade as governments rally to the aid of those domestic lobby groups whose constituent members' livelihoods are being jeopardized. Overseas allocation of work, which causes a material decline in domestic employment and thereby a resource reallocation (in that it causes job loss but reduces the costs of products to consumers), is not only a short-term phenomenon but one that has far reaching long-term implications.

In the future, entrepreneurial organizations will take advantage of all cost issues that will in turn drive the BPO segment. But the political risk will increase for those organizations whose domestic governments seek protectionism through either tariff, quotas or some form of extraterritorial taxation. Long-term declining domestic opportunities and declining salaries could drive this political intervention as the migration of work to lower cost jurisdictions continues.

Centers of excellence for highly skilled labor and services also will become concentric and will revolve around the necessary sharing of ideas, a standard of living that is expected and demanded as well as a geopolitical climate that is inviting.

Question: *How will the growth of BPOs affect the taxation policies and national and municipal revenue streams?*

Ludwig: The more offshoring occurs, the fewer taxes will be available. However, having said this, the local and federal governments are more in tune and are trying to tax organizations based on their head office location. In the future, they also will try to issue extra territorial taxation. And as the result, there will be more tax treaties with more friendly trading nations in order to share the bounty of doing business elsewhere. That is a political risk and an economic risk.

2.2

By **Marjan Bolmeijer**
CEO
Change Leaders, Inc.
New York, New York

Unraveling the DNA of the Global Leader

The board was fed up. Eighteen months into an aggressive, global corporate expansion, with five international joint ventures, eight foreign acquisitions, and a number of global BPO projects, the CEO was about to get fired. The company had run into one difficulty after another trying to build a global presence. There had been unusual tension during the joint venture negotiations, and several BPO projects had derailed. Clearly there was something going on, and it wasn't the lack of technological opportunities.

Several soft business issues had contributed to the lackluster results, not the least of which was the role the senior leadership's background played in the failure of the expansion efforts:

- *Failure to expand local ties:* Blind to his strong emotional affiliations with local cultures (i.e., Indonesia), the CEO failed to adopt regional affiliations (i.e., Asia) that would have benefited the company's global expansion.

- *Shortage of cultural curiosity:* Due to his status, the CEO traveled in his own cultural bubble. Those around him kept the bubble from bursting by adjusting their cultural behaviors.

- *Lack of top-down global commitment:* The CEO did not evaluate direct reports on global leadership attributes and wrongly assumed that lower-level operational managers would compensate for the top leadership's dulled cultural sensitivity.

The corporation was urgently trying to respond to global competitive pressures by transforming from an ethnocentric organization, with primarily a world headquarters (WHQ) power base and culture, to a geocentric organization, driven by a global network structure with local power bases and cultures.

Yet, the CEO and his team had been personally unprepared. As role models they had conveyed the implicit message that managing across cultures wasn't the company's strength and that this was OK. The resulting ripple effect could be felt throughout contentious outsourcing negotiations.

Against the backdrop of a world with fast-changing business models, intensified demands on global leaders, and increased transparency of their work, global leaders involved in outsourcing must understand two critical global leadership components to lead their companies:

- The DNA of the global leader

- Organizational design and its impact on the global leader

Understanding these global leadership components will provide a better understanding of potential outsourcing partners and allow the organization to build the necessary trust, synergy and collaboration for healthy outsourcing ventures.

DNA and organizational design models

DNA

Deciphering the global leaders involved in a potential outsourcing opportunity is no small task. The challenge is intensified by the absence of a comprehensive theoretical framework that defines global leadership and provides well-researched attributes that have a positive correlation to the global leader's effectiveness.

Different models need to be used to decipher a global leader, such as models for skills, personal characteristics, professional experiences, career imprint, cultural backgrounds, education, networks, mindsets, values, behaviors, emotional intelligence, or leadership styles.

Organizational Design

All senior executives are to some extent shaped and influenced by the organizational design and the resulting cultural context in which they operate. That is, their leadership styles, habits, traits, or skills are only partially self-determined and partially the result of unconsciously conforming to their company's cultural context. Therefore, the company's organizational design provides another insight into the type of global leaders the company produces.

The model of the ethnocentric, polycentric, and geocentric organization, created by Wharton Business School professor Howard Perlmutter, provides a useful illustration. Taking a closer look at the model's two extremes, the ethnocentric and geocentric organizations, it becomes possible to shed some light on the way organizational design influences a global leader's personal attributes, such as sense of identity, values, leadership styles, and drive for personal development.

The ethnocentric organization: The global leader in a local world

Organizational Design

"Give me a W. Give me an A. ..." can be heard at staff meetings in Wal-Mart stores anywhere in the world. Such ethnocentric organizations tend to have a WHQ organizational design with a centralized decision making process. Global corporate strategy, operational processes, policies and corporate values all originate from a single location. Basically, information flows from WHQ to the regions, and regional offices operate in a similar way as the home based WHQ.

Cultural Context

In this type of global company, the senior executive teams, most of whom are located at WHQ, are global leaders: their agenda includes global topics and they carry broad regional responsibilities. For instance: Group VP, Asia.

The leadership style and role of a global leader in an ethnocentric organization has a large, national cultural element (Wal-Mart's U.S. chant in Asia). The executives see themselves as rooted in the culture of the country where the global headquarters is situated. They perceive themselves to work for WHQ, make decisions and act on its behalf, and see units from other countries as internal customers.

DNA of the ethnocentric global leader

Sense of Identity
In the ethnocentric corporation, the global leader's sense of identity can be described as:

"I have a strong national pride. I'm a Brit. That's where my home is. I have a million frequent flyer miles, work for a multinational organization, have been an expatriate, but home is where my heart is. Because I am only exposed to a few cultures at a time and for a short amount of time, I can easily maintain my own cultural identities of country, region, company, and family."

Values, Beliefs, and Assumptions
Global leaders at an ethnocentric company show a hierarchy of values when traveling abroad. First, they represent WHQ, then the company itself, and in third place a regional headquarters. The implied notion is that if the WHQ does well the rest of the company will do well.

As WHQ sets a strong cultural framework for their global operations, its challenge is to function as the company's worldwide moral and ethical role model. As its representative, this global leader aspires to embody its values and beliefs: to walk the talk.

Leadership Style and Focus
Key elements of the ethnocentric leader's style and focus include:
- Modeling symbolic roles, behaviors and styles explicitly selected for communicating and maintaining WHQ culture and legitimacy
- Living and articulating to others repeatedly the WHQ values
- Leading as a representative of the WHQ senior team
- Sharing leadership and developing the next generation of leaders

Drive for professional growth

In the ethnocentric organization, the starting point for leadership development tends to focus on strengths and weaknesses and asks the question, "What is not yet there in terms of skills or experiences that need to be developed?"

Leadership development programs are usually designed by WHQ and include such tactics as formal assessments, cross-functional rotation, stretch assignments on the job, mentoring, shadowing, 360 degree feedback, global rotation, custom-designed or university based leadership development programs, or exposure to the senior executive team.

These approaches start with the viewpoint that leaders can be homegrown and that leadership development is a journey. Any journey requires an investment of time. For instance, the executive transferred abroad to learn to detach from strong local affiliations, develop a global mindset, and increase cultural sensitivities still needs on-going developmental guidance. Plant and build, rather than plant and run, is a more effective way for ethnocentric organizations to build global leadership.

In this type of environment the regional leader will have an interest in establishing a supportive network with WHQ executives for mentorship around developmental objectives and career planning.

Key global leadership skills for the ethnocentric leader

Staying Slightly Detached

Too little time in any role or company and the feeling of being an outside consultant creeps in (being part of the solution). Too much time in any role and the feeling of being an engrained part of a whole comes up (part of the problem).

The ethnocentric leader, especially if he or she doesn't travel or move a lot, risks getting too engrained in the company's culture. Here the required skill is to walk the fine line between getting embedded enough to be able to notice the small organizational pieces while maintaining the higher level perspective to notice the larger organizational trends (see forest and trees).

Since this emotional skill is rarely discussed in leadership development programs, it is often overlooked.

This skill has two components: the analytical and the emotional. Analytically every executive knows how to keep a detached organizational perspective. For instance, thinking about opportunities in 2010 creates this detached perspective. Emotional detachment is more challenging. It occurs, for instance, when starting a new position in a new company. The challenge lies in maintaining this emotional, slightly detached, perspective over time.

Quickly and Deeply with a Wide Variety of People

There is always some pulling and tugging for power between WHQ and local units. This creates a need for executives from an ethnocentric organization to avoid the "red carpet" treatment. When visiting a regional office for a day, where drawers have been cleaned, walls freshly painted, and presentations show a pretty picture, it can be difficult to uncover what is really happening in the bowels of the local unit.

This requires the global leadership skill to connect with very different people very fast. It is not a question of doing the "Hi, how are you?" routine, but of showing true curiosity, building substantial rapport quickly, and allowing powerful conversations to emerge while leaving egos and politics at the door.

These face-to-face meetings offer the single most important venue for dispersed units to have the meaningful conversations that build the important relationships through which work can get done effectively across the globe.

The geocentric organization: the global leader in a global world

Organizational Design

The geocentric company tends to have a complex, global network-centric organizational design, with highly interdependent local units that contribute to both local and global organizational objectives. The design is intended to enable the organization to quickly adjust strategies, policies, structure or processes to the fluctuations of regional competitive advantages on the global playing field.

Communication flows up and down through the hierarchy, both ways between headquarters and subsidiaries, and between subsidiaries. Decision-making moves less from HQ to subsidiaries but has a global, system wide approach with a collaborative style.

Cultural Context

The geocentric leaders, located across the globe, have simultaneously worldwide and regional objectives, and their sphere of influence includes corporate, regional and local headquarters.

The global leader in the geocentric company operates in an environment that is less governed by the organization's global cultural strategy and more by that of the regional offices where the executive works. The company's local corporate identity has been enhanced by a global one (Example: once known as BP, British Petroleum, it now stands for bp, beyond petroleum).

Of the two organizational designs, ethnocentric and geocentric, this one is likely to have the most culturally complex environment.

Its global leader makes decisions and acts on behalf of the organization rather than a single unit with the perspective: "Your problem/opportunity is our problem/opportunity. If we are going to do well, we all need to do well." The leader has a strong global network throughout the organization, and when traveling represents the worldwide corporation rather than its headquarters or a specific country or region.

DNA of the geocentric global leader

Sense of Identity

The geocentric leader is more likely to have a sense of regional or global citizenship, as reflected in these statements:

"I'm an American CEO living in London, leading a multinational organization. I feel more like a global citizen than an American citizen."

"Although the airplane used to make several stops, I always felt it returned home at some point. Nowadays every stop feels like home. I had to make that distinction so that I could raise my sense of loyalty to our staff at all these locations."

"I'm always around different cultures. As a direct report to the CEO and without peers at this location I am a unit of one representing a variety of cultures within the company. There were times in my career when I needed to maintain, adjust or completely change some parts of my cultural identities."

Values, Beliefs, Assumptions

Geocentric leaders tend to value the diversity that globalization brings and recognize the universal characteristics of human nature and culture. Since their ever-changing world has forced them to make numerous personal leadership changes, they believe in the ability and willingness of human beings to change themselves. This insight and optimism about human nature results in a compassionate leadership.

Leadership Style and Focus

Unlike in the ethnocentric organization, where leadership styles are more influenced by corporate headquarters, here leadership styles are more self-determined and adjust faster to meet local needs. Key elements of the geocentric leader's style and focus include:

- Virtual accessibility and availability across the globe 24/7
- Communicating comfortably with many people, at all hierarchical levels, from an equal status perspective
- Role modeling leadership values and behaviors that hold universal human truisms
- "Synergy and comfort builder" by being around, even if from a distance

Drive for Professional Growth

The absence of many structured, global leadership development initiatives originated from WHQ and the need for fast corporate growth create in this leader a proactive attitude towards personal growth: "What more is possible?"

Competition is also a driving force for this leader's growth. The geocentric company has fewer corporate policies to recruit from within and has the ability to pick its very best candidates from a larger number of regional offices (legal restrictions permitting). This increases the pool of candidates with important international experience.

Also, this leader is likely to move and travel more, which requires shedding some degree of home-country affiliations, develop cultural sensitivities, augmenting related emotional skills, and broadening his or her bandwidth of global leadership qualities — all qualities that make this leader very marketable.

Key global leadership skills for the geocentric leader

Driving a Global Network

Geocentric organizations tend to have two different executive challenges that are being addressed with a single approach that requires substantial emotional intelligence skills: global, face to face, network meetings.

The first challenge is that the global organizations need their local executives to give a percentage of their time to building operational synergies around global corporate concerns. For instance, a company's 20 regional and local CFOs need to give 10 per cent of their year to global finance issues.

Second, for the regional and local CFO, building an in-house peer network can present an unusual challenge since everyone is spread across the globe. The same is true for keeping a finger on the organization's political pulse, reading emotional currents, and understanding concerns and points of view from different key players.

As a result, regular meetings are needed to discuss critical issues face to face and build the relationship needed to get day-to-day work done. Global network meetings for all top 20 CFOs or other C-level executives offer a valuable solution.

Different from the company's annual retreat, different from regional or national operational meetings, these forums tend to address global issues affecting all attendees (making decisions only we can make). Given the large number of participants, these forums also tend to have a complex political and cultural landscape with a large number of agenda items, making it challenging to have in-depth, meaningful dialogues. Driving such global network meetings requires leadership skills in managing global networks, aligning teams across the globe, building cultural synergy, and establishing international decision making processes. Yet, even with all its complexity, this approach tends to quickly create important operational benefits.

Developing a Global Leadership Persona

Any leader, independent of the type of organizational design he or she is most influenced by, would do well to develop his or her own global leadership branding image or persona.

Executives from ethnocentric organizations can let WHQ guide their decisions around their leadership persona (Integrity is our No. 1 value! Coaching others is important! The boss should stand in the spotlight.). Since these guidelines run across geographical boundaries they provide some framework for the regional or local leaders to adjust their leadership image, style, and traits.

With less of the global headquarters influence at play in geocentric organizations there is a stronger need for individual executives to fill the gap by developing their own global personas. This is often unfamiliar territory for those who spend so much time working on the company that little time remains to think about their personal in-house or external branding image and the resulting cultural effects. The thinking seems to be, "If I read the local dress code well, the etiquettes, and manners of speaking, I'll be fine." That perspective is less likely to impress superiors, who consider a distinctly personal leadership identity as a sign of emotional intelligence.

Three must-have beliefs for any global leader

Current leadership development trends in the United States and certain European countries show that the days are numbered for assumptions such as, "you are who you are," "older people don't change," or "he can't be changed." Today, companies are increasingly intolerant of personal inconsistencies from their leaders. Their message is clearly to "fix it," and more leaders are learning how to personally develop and change fast. To do so, they must embrace three new beliefs:

• It's Possible: Changing personal leadership features (behaviors, skills, emotional intelligence or styles) is possible at any age and under any circumstance.

• It's Personal: Leadership styles and features need to be continuously re-aligned with the ever-changing needs of the organization and its global marketplace.

• It's a Process: This requires a personal systematic focus and process for regularly monitoring and adjusting one's leadership persona and its effects.

These are critical new beliefs for global outsourcing projects. Imagine a command-control leader from an ethnocentric organization who has never heard of the need to "fix-it" trying to bulldoze through a negotiation with a global leader from a geocentric organization who believes in people empowerment and a humble, low profile leadership style. Clearly, a shaky foundation for an outsourcing contract.

The ability to adjust and grow one's personal leadership features and corresponding emotional intelligence is rapidly becoming one of the key skills for successfully leading outsourcing ventures or reaching the upper echelons of the corporate world.

Conclusion

The quick pace of globalization will most likely introduce new business models faster. Shifts in global economic powers, industry reconfigurations, technology and cost inequalities will continue to create and fuel changes such as the global outsourcing phenomenon.

Given these circumstances, it is critical that more global leaders take a closer look at organizational design and global leadership attributes, since both contribute to the success of outsourcing projects.

Even more critical is the need for global leaders to take a closer look at how and what they need to change in their own leadership attributes to adjust and succeed on the fast changing global stage. Possibly, the most important global leadership competency is the ability to affect personal change. "You are who you are" is no longer good enough. Self-awareness alone is no longer good enough. Ultimately, the will and the ability to create one's own personal leadership changes may well prove the difference between success and failure at the highest levels of a global business world.

DNA BUILDING BLOCKS

Globalization has put pressure on leaders to develop new skills and experiences, and to adapt personal traits. Some experiences and skills must be developed; others the leader can draw upon from earlier in life.

Early Childhood Experiences - Family diversity, linguistic skills, cross-cultural exposure, study abroad, international family moves and travels

Career experiences - Exposure to the global strategic agenda, international mentors with global mindsets, cross-cultural stretch assignment, international operational P&L responsibilities, performance appraisals with emotional intelligence criteria, experience working in a 'cultural mosaic' office environment

Business know-how - Global finance, global macroeconomics, global strategy, global brand management, global marketing, regional human resources

Personal skills - Intelligence, physical stamina, emotional intelligence, motivation to work in a truly international environment, readiness to act when opportunity strikes, decisiveness, self-awareness, curiosity, optimism, empathy, social perception and judgment skills, ego management, tolerance for ambiguity

References

1 Perlmutter, Howard V. 1969. "The tortuous evolution of the multinational corporation," *Columbia Journal of World Business* 4(1): 9-18.

Rustam Lalkaka
President, Business and Technology
Development Strategies LLC
New York, New York

Here Come the Incubators

Question: *What exactly is an incubator?*

Lalkaka: Business incubation is the process for nurturing early-stage entrepreneur-groups in taking their innovations to the market. These groups are carefully selected and given focused counseling, training, mentoring, networking and facilitation services, as well as workspace and shared office facilities. They must leave the incubator in two or three years.

Question: *How would you assess the success of incubating?*

Lalkaka: Incubation, in general, has led to positive economic impulses in many countries, developed and developing. Silicon Valley, California, for instance, is a kind of vast incubation system. Stanford University Professor Frederick Terman had given a small amount of money to his students Hewlett and Packard to develop their innovation; from that point on, things began to come together—a strong infrastructure, sound knowledge base and ethnic mix, venture capital, legal and other services. Everyone wants a Silicon Valley in their own country, but until those conditions are created,

you don't have it. Incubators in many countries have had problems. The trick is for incubators to secure supportive public policies and seed government funds without excessive government interference.

There are about 5,000 incubators around the world today. China now has about 500, second to the United States, which has 1,000. We helped establish the first one at Wuhan in 1987. Under strong technocratic leadership and with a public investment of $1.5 billion, China has used incubation effectively to leverage the transition from a centrally-planned economy towards a more open market system. In 2005, the number of incubators in the developing countries exceeded those in the developed. But whereas in the developed countries the majority of incubators are not technology-related, in the developing countries 80-plus percent are technology-focused.

Question: *What are the future trends in business incubation?*

Lalkaka: An emerging trend is "co-incubation." Incubators will link-up with each other, sharing and expanding their capabilities, performance and impact. Multinationals have an important role in this endeavor. Some already have discovered that the big market is at the "bottom of the pyramid," not the top. They begin to combine market opportunities with corporate social responsibility, in public-private partnerships.

In both developed and developing countries, what we now need is not just more incubators (the work places), but better incubation (the process). Incubation focused on technology ventures and with limited outreach is not the best option. In most countries, the critical problems are unemployment and poverty; so, we need more social entrepreneurs and civic innovations, incubators for empowerment, for youth and women, for rural communities. On the incubation platform you could have an in-house management consulting capability and a seed equity-capital company. For the future I see co-incubation for co-innovation, e-incubation with e-counseling, e-learning, international partnering, social inclusion and accredited incubator managers. The galloping pace of technology and the megatrend of globalization are making the earth flatter, but not quite flat yet.

Question: *What do you think is the relationship between incubation and outsourcing?*

Lalkaka: Incubation can lead to powerful outsourcing clusters. In the past there was little specific outsourcing activity at incubators. In 1996 China pioneered in converting eight of its incubators into international business incubators (IBIs) for attracting foreign high-tech ventures and facilitating their entry in to the complex China market while also orienting local ventures for world markets. Now they are establishing Chinese incubators abroad. There is growing interest in participation by incubator ventures in the global supply chain. In 2005, the Asian Association of Business Incubation (AABI) invited nominations and selected six incubators to become accredited international incubators to help "soft-landings" by foreign companies.

Question: *Politicians in the developed world are trying to oppose outsourcing to protect jobs back home. What can be done to stop the erosion of employment?*

Lalkaka: Understandably, people who lose their jobs in developed countries due to offshore outsourcing are very upset. The primal scare of a vast loss of jobs is somewhat exaggerated, partly politicized. China, India and others in South America will continue to advance. This is their opportunity, their time in history. "There is a tide in the affairs of men," wrote Shakespeare, "which, taken at the flood, leads on to fortune." These nations are riding that tide. It's up to the U.S. to put enormous investment in its engineering curricula and schools. America is a vast resilient economy, and the political and business people can come together to meet this challenge so everyone wins in the longer term.

Question: *What is the role of culture in the innovation process?*

Lalkaka: Culture has such a tremendous impact on risk-taking and business practices. But culture also changes. People do not want to be forced to change, but they will change given the right motivation and the demonstration of benefits. For instance, the amazingly fast spread of cellular phones, computers and the so-called "simputer"—a $200 computer developed in India that is used in villages. Then there are the "necessity entrepreneurs"—people who start businesses not because they have some great idea or market opportunity, but are forced into entrepreneurship because they have no jobs—and they do well.

Another significant factor not often mentioned are contributions made by the diaspora of overseas Chinese, Indians and Philippinos to their countries of origin. Korea pioneered this. In 1976 we helped start a program in Turkey called TOKTEN (Transfer of Knowledge through Expatriate Nationals) where UNDP covered travel and living costs for those willing to work as volunteer short-term consultants in countries of origin. It was adopted by many countries, became one of the longest running and most successful programs in the UN development system. Today expatriates are sending more than money, including their contacts and their technology. Two-thirds of the direct foreign investment in China comes from Chinese overseas, and there are special incubators meant for them.

Question: *What is the future of work?*

Lalkaka: New technologies are radically changing the nature of work. We see a lot of convergence, multi-tasking, unprecedented and near-costless access to information, knowledge, and some day, we hope, to wisdom. People are increasingly working from their homes in virtual modes, more comfortably in pajamas, less distracted by traffic and office gossip. We are adding a billion new workers to the world economy (mainly from Eastern Europe, China and India) whereas the financial base remains much the same. This puts pressure on productivity and on wages.

And there is the demographic imbalance—populations in the rich countries are getting older while in many developing countries the proportion of youth is rising. That poses the dilemma: *Do you export the work or do you import the workers?* Globalization is irreversible; the challenge is to prepare to make it work for all, as an instrument of opportunity and equity—not of fear and insecurity.

2.3

By **Eugene Goland**
Founder, DataArt
Founder and Chairman of OOBP.org
New York, New York

Outsourcing:
Not Just for the Big Guys

In January 2003 at the annual strategy board meeting of my 200-man software outsourcing and consulting company, we were reviewing the performance of our top management team in comparison to strategic objectives of a previous year. We noticed that objectives that require little time were mostly on-target, while those that require a serious time commitment were often neglected because there was "not enough time."

It also became clear that activities related to investments into our company's core competence are mostly long-term and time-consuming. For example, we had launched a knowledge-sharing portal, but little effort was done to make knowledge sharing effective company-wide. Additionally, we held seminars to educate employees on career paths and professional choices, but little mentorship took place. Our efforts to get to the bottom of the problem only submerged us in multitudes of smaller problems and issues—none of which was related to our company's core competency and value to our clients. Our top management's time—our most precious resource—was consumed by things that could be done by an outside expert at a fraction of the cost and probably with better quality.

We asked, "What would be an ideal scenario for our next annual meeting?" The picture was quite clear. We wanted to spend our time talking about issues that focused on growth—client satisfaction, core competence and competition. Naturally, we agreed that non-core activities should be outsourced to experts. "How do we know that outsourcing will be effective?" somebody asked. "We'll have to learn to measure," I replied. "What do we need to do to become good at measuring and outsourcing?" The answer was apparent: outsourcing must become one of our core competences.

Today, 18 months after our strategic shift towards outsourcing, we already see some benefits, although we still have much work ahead of us to reach our goal to become a core-competence-only company. Today, our top management is primarily motivated to achieve effectiveness, to reach end results of strategic initiatives, and they are far less involved in the tactical steps. Most of the educational activities, many back office functions, and even some of the marketing functions are now outsourced. Some are accomplished by spending less money than before; some are at the same price. But overall users of those outsourced functions are reporting higher quality. Our client satisfaction rating is on a healthy upward-looking trend while our revenues and profits have more than doubled.

As I collect opinions on outsourcing from members of the OOBP.org (Offshore Outsourcing Best Practices) community of small and medium enterprises (SME) and with management consultants focused on smaller companies, I confirm my assumption that while today only a small fraction of SMEs view outsourcing strategically, the benefits of outsourcing are so appealing that it is readily acknowledged by most companies of that sector. (Note: According to Gartner, "Small businesses account for only three percent of the U.S. IT outsourcing market.") As globalization and advances in telecommunication technologies reshape the business world into a truly global marketplace, I believe the stage will be set for a new breed of companies—relatively small in size, highly focused on their niche, and outsourcing everything but their core competence.

Segments by size and their differences

There are distinct features of small companies that make their outsourcing practices different from those of larger ones. The distinction that matters most when comparing smaller and larger companies is their ability to formulate the requirements and to deal with multiple vendors systematically. Other distinctions include the degree of stakeholder involvement in outsourcing, organizational maturity, planning horizon and access to capital.

Those distinctions affect the buying behavior of outsourced services, creating separate market spaces with distinct structures and dynamics, and direct the evolution of outsourcing to follow a somewhat different route.

Large companies tend to measure outsourcing relations by compliance with formal requirements, market pricing, service levels and an overall focus on the process and metrics. On the other hand, smaller companies tend to be more results-oriented on the strategic level, and on a tactical level they are often more relationship-oriented. This is not to say that larger companies neglect the end result, but rather to acknowledge the separation of the function of high-end planning by top management and the tactical execution by mid-management. The project manager in a large company does not have a full picture of the strategy, and his performance is measured by tactical outsourcing metrics. Unlike large companies, where the CIO buys reports, routinely listens to vendor presentations, and asks his procurement department to run RFIs (requests for information) from dozens of vendors, smaller companies are not equipped to do all that and subsequently are often left unaware of what is going on in the market.

The skill set of an outsourcing officer from a larger company needs to be different than that of a smaller company. The most important skill of an outsourcing officer (OO) of a large company is "packaging" the outsourcing requirements, which includes specification, measurements and formal coordination with other in-house and outsourced activities. Dealing with vendors is relatively easy and a formal process since the work is packaged in such a way that it is easy to measure, and because large companies tend to deal with established vendors. Large companies also rely on legal protection to cover risks, and therefore relationships with partnering organizations will be of less importance. The most important skills of the OO working for the smaller company are people and project management skills. Outsourcing practices for this sector is mostly relations-oriented. Buyers and vendors tend to form long-term strategic dependencies much more than with larger companies. The nature of the work is more dynamic, requiring frequent adjustments, and vendors often work in groups to deliver a variety of skills. Selecting the right vendors and maintaining long-term mutually beneficial relationships are of the utmost important for SME companies.

Vendors serving one market are not effective for the other. More than 80 percent of small and medium business that are members of OOBP.org regularly express concern that their outsourcing needs are significantly different from the market of larger companies and that vendors serving SMEs must take into account these variances. The most visible technical obstacle to outsourcing by a SME is the ability to formulate the requirements and to "extract" an internal process in order to make it external. Vendors need to understand this and have the necessary skills to make this possible and cost-effective. Vendors focused on the needs of large company are optimized to work on well defined specifications and are unlikely be effective in the fast changing context of a small company. Interfaces between companies also require consideration. In the SME sector stakeholders or top management are frequently involved in the process, and they feel awkward when they interface with mid-level project managers from the vendor side who have mediocre communication skills and are focused on contract wording instead of the business objectives.

There are developing business models that are feasible for one sector, but not the other. For example, vendor due diligence and rating are services that are badly needed for the SME sector and are not likely to be used by larger businesses. Larger companies are likely to work with established vendors and/or have internal due diligence and audit resources, while smaller companies cannot afford this expense. Members of OOBP.org often complain that selection of a vendor is like "fishing with a rod in the dark waters instead of ordering a fish from the menu in the restaurant," as a CEO of a small medical technology startup puts it. The only tools available to a researcher are Google during the first selection stage and conference calls in the second stage. Experienced buyers usually use a third selection stage with a test project undertaken by multiple vendors, but this is expensive. Availability of rating services significantly reduces the cost of vendor selection, while it increases the success rate and overall industry effectiveness.

SME outsourcing drivers and inhibitors

The fundamental drive to outsource is the same for SME's as for larger companies. It is the same basic reason that pushes companies to innovative changes and overall cost and quality improvement. It is competition. To compete firms must specialize. This, by definition, means that they need to limit the scope of their functions. Outsourcing is a tool that allows firms to specialize.

Practical reasons to consider outsourcing include access to the infrastructure and expertise unavailable within an organization (the alternative would be a capital investment into such capabilities); lower costs (outsourcing companies might have access to a lower cost resource, such as offshore labor); and management bandwidth (outsourcing saves management time).

If a firm decides to keep a particular function in-house, it must figure out the best way to execute that function very efficiently. Otherwise the firm will find itself less competitive than others vying for the same space on the market who do chose to outsource this function.

For large commercial enterprises outsourcing often is counterbalanced by leveraging assets of their holding companies to enhance their competitiveness, or by the fact that there are economies of scale to justify investment into the firm's infrastructure. This is almost never the case for SMEs. Outsourcing of noncore activities is the most feasible strategy for SME.

OOBP.org members list the following limiting factors and technical difficulties in the order of importance.

Limiting factors:
• Fear for vendor performance

• Fear of loss of IP

• Uncertainty

• Fear of loss of control

Technical difficulties:

• Lack of experience (especially task formalization)

• Internal resistance

• Difficulties in vendor selection

Fear of poor vendor performance is an inherited fear for most service-oriented engagements on the client side. In exchange for hard cash or pre-payment and investment of time, as well as other resources, clients are promised a deliverable of something in the future. Traditionally, consulting firms were investing a fortune into a brand to address the issue of credibility. The logic behind a brand investment is to demonstrate to a potential client that the vendor has too much at stake to risk a low-quality service. The nature of brand equity is such that it is expensive to build and easy to spoil, and therefore every disgruntled client can bring too much harm. Theoretically, it is cheaper for a vendor to keep clients happy than to sustain damage to a reputation or brand. While brand investments are effective, they also are very costly, and at the end of the day this cost is being transferred to clients. New, more cost-effective ways to address the credibility issue are emerging. From the buy side, techniques are being explored to shift non-performance risk to the vendor, and knowledge is being accumulated on how to best manage an outsourcing relationship. From the sell side, there are signs of increasing transparency, willingness to take on some of the risks, emerging rating services and, most importantly, ever decreasing cost of services due to offshoring.

Fear of loss of intellectual property (IP) or sensitive data by SMEs is mostly overrated. Internal personnel are likely to act more as a bridge than a vendor. While vendors are usually focused on their business model, an insider usually has a much better grasp on the market and necessary network to take advantage of know-how or IP. Some common sense precautions coupled with a legal contract can work very effectively to address the IP issue. For example, one of my clients, a market research company, was able to eliminate most of its relevant risks by populating the system with fake data and splitting the work between three independent vendors.

Loss of control and flexibility through an outsourcing relationship points to inadequate planning and/or a weak outsourcing contract. If done right, outsourcing greatly increases flexibility, strengthens control and enhances the effectiveness of change management. While it is true that management can change the course of an internal project immediately and without contractual penalties, this kind of flexibility doesn't account for internal costs of switching gears and often is misused to substitute for the lack of good planning in the first place. Consider the range of available options when a project is planned for internal execution, versus a project considered for global sourcing. Internal considerations include limitations of available personnel, their skills and schedules, and perhaps some equipment with specific features and associated costs. Suddenly you are faced with the task of how to best utilize resources on hand rather than how to best get the project done.

Flexibility gained through vendor scale-up capacity and access to a global pool of vendors gives a drastic increase in flexibility.

Growth and maturity of SME outsourcing segment

Today SMEs do not use information technology as well as other outsourceable technologies nor as intensively as larger enterprises. The main reason is that economies of scale for the SME are often not there yet. For example, the economics of investment into electronic medical records for a 300-bed hospital is very different than a two-doctor medical practice. Surprising as it may seem for an IT person, I have come across dozens and dozens SMEs that still use paperwork in a literal sense. While in some rare cases there is a healthy dose of management ignorance, in most cases there is a calculation that investment doesn't make financial sense. Two factors account for relatively expensive IT solutions for SMEs—lack of off-the-shelf solutions for some niches and expensive consultants who compensate for lack of SMEs' IT skills.

Another strong limiting factor for market growth is a relative market inefficiency and plenty of negative experience. According to Gartner's report for the year 2003, half of all deals were classified as a failure by the buyer. According to my personal observation, the SME segment experiences an even greater magnitude of failures. It is also quite visible that the ratio of successes and realized benefits is skyrocketing to greater acceptance of outsourcing.

The tiny existing size of the SME outsourcing market is shaped by limiting factors on one side, and benefits on the other. As the market matures, limiting forces are bound to weaken, and, as globalization takes further shape, benefits are bound to become more valuable. There is no doubt that the market will expand, and it is very likely that it will be expanding faster than other segments consisting of larger companies.

As the demand from SME for outsourcing grows, the supply side will grow and become more effective. An increase in effectiveness will be driven by experience accumulated by individuals and by companies; by emergence of best practices and relevant methodologies; by standardization of services; and by emergence of sector-specific and task-specific service level metrics. Vendors will become more transparent to address concerns of uncertainty and the international legal framework.

As SMEs transform to embrace outsourcing, more and more vendors will focus specifically on this segment. These vendors will need to be sensitive to SME specifics and are likely to demonstrate the following features: access to worldwide resources; reputation-based marketing for non-commodity products and services; the ability to work with other vendors in a team; and marketing as expertise-based outsourcing.

Knowledge management and relevant skills will become increasingly important. As we learn more and more about what we do and what surrounds us due to science and innovation, as data is being exchanged freely and instantly due to ever-improving information technology, as management decisions require more and more context data due to quality demands, the ability of an enterprise to convert data into knowledge and effectively manage it becomes critical.

As SMEs grow in number and variety, and the political arena stabilizes, the HR market will become more fluid, transparent, and ever more competitive. Automation and offshoring will eliminate some jobs, but they will surely create new opportunities. Employment in general will become more project-oriented, and individuals will market their skills in a manner similar to SME companies.

In general, jobs in the SME segment will become more challenging. Consider a payroll specialist who was employed as an internal employee for a back office function; that same person now will work for the firm that specializes in payroll processing. This same person suddenly will be bumped up on the front line, and become involved in a core firm activity delivering customer value.

There will be less "buying" and more "hiring" in business-to-business engagements. For example, when a small apparel business engages in an IT outsourcing relationship, it will be more appropriate to say that apparel firm is hiring a CIO together with its IT department rather than to say that firm is buying outsourcing services.

John Furth
Senior Vice President
International Strategic Planning
Discovery Networks International
Washington, D.C.

Media's Appetite for Innovation

Question: *Media companies have a vast appetite for innovation. How does globalization impact innovation?*

Furth: A good friend of mine in the media industry once said, "Strategy or transformation in media companies does not look the same as it does in other companies." Media companies tend to be very tactical because they are, in a sense, fashion businesses and move very quickly. Outsourcing is a challenge for media companies because of their tactical nature.

The media industry does not face the same troubles you find in the manufacturing industry or in engineering-oriented companies. In many cases, margins at content-driven media companies are high, but that is not true across the board. Content, in itself, is not open to transformation or changes. It is always about getting the best, most creative, most talented people and putting them in a room and having them create something.

Media companies that are engineering-driven face problems because of the need to improve shareholder value. These companies must think about transformation. For them, out-sourcing is a way to optimize their operation, improve the supply chain and improve shareholder value.

Question: *You've worked in Europe and Japan. What outsourcing model do Japanese companies take?*

Furth: Japanese companies still take the lifetime approach to employment. Outsourcing requires the ability to scroll down employment in different parts of the world with high costs or less innovation, and build resources in another country that has lower costs or higher innovations. But this lifetime employment is so engrained and such a sacred cow in Japan that it will be very difficult for Japanese companies to become flexible enough for widespread adoption of outsourcing. However, several leading Japanese executives are very aware of the growing movement to outsource to China and less so to India. Even homeshoring, which would raise the employment rate in Japan, is not widely adopted.

Question: *Which countries will be the dominant players in the next 5-10 years?*

Furth: India is on the forefront and that will not change anytime soon. Large Indian IT outsourcers, such as Infosys, Satyam and Tata, will continue to grow. India has respect for IP, the ability to attract foreign investment, excellent engineering and software capabilities, and an excellently trained and very hard-working workforce. China is strong. Russia is up and coming. However, there are legal issues with both countries.

In Japan, Europe and the United States, you have an excellent, trained workforce and legislation to support business. However these countries have cost issues. And since outsourcing is driven by reduction of cost, a drive for more flexibility and efficiency, these higher cost countries do not seem to be the appropriate location for lower-level business processes. However, that is not to say they are not outsourcing destinations. Reverse outsourcing is occurring. These countries are, and will be, destinations for outsourcing of research and development, thought capital or groundbreaking innovation. This reverse outsourcing is for companies that really want to harness the best and brightest minds that are on top of the newest technologies and innovations. We could see countries such as India, China, Indonesia or Brazil really make an effort to generate more thought capital through the intellectual property in more developed countries, where they have excellent educational institutes, support from the government and strong protection of that intellectual property.

The overall outsourcing trend will have more generic, more process driven aspects as business goes to less developed countries, which are home to lower costs. Higher-end outsourcing, involving innovation, will be "outsourced" to the developed nations.

2.4

By *V.N. "Tiger" Tyagarajan*
Executive Vice President
Genpact
New York, New York

Disaggregated Corporations

The assembled board members give Dr. Stanford Lane a standing ovation. Beyond the panoramic windows of the 50th floor boardroom, the view of the Manhattan skyline is stunning. It has just rained and beams of sunlight streak from behind the clouds. Dr. Lane feels a lump in his throat. It is a special moment in his professional life. He has built one of the most unique and successful businesses in the healthcare industry.

The year is 2015, and in just five years the chain of neurosurgery hospitals Dr. Lane founded—Recovery Hospitals—has grown to the point that it generates $3 billion in revenues with $500 million in net income. Recovery Hospitals had decided on day one to be a disaggregated corporation. All its functions, except surgery and a few pre-surgical procedures, are outsourced.

Halfway around the world, above the busy streets of Tokyo on the 35th floor of Shinjuku Park Tower, Mr. James Wang, CEO of Wang Motors, signs a contract to outsource his company's last in-house manufacturing activity—the production of engines and transmissions. By any stretch of imagination, producing engines and transmissions is the core competency of an automobile company. But Mr. Wang wanted his company defined differently. He wanted Wang Motors selling the most technologically advanced and efficient cars. Based on that principle, the company concentrated all its resources on innovating new products and owning the intellectual property. The strategy paid off with Wang Motors nearly two years earlier than expected in cutting-edge hybrid-car technologies and mass-producing solar-powered vehicles ahead of competition.

Eleven time zones away, facing a picture window revealing London in late afternoon, Sarah O'Conner gazes past her personal banker while he enters the information she has requested into a computer, and her eyes follow the Thames toward the Tate Gallery. They fix on where she will join her husband in one hour—at "The Crown," a Victorian pub with splendid views of Parliament, Lambeth Palace and the numerous wharves that line the riverbanks.

O'Conner had decided to shift her account to the Global Bank based on its excellent J.D. Power and Associates ratings. In 15 minutes, she received new credit and debit cards, a checking account and an investment account. The bank also gave her car, home and life insurance quotes that were 25 percent below the rates she paid previously. Global even offered a one percentage point rate increase on her savings account, a 0.5 percent reduction on an existing mortgage, a 1.7 percentage point reduction on her car loans and free online stock trading.

An hour later, the Global Bank CEO's computer screen blips as O'Conner's 5 million account is transferred. She is one of several customers moving accounts to Global Bank due to its superlative service, better rates and superior investment solutions. Global Bank today has assets of £240 billion, up from just £11 billion just 10 years back.

The secret to the success of the three companies is total disaggregation.

Steps to the future state

Recovery Hospitals, Wang Motors and Global Bank reached the state of total disaggregation from different routes. The bank and automobile company were consolidated corporations that disaggregated one step at a time over the course of 10 years. Recovery Hospitals, on the other hand, launched as a disaggregated corporation.

In 2010, when Dr. Lane set up his chain of hospitals, he hired an outsourcing management firm—Optimal Sourcing—that selected vendors (he called them business partners) to manage and assume responsibility for individual non-core processes such as:

• Customer service operations for scheduling patient appointments and handling doctor referrals

- Transaction processing to handle billing and insurance functions
- Human resources
- Finance and accounting
- Medical transcription
- Information technology
- Hardware maintenance
- Medical diagnosis
- Legal processes
- Document management
- Purchasing

To get best-in-class service, vendors were selected from all over the globe with the goals of achieving cost-effectiveness and domain expertise. For instance, the software vendor is based in India, the mecca of IT outsourcing. A Chinese hardware maintenance vendor posts employees at all Recovery Hospitals' sites in the United States.

Medical diagnosis is conducted from Russia, India and off-site U.S. locations through the use of automated systems. Robots and robotic devices conduct such routine diagnostic tasks as taking X-rays and drawing blood. Medical doctors in the three countries diagnose the blood samples and other results remotely and send reports to the on-site doctor. Still and motion data are transmitted to offsite doctors with the use of tele-radiology.

Based on the reports from the offsite doctors, the onsite physician makes a decision on the course of treatment. The most tangible benefit to the patient is the speed of service. Usually hospitals take about two weeks to get a patient through surgery after being referred. At Recovery Hospitals the process takes 48 hours. The intangible benefit that the patient does not notice is the quality of service provided by the best minds across the globe.

Wang Motors realized that to offer the top product to its customers, it had to concentrate on what it does best—automobile engineering. In 2010, it had several external suppliers providing parts from electric switches to fuel-injection systems. Step by step it outsourced the production of safety systems and embedded software that controlled the car to best-in-class providers. With the outsourcing of engine and transmission manufacturing, the only function that Wang Motors has in-house is the research and development facility for the most proprietary parts of the car.

The supply chain of the company scattered across the globe consists of best-in-class manufacturers, delivering parts to car production facilities on five continents. Even the car assembly plants are not owned by Wang Motors. What the company owns is the intellectual property that creates several unique car components and the powerful Wang Motors brand name.

Westminster Bank re-branded itself as Global Bank in 2010, five years after it began disaggregating. The process of disaggregation turned it from a local bank to a one-stop financial services powerhouse that operates across the globe. From an asset base of 11 billion in 2005, Global Bank has assets worth 240 billion in 2015. The secret of Global Bank's success is scale, which disaggregation provided.

The bank first outsourced outbound call centers to India. The success of direct market campaigns put a major burden on the bank's back office operations as customers grew exponentially. To prevent the small-sized back office from hurting customer growth, the bank outsourced functions such as credit decisions, F&A, risk profiling and customer analytics, one step at a time. This improved efficiency and added scale to the operations.

Then customers demanded more financial services such as insurance and investment banking. Given the fact that it had no experience in these areas, the bank acquired mid-sized insurance companies and brokerage firms. Next, it outsourced insurance and investment banking back office functions to add scale to the newly acquired operations.

Finally, confident of servicing a large customer base through outsourcing, the bank tapped global customers. To supplement its existing asset and liability acquisition channels, the bank outsourced part of the deposit taking and credit disbursement functions. The year is 2015, and the bank provides customers across the globe through a blend of personal, online, telephone and agency banking with back-office support from China, India, Ireland and Russia.

Disaggregation is a complex process, and all three companies took a series of similar steps to achieve optimum organizational efficiency and effectiveness. They began by selecting best-in-class vendors through an intricate selection process. Then the vendors and their customers worked to transfer knowledge and baseline processes, and to achieve the steady state of continuous improvements. During the initial stages of outsourcing, the companies coordinated activities among vendors and dealt with several tactical issues. With the maturing of global sourcing, vendors work with each other and look to the customers only for strategic direction.

For instance, when Wang Motors wants to improve software technology in cars, it calls a meeting of the chip supplier and the IT provider and tells them what is needed. The two organizations work together to fulfill Wang Motors' requirement.

The year is 2015 and disaggregated corporations are for real.

Will Recovery Hospitals, Wang Motors and Global Bank be fact or fiction in 2015? Is the term disaggregated corporations, or modular companies as Carliss Baldwin and Kim Clark described computer manufacturers in 1999, an esoteric management concept or an attainable goal? A look at the outsourcing landscape today proves that businesses in dozens of industries are rapidly moving toward the goal of being disaggregated corporations.

The present state—progressive disaggregation

The continuous quest for best-in-class service and products is changing the construct of the corporation. Disaggregation has reached new levels. Initially, companies outsourced only manufacturing activities, and now they are moving to services. Outsourcing of car parts is nothing new for Toyota. The same is true for Boeing, which boasts a host of suppliers providing critical aircraft components.

Wang Motors is an advanced Dell Computer, Toyota or Boeing as it manufactures and assembles nothing in-house. All the company does is engineer innovative products and partner with external suppliers to manufacture them. Wang Motors also coordinates activities of various suppliers to induct new products into the supply chain.

Now services outsourcing has accelerated disaggregation. As the world focuses on the politics of globalization, corporations driven by the desire to maximize customer and shareholder value form unique global partnerships so they can access and deliver best-in-class products and services.

Consequently, global sourcing dramatically changes organizational structures. Increasing the shedding of non-core processes, it is making client corporations lean, agile and interdependent on their service providers as suppliers become experts in the outsourced functions. The end result is the move toward the creation of sharply focused disaggregated corporations. The change in organizational structures is also creating new rules of engagement among suppliers and clients. These are the initial links of an emerging global services value chain.

The process of global disaggregation that began in the mid-1990s also led to the rediscovery of the corporation. Companies have been asking themselves what their ideal construct is. They have been continuously redrawing boundaries to decide what is core and non-core to their business. Today, the corporation is fluid, still finding itself. Organizations decide on a global level whether to make or buy products and services. Future corporations such as Wang Motors and Recovery Hospitals create next to nothing in-house.

Earlier, companies would generally decide to make everything. That slowly changed as outfits sought greater efficiency through sourcing. As national talent pools dried up due to the increased sourcing demand and costs began to rise, corporations switched to global sourcing. This phenomenon resulted in the greatest efficacies in terms of cost, quality, innovation and speed to market.

Corporations are looking to achieve the future state of excellence today. Disaggregation has made that possible. GE uses tools such as Six Sigma to gauge what is critical to quality (CTQ). CTQs are the key measurable product or process characteristics whose performance standards must be met to satisfy the customer. Simply put, CTQs are what the customer expects of a product. In the process of disaggregation, companies continuously strive to define their core competencies by asking few simple questions:

- Is this process that runs in-house CTQ for the ultimate customer?

- Is this process or product the secret sauce of the company's success?
- What should the company be known for?

If the process is not CTQ to the ultimate customer, not the critical secret sauce for success and is something that the company does not want to be known for, the function is outsourced.

Let us take the example of Coca-Cola. Its secret sauce is the closely guarded Coke formula, which is CTQ for the ultimate customer. So producing the formula is kept in-house, but bottling the drink is outsourced. Since the company does not want to be known as a bottler, but as a producer of superlative soda, it will not manufacture the bottles or its labels, as a best-in-class bottle is less critical to Coke's success than its secret formula.

In the case of Global Bank, running non-scalable, non-core back office functions in-house posed a risk to growth. Back-office processes like customer risk profiling and credit decision-making, though important, are not critical to customer acquisition. Better service, products and rates are the key. Disaggregation cuts Global Bank's intermediation costs that are passed on to the customer through better rates. Best-in-class providers improve turnaround times, which provide faster service to the ultimate customer. And finally, global sourcing provides the back office support that enables the bank to expand operations.

Global sourcing has resulted in a refocus on core operations. Companies are still a long way from achieving the future state of disaggregation, but several of them have made significant progress toward that goal. GE is a classic example. In the past, GE created value through operational excellence. Now with many of its non-core processes outsourced to Genpact, its BPO unit, and with operational excellence reaching a state of steady and continuous improvement, GE's mantra now is "innovation" and "imagination." At a very fundamental level, buy-side organizations excel in core competencies due to the specialization that disaggregation enables. They attain best-in-class status.

The process of disaggregation not only changes the essence of client organizations, but also of their service providers. As the customers specialize in their core competencies, so do the service providers. Processes that were non-core to the customer become core to the provider. The transformation is fundamental. In the lexicon of the Corporation of the Future[SM], the term "non-core" will not exist.

Consolidated corporations had a few core functions to which a majority of resources were devoted, and the other supporting processes languished with little or no attention. Disaggregated corporations democratize business so that every function gets the attention it deserves. This genetic evolution of businesses has created best-in-class players partnering with each other to create value never achieved before.

Birth of a global services supply chain

Companies have sourced globally for years. But the process of disaggregation has created a whole new phenomenon—a global services supply chain. Toyota's version is famous for its efficiency. It sources several parts from best-in-class suppliers based across the globe. The same is true of aircraft manufacturers such as Boeing and Airbus, which have strong supplier relationships to provide precision parts. However, a services supply chain is very different from a manufacturing value chain in terms of complexity and flexibility.

First, manufacturing supply chains converge to the point of production of the finished product. The final product has to be built at a single location on an assembly line and then shipped to customers. This is true of all manufacturing, from computers to cereals. Let us take the example of China today. Wal-Mart sources toys from Chinese manufacturers that procure plastic pellets from the U.S. and other parts from Europe to make toys in Asia that are eventually shipped to every continent.

Second, because setting up manufacturing facilities is capital intensive, disaggregating the supply chain has cost implications. For instance, if Wang Motors wants a supplier to move manufacturing to a different part of the world, it is very difficult given the time and costs involved.

The emerging global services supply chain is fundamentally different. Services are knowledge intensive and people dependent. Technology enables processes to be broken up and executed anywhere in the world to take advantage time-zone differences and access to the best talent. If Recovery Hospitals finds a new and more cost-effective pool of radiology talent in Ukraine, the function can be migrated to the new location and plugged in in an instant to the supply chain using information technology.

As the services supply chain breaks up a process for execution in different countries, value is continuously added as it moves from one location to the next. For instance, one of Genpact's U.S.-based customers has three steps of a single transaction executed in three different countries. Genpact's supply chain has a global footprint with operations in India, China, Hungary, Romania and Mexico, which enables slicing and distributing different aspects of the process across these locations to deliver best-in-class services.

The customer generates paper-based invoices in the United States, and the first step of the transaction is to ship the invoices to Mexico, where they are digitized. Then the information is electronically shipped to India for more value-added processing such as accounting entry, pricing and profitability analysis, and customer segmentation. The final leg is executed in China, conducting customer contact and follow-up with suppliers. The beauty of the supply chain is that the customer can access information wherever the transaction is across the globe.

The scattering of the services supply chain is made possible by advances in information technology and telecommunication systems as well as the nature of the product. Unlike a manufacturing supply chain where parts of the final product are physically shipped to the point of aggregation, service products are moved virtually. Virtual shipping is inexpensive, and the cost per unit falls exponentially as volume goes up. The end result is an extremely opportunistic and flexible global services supply chain.

People drive global sourcing of services. It is a given fact that technology advances have made it possible to have a seamless global financial market, where investments flow to assets that provide the maximum returns. Telecommunication advances have made the same possible for global services sourcing. Companies can today seek the best talent clusters anywhere in the world, enabling the creation of a global service delivery for the first time.

The new rules of engagement

Measuring is the discipline of disaggregated corporations, which has resulted in writing new rules of engagement. Consolidated corporations had a group of people running non-core functions that were never measured. Disaggregation has created the mechanisms to measure non-core processes as suppliers apply tools such as Six Sigma. The measurement of non-core processes has created new levels of partnering between suppliers and customers, as vendors and their clients look at creative ways improve processes.

This partnering has also created a new phenomenon—a governance system to monitor and supervise the outsourced processes. Disaggregated corporations build governance models to track:

- Adherence to mutually agreed principles and resolving disputes
- Monitoring and correcting the progress of the relationship
- Mitigating risks associated with global sourcing
- Finding ways to maximize returns of global sourcing

Genpact has a three-tiered governance model built like a pyramid. At the foundational level is the operations governance team, followed by the strategic management team on top of which sits the executive board team. The responsibilities of the individual governance teams, with equal representation from the customer and Genpact, become broader and more strategic as they move higher in the pyramid. The lowest level focuses on improving single engagements, and the executive board looks at multiple engagements. Genpact's model aims to create greater value, be more successful and make the relationship more meaningful for both the client and itself.

Another important creation of disaggregated players is the service level agreement (SLA). Essentially a tactical tool, SLAs sit at the center of achieving the promised efficiencies of disaggregation. SLAs clearly lay down roles and responsibilities of both the provider and vendor. They create absolute and measurable targets that non-core processes must achieve. With these fundamentals in place, providers of non-core services are in a position to deliver best-in-class services.

Essentially, disaggregation has put in place practices that never existed before. From loosely structured internal interactions in consolidated corporations, disaggregated corporations measure processes, construct governance models and build tightly structured working practices to the mutual benefit of suppliers and customers.

The discipline of measuring leads to continuous improvements in efficiency. Genpact increased productivity in a SG&A centralization initiative of a pan-European customer by $300 million in three years through constant measuring of the process.

Advantages of disaggregation

Disaggregation delivers multiple benefits to corporations including:

- Global best-in-class services
- Cost savings
- Shift to variable cost structures
- Improved top line
- Reduced losses
- Increased speed to market
- Better focus and decision-making
- Shorter cycle times
- Continuous improvements
- Specialization
- Innovation

That global sourcing delivers cost savings is a part of the stakes on the table. Outsourcing cuts the cost of running a process by about 35 to 45 percent. But business impact created by operating the process more efficiently through global sourcing is far greater than the initial cost savings. For instance, in a billing project implemented for an $18 billion global energy-services customer, Genpact delivered an immediate cost arbitrage benefit of 28 percent. The goal of the project was to improve billing processes, reduce invoicing errors and control revenue leakages.

The ability to deliver faster service through best-in-class talent and continuous quality improvement are the key drivers. Genpact's heritage of Six Sigma that it brought from GE assures process improvements that deliver business impact far higher than the initial cost benefits of outsourcing. In a project to reduce accounts receivable (AR) delinquencies, Genpact achieved a 15 percent productivity gain and $2.5 million savings in collections through process improvements driven by Six Sigma methods. The streamlined, more effective processes lead to several other gains including:

- AR delinquency reduction of $403 million in six months
- Client settlement steps reduced to seven from forty-six, resulting in a 35 percent productivity gain
- Process reengineering that generated $200 million in cash flow, improved invoice accuracy to 99 percent and cut cycle time by half

Disaggregated corporations will achieve maximum customer impact through an extreme focus on core. While the focus on core has increased with the advent of global sourcing, it will reach an extreme level with companies continuously rediscovering themselves and identifying their core competencies. The high degree of specialization will enable process innovation and continuous improvement in efficiencies. Service providers will continue to seek the best and most cost-effective way to deliver services on a global basis.

Peeking into the future lets us examine how Global Bank performs. To access liabilities cost effectively on a daily basis, analysts employed by the bank's supplier search the markets for wholesale funds at the lowest available interest rates. Based on analyst information, the bank optimizes interest rates daily to take advantage of fluctuations. Accessing cheaper funds on a regular basis through its outsourced deposit collection storefronts enables the bank to keep its total cost of liabilities two percentage points lower than the competition.

One of the most important aspects of global sourcing is the shift from a fixed to a variable cost structure. Customers no longer have to invest capital to maintain supporting processes; the service provider does that. The freeing up of capital enables buy-side organizations to invest resources in their core functions, providing better return on investment. For instance, Wang Motors gets better returns by investing money in R&D for solar cars rather than by setting up HR functions for its operations across the globe.

Disaggregation is a continuous process. After the low-value functions are outsourced, higher value functions can be migrated, giving much better returns. A company can start with the outsourcing of its direct marketing campaigns, as Global Bank did, and later shed higher value functions such as customer analytics. A manufacturing company that outsources parts of its supply chain can start by delegating receipt processing and move on to procurement and logistics management outsourcing. The global sourcing of high-value functions is not to take advantage of cost differentials but to increase business impact by accessing best-in-class providers that improve processes and take new products to market faster.

The future of disaggregation

Recovery Hospitals, Wang Motors and Global Bank are the disaggregated corporations of the future, when business entities will be lean and agile and operating in extremely delimited areas of expertise. Are corporations on the right track to achieve the future state? Yes, to a large extent. Client organizations are shedding non-core functions and sourcing them to best-in-class providers. The telecommunications infrastructure is making giant leaps with robust 3G (voice, data and video) services likely in the near future. Cost-effective 3G will be the next catalyst to global services sourcing.

Today's service providers tap clusters of talent according to the geography where they reside. But that has limitations, because individual talent in a different location cannot be harnessed. Increasingly, technology is dissolving geographic boundaries. Cost effective 3G connections will enable total disaggregation of the workforce. Talent based anywhere in the globe will be able to connect remotely to a virtual office and collaborate seamlessly.

The vendor landscape will also see disaggregation. Today, single vendors provide services for all types of transactions, such as HR, finance and accounting, customer service, etc. These services are offered across all industry verticals. Total disaggregation will demand that vendors specialize in specific processes and industries.

Disaggregation will also lead to new kinds of collaboration. Currently, outsourced manufacturing activity generally functions independently of outsourced services. A collaboration of the two supply chains is inevitable in the future. For instance, Wal-Mart buys several goods and services from Chinese manufacturers and runs a billing department in-house. Later, a services outsourcing company may take over the billing function and work directly with the Chinese manufacturers.

The future market will continue to have consolidated players both on the vendor and client side. But it will be the highly specialized and disaggregated corporations that will win.

So what will be the characteristics of disaggregated corporations and the future market? Speed, not size, will define winning corporations. It will not be the number of employees but the size of the customer's mind share, the portion of his wallet and the company's position in the marketplace that will define the future corporation.

Disaggregated corporations will own the customer through a powerful brand. They will seamlessly manage global sourcing operations to bring the best products and services to that demanding customer. They will introduce innovative products at the speed of thought, leveraging plug-n-play supporting processes that shorten time to market for new ideas.

Mitchel Lenson
Retired Managing Director and Group CIO
Deutsche Bank
London, England

The Strategic CIO

Question: *At a time when so many business processes and major projects are being outsourced around the world, how do you perceive the role of the CIO?*

Lenson: The role of the CIO is evolving now to someone at a very senior level—somebody who helps drive change and transformation. It is the person who actually recognizes that negotiations are required with internal and external parties to optimize the resources spent—and in many ways to create the leadership around those processes and thoughts. A mistake technologists often make is assuming change and transformation can only occur through technology. I believe it is one tool, but you must be careful that it does not become the only arrow in your quiver.

Question: *Has outsourcing and offshoring become a central part of corporate strategy?*

Lenson: Yes, it has. As such the trend for outsourcing has become more public and high profile, and therefore more structured and far more strategic in the way it's approached. At Deutsche Bank, we call it "smart-sourcing," not outsourcing. To say outsourcing is a new phenomenon is not true for us. We always had developers in multiple locations, including low cost ones. We look at smart-sourcing from a number of perspectives, whether we are insourcers of business processes such as prime brokerage or white labeling or the outsourcers of processes to low cost locations, together with a combination of whether we can do it internally or externally, and we'll source it from wherever it is the smartest to do so—considering both location and organization.

Question: *What is your view on the future of outsourcing?*

Lenson: By nature I have a fairly laissez faire/Friedmanistic type of approach to economics. Technology is just following the way of its predecessors. Products are not manufactured in England any more. The same is true for the United States. China produces more refrigerators and washing machines than either country. The reality is, economically it is an undeniable trend. Not much gets manufactured onshore anymore; the world has started to wake up to the fact that knowledge work can also go the same way. We are at a place with technology that where there is political stability and a willing and able labor force, anything can go to other places.

Question: How can CIOs create value?

Lenson: There are three challenges: One is to convince the CEOs that they don't need to spend as much as they want to spend. With all the money some people want to spend, you end up being less efficient. And in a world where margins tend to collapse, you have to be more efficient and more effective every day, every week, every year because if you're not, then your revenues will shrink and you have to run faster just to stay still. Two, when you do spend money, realize what you are spending it on and the benefits of it. Finally, when you do spend money, recognize that it is going to be spent on a very specific thing and you won't continue to expand the scope because people will come up with better and brighter ideas of what to do. So, the bottom line is, be disciplined around the execution of your spending.

Question: When you select a global outsourcing partner, what criteria do you consider as you make that selection?

Lenson: At the moment, because the economics work, the intellectual side works, the long-term supply works, India is where the very best partnerships are forming. They have hundreds of thousands of engineers coming out of universities in a very good educational system. The laws are somewhat difficult at times, but because they were developed based on the Anglo-Saxon principle of English law, they

do recognize such concepts as intellectual property rights. But I wouldn't get hung up on that. Also, you want to make sure the organization you're working with is financially stable and has some degree of depth, which quite often means that large firms like ours are less willing to go to a smaller start-up because they don't have the proven track record of being there for the long-term.

Question: Do you see more Chinese and Indian companies acquiring companies in Europe and the U.S.?

Lenson: The Chinese have just bought MG from Rover after the collapse of the car company in the U.K. They are taking all the production to China. Ultimately, the only thing they bought is the intellectual property right with the MG motors name. India was one of the first countries in pharmaceuticals to produce and clone drugs. I predict that in the next 20 years, they will own 30 to 40 percent of the patents on new technology related to pharmaceuticals. So, whether its India or China, I think more and more they'll start with a manufacturing base, then take over the basic commodities and build up research and develop to a point where they start saying, "Well, actually, we can clone other ideas." Japan did it with cars and music products in the '70s and '80s. So, I think China and India and others will do the exactly the same thing—it's as inevitable as breathing the air itself.

Question: Is there anything the developed world could do to better compete with China and India?

Lenson: I think the way we will make sure our economies carry on is by being open. One of the biggest dangers in the world now is the response to terrorism, the closing down of borders. People came to the big western countries not necessarily for the education systems, but because it gave them the chance for free expression and it gave them the chance to develop their ideas. From those ideas we became great. If we close our borders to those very things, then actually, the biggest risk for us is that we stagnate, and then we don't have a chance to compete with China and India. But our advantage always has been that we own the intellectual property rights.

Question: *What will a company like Deutsche Bank look like in the next 20 to 50 years?*

Lenson: That's a difficult question to answer. Compare the number and size of truly super banks today to 25 years ago and who would have predicted the winners' and losers? When I started 25 years ago there was virtually no such thing as investment banking, as we know it today. Now look at the top 20 banks in the world and how they operate. If you thought 20 years ago we would be trading credit derivatives and other structured products at all, let alone in the volumes we do today, without risk management techniques and the technology to manage them and the systems in place to handle the scale processing, none of this would have been possible. In 50 years time, we will see a totally different landscape, banks will be disintermediated, so to a very great extent a lot of the things you walk into the bank to do just won't exist any more because they will be commoditized out of existence by more peer-to-peer,

consumer-to-consumer products. In fact it is not clear that it will be banks that will be providing many of these consumer services. A combination of: capital requirements and size of technology spend, together with the continuing forces of globalization will continue the trend of consolidation, thus reducing the number of banks in existence. As for all the names you associate with greatness in banking today, very few will exist in the same way in the next 50 years. Those who remain in existence will no doubt operate in a virtual world where geography and national boundaries will no longer define who a bank is or which country it or its labor force operates in This will no doubt present many interesting challenges for governments and regulators.

2.5

By *Randy Terbush*
Vice President and
Chief Technology Officer
ADP Employer Service
Roseland, New Jersey

Outsourcing and the Open Source Software Model

Outsourcing and open source software (OSS): of all the challenges facing information technology leaders around the globe, these two topics may be the most controversial. The evolution and adoption of both of these practices have drawn fire from all parts of the corporate and vendor communities, as well as the public at large. It may come as no surprise that these two issues offer some of the same risks and rewards.

Today, shrinking IT budgets and an increasingly competitive marketplace have forced most IT shops to begin exploring outsourcing as a method to decrease costs and improve time to market. As offshore outsourcing services have matured, businesses have found offshoring to be a very natural evolution in the way they deliver software products and services. It is the author's belief that there are strong similarities between offshore outsourcing and the adoption of OSS solutions. These similarities will lead to wide spread adoption of open source technologies and an increasing trend towards acquisition of software through a services model focused on delivering OSS into the enterprise.

Embracing OSS could offer benefits other than the economic. For example, adopting OSS for the commoditized components comprising a large part of today's standard infrastructures could allow R&D organizations to focus their innovation efforts on harder problems. Conceding the more mundane parts of the software stack could actually provide a true standard base, which has been a long and unrealized promise over the past decades of the computing evolution.

In the near future, it is quite possible that the term "open sourcing" may instead represent the concept of sourcing software solutions through "open" communities—perhaps known as "open outsourcing."

Since 2001, the information technology sector has seen an unprecedented belt tightening and subsequent reduction in force. Out of that forced diet three trends have emerged: outsourcing has been widely adopted as a means for companies to control costs; Generation-X IT professionals have driven a rediscovery of OSS in the corporate IT department; and many organizations have reached the limit of innovation that they can reasonable support. This confluence of trends has created a new paradigm—one that I refer to as "open outsourcing."

Open source origins

The "rediscovery" of open source in the early 2000s was long overdue. The collaborative processes, which serve as the underpinnings for OSS development, are the same processes that the scientific research communities have relied upon for centuries to advance the current state of the art. In fact, the scientific community spawned one of the most important OSS "products" of all time: the Internet.

Early adopters of computer technology had no choice but to use the software that was delivered with these new and rapidly evolving computing platforms. There were no commercial alternatives. Researchers and early IT workers knew this software to be the current state of the art and saw no reason to challenge the existing software/technology development processes. Likewise, there was no reason for the science and research communities to hold this development process up as a superior methodology as there were very few formal commercial development processes for comparison.

Along came the 1980s, the advent of the personal computer, and the Gen-Xers. Many of these Gen-Xers are the sons and daughters of the research technologists who had been creating the computing technology and refining the collaboration processes required to deliver and advance the technology. With early access to computing technology and a now growing commercial computer business environment, these Gen-Xers began emulating their parents, peers, and mentors and formed their own communities of alternative software solutions. A few of these alternatives aimed squarely at defeating some of the commercial solutions in the marketplace, producing a very aggressive and sometimes malicious message that has not been welcomed by corporate IT. Consequently, a generational divide had developed in the IT community. This divide has survived through the '80s and '90s and is only today beginning to disappear as the Gen-Xers take their rightful place in the IT workforce.

In the 1980s, as commercial software vendors began figuring out how to capitalize on the rapidly growing market for software technology, consumers received the message that only commercially developed software would satisfy their business requirements. The competitive nature of the IT industry during this time led to many different customer acquisition and retention strategies. Many proprietary "standards" were developed, resulting in a serious fragmentation of operating systems, networking solutions, data storage formats, and document formats. The painful and expensive lessons learned from these investments in proprietary solutions have helped establish a strong commitment to open standards in IT. The success of these open standards led to the commoditization of a large part of the IT computing infrastructure, causing a paradigm shift in how businesses acquire and maintain their computing infrastructures. This devaluing of software technology, along with the maturation of Gen-X into today's IT workforce, is leading to the broad adoption of open source in IT. If you look back at other industry evolutions, most have gone through this same cycle, ultimately settling back to a commodity service model.

One of the fruits that could come out of this transformation is a reduction in overall maintenance overhead and cost and a refocusing on innovation in our businesses. Today, we are suffering through the cleanup of a technology birth. As we move into the adolescence of the technology age, we should take care to build a lower maintenance foundation and allow ourselves some resources to create innovative solutions in the new millennium. Taking a closer look at the similarities between outsourcing and open sourcing, we might find that the latter offers a way forward that could free valuable resources to allow us to go back to the business of innovation.

Innovation, quality of life and competitive advantage

What does it take to innovate in a technology driven world—one that must support 30 years of innovation legacy and consumes trillions of dollars globally just to maintain the status quo? To create another layer of innovation on this growing techno-cake, organizations will need to hire the next wave of innovators and invest in the technology du jour to continue to grow the stack.

But many organizations have reached the limit of innovation that they can reasonably support. With IT budgets shrinking and business fundamentals under increasing pressure from more and more regulation, budget dollars available for creating innovative new solutions have disappeared. CEOs, CIOs and other leaders will be forced to find creative new ways to stretch budgets to stay competitive.

Those leaders looking to create tomorrow's innovative environment should pay heed to the history of the most notable inventions: computer networking, space flight, the transistor, television, atomic energy, computers, airplanes, automobiles, radio, telephone, light bulb, compass, paper and print, cannon, gunpowder, metal working, agriculture, ceramics, controlled fire, and stone tools. Two trends drove the creation and adoption of these innovations: quality of life and competitive advantage

Many emerging world economies have taken these two drivers to heart and are successfully reaping the same benefits for their own economies by offering competitive outsourcing services. China is one of many countries that recognize the value of innovation toward building an economy and are working to create an environment that is conducive to innovation.

At the opening ceremony of the "2005 science and technology week" in Beijing, Chen Zhili, Chinese State Councilor stated, "Improving capacities for independent scientific and technological innovation is the key link in pushing economic restructuring and improving national competitiveness, and the top task of the country's scientific and technological progress."

But it is not enough to simply fund the creation of more research projects, joint efforts and federal programs to attempt to spark an innovation bonfire. Many countries like China have recognized that it takes more and are embracing the fruits of open source development communities, thereby avoiding the creation of costly proprietary technology infrastructures. By embracing these commodity technologies, they conserve valuable monetary and intellectual resources that can be focused on more difficult challenges.

Collaboration, outsourcing and open sourcing

The concept of outsourcing, as it has evolved over the past decade, is to obtain goods or services from an outside supplier: to contract work out. The process often includes the transfer or creation of intellectual property through a third party for development, maintenance and expansion of product and service capability. Globalization has accelerated the adoption of outside third party sourcing, which has led to a maturation of these outsourced labor pools and an increased acceptance of the risks and benefits of this development model. In the early 21st Century, many businesses are finding an outsourced workforce to be a prerequisite to delivering a competitive product in a timely manner that serves the broadest possible market. Better communications technology, a global understanding of challenges and the requirements to meet them, increased market size, more competitive cost structures, along with disappearing language barriers, have led to this acceptance.

Over two decades before the term open source was coined to describe software products that were available and distributed in source code form, the altruistic and collaborative individuals responsible for the development of this technology were hard at work creating solutions that represented the state of the art of their techno-craft.

Yet, despite collaborative efforts found in outsourcing and open source, one fundamental difference exists between the process of outsourcing and open sourcing. By definition, the word open dictates that technology developments created within the open source model are open to the public. The core similarity between outsourcing and open sourcing are the key effects that globalization has had on their acceptance and proliferation respectively: a more globally distributed work force, shared global challenges, a common language and increasing size of the work force.

While most corporations have become comfortable with the issues and benefits of increased globalization, the idea of giving away intellectual property to the public and ultimately their competitors is one that must be carefully weighed. In the end, it all boils down to the cost of maintaining the intellectual property versus the revenue and competitive advantage that it offers your business.

The open source egg or the outsourced chicken?

With globalization, innovation and outsourcing, one must ask, "Which came first? The chicken or the egg." Or in this case, the open source (globalized) collaboration model, or outsourcing? Open source collaboration or an outsource relationship with an outside service provider? Both are more alike than they differ. Both offer an opportunity to reduce costs. Both offer the ability to increase labor resources. Both offer a likely place to delegate maintenance and development of some of the more mundane parts of the technology stack.

But as the evolution of business operations progressed over the past decade, outsourcing has clearly come first as businesses began to test the waters of having an outside contractor, often in another part of the world, take over the development and maintenance of company technology assets. Now that outsourcing has become mainstream and even a requirement to remain competitive in today's market, many companies have taken the next step in the evolution and have released technology that is no longer seen as a competitive advantage. Technology candidates for release to an open source development model often consume greater maintenance cost than their competitive value. By opening these software technologies to the public to allow further enhancement and maintenance of common infrastructure components, these companies have freed some of their intellectual capital and are able to spend these valuable resources on challenges that offer a greater return on investment.

Trusting the chicken and the egg

Through the past few decades, the growth and adoption of outsourced labor pools has been gated primarily by cultural issues, communication, and trust. Communication is easily solved in today's world, and I believe that younger generations are embracing the cultural differences and hopefully learning from shared experiences.

Trust, on the other hand is at the core of human comfort. Trust is a fundamental ingredient required to cross any boundary of human relationship. Business relationship or personal relationship, trust is at the core of any of these bonds.

Some level of trust in business relationships is backed by legal agreement that MAY provide some additional comfort to participating parties. That same legal agreement exists in open source communities in the form of license agreements, contributor agreements, etc. These legal agreements are little more than a public statement of conduct and should be seen by any business wishing to outsource to these open source communities as a declaration of the rules of engagement. This is not unlike the purpose of commercial legal agreements.

Free the mind, innovation will follow

Innovation in this century is not just about being open-minded. Most organizations are now supporting at least 20-30 years of legacy technology. With global IT spending in the trillions, it is clear that many organizations are significantly burdened by just maintaining their current technology standards, let alone creating innovative new products and services.

Over the years, we've all lived through multiple attempts to establish industry standards in computing hardware, operating systems, middleware and data formats. As the technology industry begins to mature, it is time to begin forcing the requirements for those standards onto technology vendors. In doing so, we begin to free the minds of our most precious company asset, thus allowing us to begin a new innovation cycle. Through adoption of standards based technology stacks, we reduce integration efforts within our own organizations. By driving vendors towards a common and commoditized technology infrastructure, we force their innovative efforts further up the stack to more difficult and rewarding challenges while driving our costs for the basic infrastructure down. By embracing the commodity of the technology stack, we increase the labor pool available to maintain the foundation of our businesses as technology skills crossover more easily.

Much of the infrastructure technology needed to run our businesses is available as open source through globally distributed communities of developers. Much of the software being developed by these communities is unencumbered by the years of software features developed by competing companies driven to repeatedly outdo their competition—thousands of lines of code that offer little more than additional bugs, security risks, poor performance and vendor lock in. And all of that open source technology is available through third parties whose entire business model survives on providing the best support available for freely available technology stack.

Every open source community is born out of the same fundamental gifts that are provided by globalization: better communication, lower language barriers, common challenges and an increased talent pool to facilitate solving those shared challenges. Those same globalization gifts have enabled our acceptance of outsourcing and will ultimately lead to a fundamental shift in the way we source the information technology we use to build the foundation of our growing businesses.

References

1   Embassy of the People's Republic of China in India, 2005.

2   "History of the OSI," Open Source Initiative, 2005.

3   O'Reilly, Tim, "The Open Source Paradigm Shift," May 2004.

4   Kenwood, Carolyn, "MITRE: A Business Case Study of Open Source Software," July 2001.

5   The Dravis Group, "Open Source Software: Case Studies Examining Its Use," April 2003.

6   Koch, Christopher, "Your Open Source Plan," CIO Magazine, March 2003.

7   Moglen, Eben, "Questioning SCO: A hard look at nebulous claims," October 2003..

8   Fink, Martin, The Business and Economics of Linux and Open Source, Prentice Hall 2003.

9   Wheatley, Malcolm, "The Myths of Open Source," CIO Magazine, March 2003.

10 Shankland, Stephen; Kane, Margaret; Lemos, Robert, "How Linux Saved Amazon Millions," News.com, October 30, 2001.

Valerie Orsoni-Vauthey
CEO and Founder
MyPrivateCoach
San Carlos, California

The Global vs. Classical Manager

Question: *How does the development of the knowledge economy impact the role of the manager?*

Orsoni-Vauthey: Until recently a company's resources were easily identified with tangible assets like machines, manufacturing plants and cash in the bank. With the evolution of our local economy toward a global economy, the company's "classical" assets have transitioned to intangible assets like knowledge. This is the fundamental economic change of this last century: the most important asset of a company is the brains of its employees, and consequently the most difficult to evaluate.

In advanced economies like the United States, 60 percent of the workers are knowledge workers, otherwise called symbolic analysts. Whereas in developing or transitioning economies, as little as 10 percent of the workers—usually an elite body of the population—are knowledge workers.

With the acceleration of the development of new technologies, the increased velocity of migratory flows and the emergence of highly educated economies in transition, knowledge clusters and poles of competence moving from advanced economies to transitioning economies are setting a new challenge for today's managers.

All managers from around the world are thus confronted with a rapidly changing economy, and what was true five years ago may not be relevant anymore.

Let's look at the critical survival skills managers must develop as they face this globalized economy. They must first remain efficient, then grow in their position and finally support the expansion of their company.

I'd like to note that I use the word "globalized." I do that because globalization implies something happening, and I believe the market is already global; globalization has already happened. In some countries like France, for instance, we can see movements or read articles claiming globalization can be reversed or fought against. To me this is a sterile fight. Managerial forces will be better utilized if we accept, embrace and use for our own good the new geo-knowledge economy.

Facing this erosion of knowledge-based geographical boundaries we have two types of managers: the "global manager" and the "classical manager."

The "global manager" is typically younger, tends to have studied abroad, has more of an international exposure, and usually has traveled more extensively than his classical manager counterpart.

This global manager already recognizes that knowledge is a public good that travels as fast as technology permits. This manager knows how to identify and tap into knowledge clusters around the world and knows the enablers of change in the knowledge economy. And finally, the global manager embraces new technologies and updated management techniques, is a highly skilled adaptive worker, and has well-developed international networks.

Today, larger corporations tend to exclusively hire global managers, but they are plagued with a large number of classical managers—from the old days—who need to learn the new ways to become competitive, or disappear.

Acquiring new ways means those prehistoric managers need to quickly learn how to tap into internationally located knowledge clusters to achieve several goals: reduce costs, increase efficiency, and develop competitive intellectual property—the ultimate purpose being to augment the company's bottom line.

Question: *Are managers resistant to globalization?*

Orsoni-Vauthey: Global managers, no. Classical managers, yes. This resistance is the essence of the categorization of "global" versus "classical" managers.

Indeed, as business and executive coaches, we are often confronted with a resistance to diving into the knowl-edge economy. Why is this so frightening?

Several reasons can explain it: fear of not mastering all the facets of a new business reality, fear of not being the sole focal entry point or reference point in a particular field of knowledge, fear of simply losing power, fear of being taken over by better trained, more responsive, less expensive and often younger top managers from around the world. Add to this a lack of confidence in the general quality of foreign resources, the fear of not understanding the culture and the fear of not being able to communicate optimally because of the language barrier and you will have a pretty good image of the classical managers and their difficulties when it comes to bringing the new borderless knowledge economy into their business model.

Question: *How can multinational corporations support the evolution and development of their managerial resources in the knowledge economy?*

Orsoni-Vauthey: We know that a manager's survival and success depends on the ability to cross the chasm and to change the vision from local to international, from small to large and from being a human manager to a mutant "octopus manager" with arms reaching in all the corners of the planet.

This is where an "international business coach" with a non-judgmental sounding board attitude and extensive global business experience can coach "top-local-thinking managers" into becoming "top-managers-with-a-global-vision." It always comes down to a very simple equation: where can I find the best resources at the best price?

That means you've got to follow these steps:

- Demystify the new economy with in-house workshops.
- Work at the top of the pyramid within the corporation to develop new career paths and matrices to motivate classical managers into becoming global managers.
- Develop talent management procedures endorsed by all the top management team and extensively communicate on this subject.
- Comfort managers in their position (usually done by those at the top of the pyramid, who also need to set good examples).
- Praise human capital and avoid placing too much emphasis on how better foreigners are, how cheaper or better trained they may be.
- Improve the general level of education within the multinational corporation:
  - Better on-the-job better training
  - Learning how to share knowledge
  - Foreign language courses
  - Courses on the culture of the knowledge clusters with which the manager will have to work and exchange will help avoid cultural faux pas and increase self-confidence when exchanging with teams from around the globe.
  - More travel to knowledge resource centers around the world goes hand in hand with the demystifying efforts.
- Improve the communication process among all the actors of a particular business process: phone, VoIP, instant messenger, webcams, tele-conference, etc.

As the managers progress on this path and see positive results they will enter the virtuous circle of a successful knowledge economy experience.

Question: *Finally, would you say it is possible to transform classical managers into global managers?*

Orsoni-Vauthey: I would say that not only is it possible, but it is critical to help the vast majority of the classical managers to transition up to global managers using simple but proven communication, education, coaching and management tools.

Part 3

Globalization's Larger Implications

The world has a stake in the success of everyone else in it. Better standards of living, greater freedoms, greater respect for human rights, the rule of law and personal dignity to a large number of people are just some of the benefits of development and globalization.

Real globalization is a fact—not a mirage. It has an enormous impact on the way in which nations interact with each other today.

As we go through this renaissance, whereby we are driven to achieve the best that can be achieved, it is more critical than ever before that we build networks among countries to share ideas and strategies. Never before have so many people maintained as many international contacts as we have today. Never before have events at a distance of several thousand miles had such an effect on people locally. Never before have so many people been politically involved in foreign policy as today. Never before was the world such a village of global information and opinion.

The world today is full of flux, and competitive advantage is very thin. The advantages accruing from international trade start with outsourcing and globalization, and many believe that which can be done better by outsourcing should be outsourced. But don't be fooled. Free trade does not imply a flat world. Nor does it hamper the United States' long-held position as the leading country for innovation.

As you'll read in this section, outsourcing is first and foremost the result of a strategic business decision. Such a decision is not fundamentally different from those leading to foreign investments, joint ventures or cross-border mergers and acquisitions. The variables, parameters and criteria to be taken into account by decision makers include their own assessments of (1) market prospects (at home and abroad) for a specific range of products, (2) cost/benefits of various ways of combining production factors (at home and internationally) to produce and deliver relevant goods and services, and (3) the possible strategies on which their main competitors may embark.

Beyond their roles as "guardians of sovereignty" and "custodians of the taxation panoply," modern governments have started to play crucial roles in shaping the future of outsourcing and more generally of "global sourcing." One can ideally represent five areas in which governments have critical roles to play. These roles and corresponding sets of activities are to provide:

- Access
- An enabling environment
- An ICT-friendly education policy
- Vision
- E-government applications

While the decision to outsource is strategic, some arguments focus on the policies of foreign countries that do not share similar protections for intellectual capital. In his article, "Bring Back American Jobs and Technology,"[1] Carlton Delfeld wrote, "Having research, development and production closer to headquarters better protects proprietary technologies.

"Unfortunately, here in America, the outsourcing trend does not appear to be reversing, even in capital-intensive products. Many of the new high tech jobs are for managers to manage the outsourcing process. Microsoft, Intel, IBM and Motorola all have large and growing R&D centers in China to take advantage of Beijing's cheaper pool of talent.

"Given China's disregard for intellectual property rights, perhaps American executives should pause and reconsider the long-term costs of growing outsourcing programs. Their offshore R&D

staff may very well walk off with proprietary knowledge and the company's future.

"This is not a call for isolationism or rolling back globalization, just a reminder that outsourcing has its downside. How about a little common sense and balancing short-term cost savings against long-term strategic risks?

"Instead of just taking the comparatively easy step of lowering labor costs by outsourcing, let's roll up our sleeves like the Japanese, improve manufacturing techniques and reap the benefits of keeping more production and technology closer to home."

What does the global society look like and who will assume the mother power? What are the compelling challenges we face as we become globally more interdependent? Is it possible for the United States' long-standing "most powerful country" status to become obsolete in the 21st century? What exactly should a better world look like, and how do we recognize it or know we're achieving it?

In this section, you'll come to understand why "Peace through economic interdependence such as global and regional outsourcing" is designed to effect stability through the peaceful economic cooperation of a broad range of diverse countries. You'll also see how global and regional outsourcing has considerable non-economic benefits for countries and how it is in the best interests of countries to reduce barriers to trade and investment.

1   Delfeld, Carlton, "Bring Back American Jobs and Technology," *Forbes*, August 10, 2005.

Jagdish Bhagwati
University Professor
Columbia University
Senior Fellow
Council on Foreign Relations
New York, New York

The Economic Impact

Question: *How does outsourcing impact economic growth?*

Bhagwati: Outsourcing is part of international specialization that has been going on for decades and centuries. It has just gotten more accentuated in recent years because many services are now becoming part of the tradable sector. We have been discussing international specialization of manufacturing for years—and we are now witnessing an increasing division of labor in services as well. In my judgment, such outsourcing of services (also of goods) is completely desirable. Basically, we're talking about the advantages accruing from international trade.

Question: *Is international trade something people have to worry about as workers are losing their jobs to the developing world?*

Bhagwati: Trade unionist John Sweeney would answer this question in the affirmative. He and other representatives of the union movement warn that we have to worry about having more international trade with poorer countries like India and China, and we have to worry about investment going out into these countries.

However, there is no evidence that the wages of our workers have been adversely affected by trade as distinct from technical change that economizes on unskilled labor. Nor is there any evidence that international trade has led to a "race to the bottom" of our labor standards. The same objections apply to the fears about the effects of outward direct foreign investment, an analytically separate issue from trade.

Question: *Does free trade imply a flat world?*

Bhagwati: Unions are terrified by trade because they think it means their income will collapse, as they won't be able to compete. They believe in Thomas Friedman's idea of a flat world, meaning that Indians and Chinese can, and will, do everything. I don't think this is true—just travel to India and go outside Bangalore and you will see the world is not flat. The claim of a flat world now is as wrong as it was in the time of Copernicus. There are mountains of problems on developing nations' path of economic development. In New Delhi, for instance, every night electricity goes off and only rich people have their own generators. The poor people are suffering from these electricity blackouts but so are factories and businesses. Comparative advantage still works. Besides, even as India develops, it is going to take years before India can aspire to the current U.S. income per capita level; and while this happens the United States won't sleep! It will keep innovating, building on its strength that comes from a highly sophisticated and problem-solving culture that thrives on continuous innovation.

Question: *How can the U.S. spur innovation to remain competitive?*

Bhagwati: There are two reasons why developing countries that have gotten their act together are growing much faster than the OECD world. They've gotten their technology off the shelf, which means they save much more and, therefore, invest much more. The United States is very dependent on innovation—as a result, consumers don't save very much. I am not worried about innovation in this country because we still have this creative spirit and a lot of R&D happens continuously. In my judgment, that is where a number of countries have to catch up. The unions prefer to push for protectionism instead. But how can you really shut yourself off? This is like putting a finger in the dike. You may be able to do something on one dimension, but there are a hundred dimensions on which competition is arising. The unions' strategy is leading nowhere.

Question: *What are the alternatives?*

Bhagwati: Unskilled labor has little future today: brawn can earn you only

so much. Technical change has meant that there are no more assembly lines. The only way to improve one's income today is to get a better education, to add to what economists call the human capital. Governments should make education cheaper and accessible for everybody.

Question: *How does Europe cope with the challenges caused by globalization?*

Bhagwati: Let's talk about France as a synonym for Europe. You can work there 35 hours per week, drink a good glass of Bordeaux and live the good life. Some Frenchmen seem to think work and leisure is a one-off choice. Unfortunately for them, this is a choice that has long-run consequences. The French competitive advantage will move away from areas where continuous attention is needed, as in the IT areas. But these also are areas where technical change is the most intense. So, France could fall steadily more behind. In 30 years time, France might then experience a gigantic trauma as the economy may have lost ground to many others.

Question: *If you met tomorrow with President Bush, President Chirac, and President Hu Jintao in one room, what recommendation would you offer on improving global economic growth?*

Bhagwati: The governments of France and the United States are currently not really strategizing when it comes to economic policies. They are lurching from one kind of protectionism to another, and they are not addressing the issues. I would tell Presidents Bush and Chirac that trade and investment—outbound and inbound—are good for their countries. They should also understand that comparative advantage has not disappeared, as Tom Friedman implies; it has become more volatile. The world today is full of flux, and competitive advantage is very thin. Today, Boeing might win; tomorrow, Airbus might take over. In every industry, there is somebody from somewhere, not necessarily from China, who is coming close to the incumbent. I call this "kaleidoscope competitive advantage," meaning that patterns of trade will just turn around very quickly. Countries might end up losing whole industries.

Question: *How should nations cope with this kaleidoscopic competition?*

Bhagwati: All endeavors have to add to economic flexibility. We must ensure that technical education does not get too specialized. In the Soviet Union, where there was no flux at all, engineers were specialized by diesel engines, aircraft, tractors, etc. In today's world, we need engineers who can shift from automobiles to aircraft, depending on which activity goes down and which comes up in the international struggle for markets.

3.1

By **Dr. Bruno Lanvin**
Lead Advisor, E-Strategies
The World Bank
Geneva, Switzerland

How Governments Shape Global Sourcing

Outsourcing is first and foremost the result of a strategic business decision. Such a decision is not fundamentally different from those leading to foreign investments, joint ventures or cross-border mergers and acquisitions. The variables, parameters and criteria to be taken into account by decision makers include their own assessments of (1) market prospects at home and abroad for a specific range of products, (2) cost/benefits of various ways of combining production factors at home and internationally to produce and deliver relevant goods and services, and (3) the possible strategies on which their main competitors may embark.

Such assessments take place against the background of the fundamentals of the firm involved—history, branding, financial structure, social and fiscal characteristics linked to the geographical location of its headquarters.

However, it would be a costly mistake to consider that, because they are based on business criteria and decisions, outsourcing strategies are outside the realm and reach of governments. Beyond their roles as "guardians of sovereignty" and "custodians of the taxation panoply," modern governments have started to play crucial roles in shaping the future of outsourcing and more generally of global sourcing.

To make a case for how this has happened, I will use the specific sector of information and communication technology (ICT) and its impact on e-government to show just how important it is for modern governments to play a crucial role in the future of global sourcing.

The changing roles of governments

The information revolution has had deep effects on governments by changing both their functioning and their roles. Those changes open new possibilities for outsourcing public services.

The advent of information-intensive societies and networked economies has affected the roles for governments in at least three major ways. It has:

• Changed the functions and roles of government.

• Empowered new segments of societies.

• Globalized the policy agenda.

On one hand, ICTs have been instrumental in changing the ways in which governments and administrations operate. Informatization, decentralization and the advent of e-government all reflect the impact of ICTs on how governments function. On the other hand, the information revolution has encouraged and enabled governments to accept new roles. In addition to traditional roles in such spheres as economic and social policy, education, diplomacy, defense and justice, ICTs have prompted governments to articulate a vision of major socio-economic change and to facilitate this change by example. At the same time, civil society has become an organized player in local and global issues, globalization has become a major force in world affairs, and new market efficiencies have arisen.

IT has deeply changed the ways in which government functions—for example, through office automation and the growing ubiquity of Web-based services. The advent of e-government and e-procurement, in particular, have allowed greater transparency and accountability across governmental agencies. To some extent, these applications have even pushed governments and their leaders closer to real time management—that is, indirect, but more continuous, management, frequently intermediated by IT. One danger of this management is that governments may be tempted to make online services a priority because they are easy to use and often immediately appreciated by citizens, instead of longer-term and less visible efforts to increase government efficiency via back-office re-engineering. Governments have to maintain an appropriate balance between these two sets of objectives.

IT has had an even more significant impact on the roles of governments. In all types of economic systems, governments around the world have tried to directly influence the determinants of ICT supply and demand. Governments exert such influence less and less as producers or buyers, and more and more as facilitators, seeking to create the proper environment for innovation and growth in ICTs and to mobilize financial and human resources for the ICT sector. Government leaders have accordingly established ICT as a national priority, provided a national vision of network readiness, launched large ICT projects and accelerated the adoption of ICTs by government departments.

Using a two-dimensional graph (see Figure 1), in which the

Figure 1 New Roles for Government

The information revolution has had deep effects on governments by changing both their functioning and their roles.

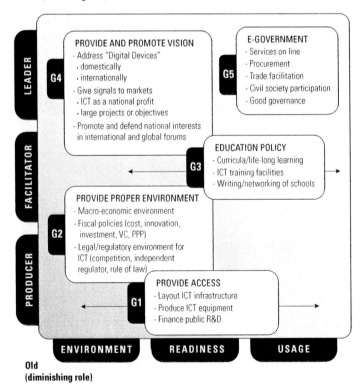

vertical axis denotes growing leadership and the horizontal axis growing facilitation, one can ideally represent five areas in which governments have critical roles to play. These roles and corresponding sets of activities are: access (G1), an enabling environment (G2), an ICT-friendly education policy (G3), vision (G4) and e-government applications (G5).

Access (G1)

In the past, building fixed infrastructure has generally been the responsibility of national monopolies. Often, these monopolies also produced terminals and various switching equipment for the telecommunications network. Research and development were often publicly subsidized, or carried out through large public projects, both civil and military. More recently, public projects have continued to be important in China, Korea (broadband roll-out), Malaysia (Multimedia Super Corridor) and Singapore (Singapore One), although such projects often involve public-private partnerships, which often are the first step on the road to outsourcing. Where large government initiatives are undertaken, they generally span the whole spectrum of ICT environment, ICT readiness and ICT usage.

Enabling environment (G2)

Providing a macro-economic, legal and regulatory environment conducive to economic growth and development is a traditional responsibility of governments. In the digital age, however, these functions imply new responsibilities specific to the ICT sector, such as spectrum management. Environmental tasks thus have significant spillover effects on e-readiness. Their effects on usage are not necessarily tangible in the absence of e-government applications.

Education (G3)

Providing the right amount and quality of human resources for a network-ready economy is closely linked to the long-standing involvement of governments in education. In this area, the emergence of a digital economy requires original approaches. For instance, changes in basic and advanced education curricula require that schools be adequately equipped and connected. Constant changes in technologies and applications also require that life-long learning and vocational training capacity be established. Although most enterprises consider education policy to be an environmental or e-readiness measure, the business sector can enjoy significant benefits from this policy should, for example, a country adopt a national policy of equipping and connecting schools on a global scale.

Vision (G4)

Large public initiatives in the area of ICT, as well as governments' ability to provide a society-wide vision of ICT development, differ from traditional public infrastructure programs financed by governments (G1). In the area of ICT, the role of governments as "vision providers" cannot be underestimated. It is the nature of the budget allocation process to pit different ministries and departments against each other. It is thus important that ICT be established as a priority at the highest levels of decision making, not simply at the level of an IT ministry. Providing an overall vision of ICT development (G4) overlaps other, more traditional roles of governments, such as ensuring social justice and equity through universal service programs.

Another new aspect of this group of governmental responsibilities is the growing importance of global issues. Governments increasingly find it difficult to address ICT issues without considering their global underpinnings. This is the case for intellectual property (e.g., WIPO and WTO treaties and agreements), Internet governance (ICANN) and norms and standards (e.g., ISO, ITU, W3C). Last but not least, over the last few years, governments have taken a leading role in formulating international plans of action to bridge the digital divide and create digital opportunities for all. Although such broad initiatives are not expected to generate massive amounts of external financing in the immediate future, their importance should not be underestimated, as international initiatives often constitute the think tanks that generate the guiding principles on which future actions and international agreements are based.

E-government (G5)

The last group of new governmental responsibilities is very closely linked to e-usage objectives. By promoting the use of ICTs in its own services (i.e., e-government), a government can acquire both experience and credibility, while leading through example. By focusing initially on activities that can generate significant savings, governments have been able to broaden the legitimacy of ICTs and generate important externalities. For example, online procurement, trade facilitation and customs automation not only generate resources, but also enhance transparency in specific government operations, thus contributing to the fight against corruption. This specific externality may even encourage foreign investors to participate in a country's network readiness efforts. Offering government services online with some degree of interactivity also strengthens the democratic process by engaging individuals and civil society in public-sector activities and reforms.

Each of those five activity groups is characterized by its own potential or absence thereof for outsourcing, nationally or internationally. Broadly speaking, the two groups (G2 and G4) which are closest to governments' environment responsibilities (political, regulatory, legal, institutional, and even diplomatic) are very unlikely to be outsourced on a significant scale any time soon: those correspond to core activities of governments, in which even the local private sector is unlikely to be called to contribute.

On the contrary, the other three groups (G1, G3 and G5) have started to be characterized by an increasing degree of participation by the private sector; this is particularly the case for access activities (G1) in which governments have started to rely more and more systematically on private initiatives and financing to achieve such political goals as universal service in the case of telecommunications; the same trend is clear for G3 (education), in which e-learning has developed quickly through the emergence of large private groups providing both economies of scale (in areas such as networks, equipment, software/middleware/courseware) and international standards (curriculum, certification). The last group (G5, e-government) is one in which progress is only starting to become measurable in terms of outsourcing; political and sometimes social obstacles have been important factors in creating a lag effect in the outsourcing of traditionally public responsibilities to the private sector. This lag is now likely to generate a watershed effect, by which e-government may become the center of a global outsourcing wave. (See Figure 2).

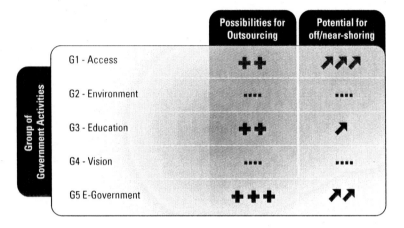

Figure 2 New Roles for Governments: Outsourcing Potential

Certain government activities have a greater potential for outsourcing.

However, before entering the discussion on how and when e-government activities may be partially or totally outsourced (and possibly offshored), one needs to take a strategic look at the ways in which the public and private sectors tend to consider the cost, benefits and possibilities of outsourcing, with special respect to information-intensive activities.

Outsourcing and information intensity: private vs. public attitudes

As mentioned above, outsourcing is basically a management decision, for which the most important parameters have to do with cost/quality ratios and market potential. In such a context, public entities such as ministries or state-owned enterprises face the same constraints and questions as private enterprises. The difference between the two sides (private versus public) is more a question of degree and complexity than of nature. Given that the public side relies on public financing and hence taxation, and that governments have responsibilities to pursue and maintain a certain number of fundamental balances in the socio-economic field (current accounts, employment, social fairness, e.g.) it is to be expected that public decisions will have to face more acceptance tests than most typical business decisions.

The private side of outsourcing

For a typical private company, the decision to outsource, whether it is inside or outside national borders, will have to pass two sets of tests, namely (1) economic and financial, and (2) legal and regulatory. The company management will first have to establish whether or not outsourcing is expected to contribute to the company's overall strategic goals in terms of cost, competitiveness and presence on the market; if this first test yields attractive prospects, the company's management will then have to ensure that this

Figure 3   **Business Outsourcing Equation**

A private decision to outsource faces two tests: economic and legal.

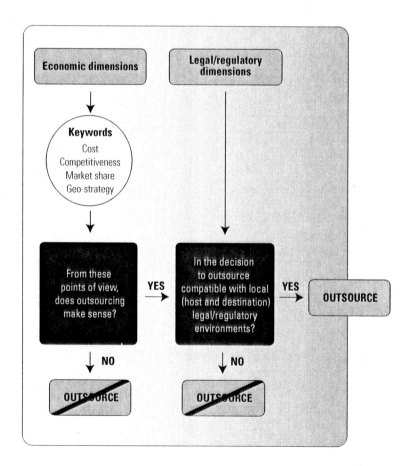

decision will not face insurmountable or excessively costly legal and regulatory obstacles, both at home and abroad. This two-stage process is schematized in Figure 3.

For governments, the basic equation that will lead to the decision to outsource or not is significantly more complex. Such additional complexity stems not only from the existence of a third test (social and political), but also from the fact that the conditions/safety nets which public entities will need to establish to ensure the viability and acceptability of outsourcing decisions will tend to be much more drastic than for private entities.

For example, the economic/financial dimension of outsourcing will need to include considerations about the potential contestability of markets. Since, in most cases, the service considered for outsourcing has traditionally been provided through a public monopoly, what guarantees/mechanisms need to be established to ensure that outsourcing will not lead to the emergence of a private monopoly, and that competition will play its expected role in keeping prices down and quality up? Another important issue in this context is that of universal service: what are the instruments required to make sure those private entities invited to take part in the provision of government services will not restrict their activities to the most remunerative parts of the market (e.g., large cities or wealthy customers), but also will contribute to expanding infrastructure and basic services to underserved parts of the country (e.g., rural areas)?

As far as the regulatory/legal side is concerned, the equation faced by governments is also significantly different from that of private companies, since the public sector is largely a provider versus a mere consumer of legal and regulatory instruments. Key objectives of public authorities will include independence, transparency, neutrality and efficiency in the ways in which pubic responsibilities will be transferred to private entities. This may imply the establishment or strengthening of competition authorities and regulatory authorities.

Last but not least, the third-level test, or political and social acceptance of the outsourcing process, may involve the investment of significant time and resources in engaging relevant stakeholders in a national debate, hopefully leading to a sustained (i.e., de-linked from short-term political objectives) support for the outsourcing process.

Once all those tests have been passed, it is still left to relevant authorities (i.e., government, independent commissions, or the private entities themselves) to define proper success indicators, proper monitoring and evaluation methods to evaluate the pace and effectiveness of the outsourcing process, and to implement the required safety nets (e.g., in the case of re-training of staff laid off from the public sector). Modalities of the outsourcing process (timing; methods, e.g., auctioning; and possible limits, e.g., through a 'golden share' that the government may wish to keep for a limited or undetermined period of time) also will need to be discussed and decided for the outsourcing decision to be eventually made and implemented.

This multi-stage process is schematized in Figure 4.

Considering the significantly higher degree of complexity of outsourcing decisions for governments as opposed to private enterprises, one can easily anticipate that the outsourcing of government services will take place at a slower rate, and remain largely constrained within national borders.

Any outsourcing decision public or private will first be considered in the context of the nature and strategic importance of the activities/services that could be outsourced. To make this point clear, and better point out differences between the business and government sectors, one needs to distinguish three levels of activities: core, strategic and non-strategic.

Core activities

It is clear that no entity, private or public, will consider outsourcing its core activities, i.e., those that constitute the raison d'être of the company/entity. Those activities will typically remain insourced; such core activities would include R&D, for example.

Strategic activities

Around such core activities, a number of services and activities exist, on which any private company or public entity will depend for its daily business and long-term viability. Such services/activities could include the staff, knowledge and equipment required to manage and optimize supply or distribution networks. For an

Figure 4   **Government Outsourcing Equation**

A government's decision to outsource is made in a logical process.

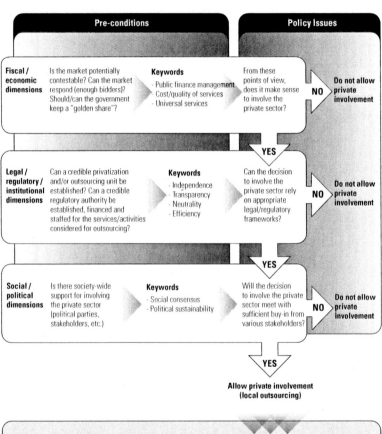

Define conditions

- Define/enforce performance indicators (configure M&E framework)
- Decide whether the government should/can keep a "golden share"
- Decide whether subsidies should be used & define relevant criteria/modalities
- Create social safety nets (e.g. for staff laid off from public sector)

Define modalities

- Asset sales (which) ?
- Public share offering ?
- "All-at-once" or by tranches?
- Auctions (direct, reverse, dutch)?

Consider near/offshoring

energy company, one could think of running a fleet of tankers, for instance. From the point of view of a private enterprise, the decision to outsource such strategic activities will basically be dictated by economic considerations and possibly limited by legal/regulatory ones. However, most companies will generally prefer to maintain such outsourcing within the geographical and economic space in which they operate. This means that, typically, transnational corporations will look for outsourcing possibilities within the markets/countries in which they have assets/interests, whereas others will tend to look for outsourcing possibilities within their respective national borders. Once a company has opted for outsourcing, the decision to consider various geographical ranges (nearshoring versus offshoring) will very much stem from economic and logistical considerations, including transport costs. Information-intensive services such as IT consulting, or any type of online service, would be natural candidates for long-distance offshoring, while manufacturing of automobile sub-parts, for example, would more naturally fall under nearshoring strategies.

As analyzed above, the ability of governments to outsource strategic activities is much more limited, largely for regulatory/legal reasons, but also for social/political ones. Hence, it is unlikely that any strategic activity will be outsourced outside of national borders. Actually, few of such activities have been outsourced at all by governments as of yet.

Non-strategic activities

Such activities, considered as cost centers rather than profit makers in most organizations, have offered the bulk of outsourcing for the last 20 years or so. They consist of ancillary services (cleaning and maintenance of buildings, payroll, billing and accounting, for example). The most spectacular growth has affected long-distance (offshored) information-intensive services such as those supplied through call centers. Yet, in this area, governments have been remarkably slow at following the path of the private sector, for the reasons mentioned above.

This topology of potentially outsourced activities, whether they are public or private, and whether they are information-intensive or not, can be summarized in Figure 5.

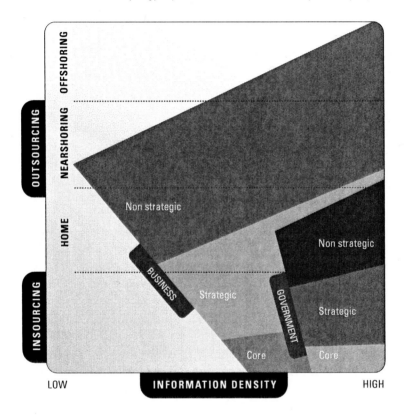

Figure 5   **Business and governments face similar outsourcing decisions**

This is the topology of potential outsourced activities, public or private.

This phenomenon, however, may be of shorter duration than most observers tend to anticipate. To understand why this could be the case, a closer look at the sector of e-government is revealing.

The example of e-government

Providing services online has been one of the directions towards which many governments have turned recently, in order to diminish costs and improve the quality of government services. In many cases, this migration from paper-based services to e-government has been made possible by a significant involvement of external private partners in all aspects involved, from basic data collection and storage-establishing interoperable data bases and resources sharable by a large number of departments and ministries to security devices encryption, firewalls, etc., and up to dedicated software, interfaces and payment systems.

In e-government, outsourcing to the private sector had to take place de facto, simply because it required expertise that did not exist in the public sector. In other words, many of the preventions outlined above, whereby the public sector has to go through a much more complex decision process than the private sector before reaching a decision to outsource, have had much less opportunities to manifest themselves in e-government than in other segments of public services. Wherever e-government services have been deployed for the provision of customs services to importers and exporters, or drivers licenses, birth certificates or land titling to individuals, or allowed businesses and private citizens to declare their income and pay their taxes online, they have generated a new wave of public-private partnerships and the emergence of new business models. In most cases, they have proved able to combine economic objectives, with most e-government activities rapidly becoming money makers, and social ones that enhance the ability of average citizens to access affordable government services.

It is likely that the interest of both governments and the private sector for e-government will continue to grow in all parts of the world. Outsourcing should play a particularly important and growing part in the growth of e-government worldwide, under the combined effect of at least three main forces:

• The triggering power of local outsourcing (watershed effect)
• The emergence of supra-national regulatory/regulatory spaces (pull effect)
• The consolidation of global commitments to a global open economy (push effect).

Force 1 - The triggering power of local outsourcing (watershed effect). In terms of outsourcing, the critical and most delicate step to be taken by governments is that of going from public monopolies to privately produced and delivered services. Once this initial step has been taken, the various modalities of outsourcing including offshoring become part of the options. In other words, the partial privatization of public services is creating a reservoir of activities that can rapidly and massively become candidates for outsourcing and offshoring. Nowhere is this phenomenon more apparent than in e-government. The opening of the outsourcing dam may be accelerated by two more forces acting respectively on the pull and push sides of offshoring demand.

Force 2 - The emergence of supra-national economic/regulatory spaces (pull effect). A major potential obstacle to the offshoring of government activities can be found in the disparities that exist among various national economic, fiscal, legal, social and regulatory frameworks. For example, governments may be prevented from allowing foreign companies or individuals to provide some services on their national territory because they cannot compel such companies or individuals to abide to the same criteria of quality. Barriers of this type tend to crumble quickly when economic and regulatory spaces start to be created across national boundaries. One of the best examples available so far of such a trend is that of the European Union. The adoption of common norms and standards in the definition of services, as well as of fiscal, legal and regulatory instruments, is creating a pull effect on e-government services: more and more governments will seek to outsource public activities within such regional spaces, hence feeding a wave of near-shoring of e-government services.

Force 3 - The consolidation of global commitments to a global open economy (push effect). Governments have also been pushed to outsource a certain number of their activities because of commitments they have made at the global level. This is the case in particular of members of the World Trade Organization (WTO), and of countries in the process of accessing WTO membership. For example, those countries that have signed the Telecom Annex of the WTO Agreement have committed to opening their telecom sector to international competition. A large number of public monopolies are hence being progressively pushed towards the arena of global competition.

How and when will those forces manifest themselves?

Regarding e-government services, a major distinction needs to be made between back-office and front-office. Many governments have tended to rush to the establishment of front-office services, typically the online delivery of documents, certificates or licenses, because they were more visible and more likely to trigger the interest and support of the public. However, it is now widely recognized that the most important benefits of e-government can be found in the rationalization and streamlining of back-office operations such as the sharing of information resources across government units. Such operations are generally close to the strategic or even core functions of governments. They tend to be regarded as less likely candidates for outsourcing, not to mention offshoring.

Yet, if the behavior of private companies is of any indication in this field, governments may show a growing interest in allowing their private partners to source some of their services globally. Indeed, if we look at the list of export-oriented foreign-direct investment (FDI) projects related to offshored services globally over the last few years (see Table 1), we can see that a number of back-office functions have been at the core of such projects.

The definitions of back-office versus front-office activities can be significantly different between the private and public sectors. However, the main factor, which has made business back-office functions outsourceable (specifically the ability to disaggregate tasks into sub-tasks and to share work across networks), may soon become even more important for government services. Whenever obstacles exist (legal, regulatory or psychological) about whether or not a particular government activity can be considered for outsourcing, ICTs will allow governments to identify and de-link outsourceable activities from non-outsourceable ones. As a result, the next wave of e-government outsourcing could hence very well affect back-office services. If this is so, it could be massive.

Relevance to the future of global sourcing

Modern governments have accepted that, to fulfill their roles efficiently and respond to the expectations of their citizens, they have to be both facilitators and leaders of the information revolution.

Because ICTs have affected so deeply the roles and the functions of governments, they have created both new opportunities and fresh attitudes, from governments, businesses and civil society as a whole. The growth of e-government services and the growing involvement of the private sector in their provision and delivery has been one of the most visible manifestations of this trend over the last ten years.

On the other hand, governments are called to play new roles in the context of the rapid globalization of the world economy: as regional economic and regulatory spaces continue to emerge, and

Table 1   **Common export-oriented FDI projects related to offshored services**
A number of back-office functions have been at the core of foreign-direct investment projects related to offshored services.

Call/contact centers (front-office services)	Shared service centers (back-office services)	IT services	Regional headquarters
Help desk	Claims processing	Software development	Headquarters
Technical support/advice	Accounts processing	Application testing	Coordination center
After-sales	Transaction processing	Content development	
Employee enquiries	Query management processing	Engineering and design	
Claims enquiries	Customer administration processing	Product optimization	
Customer support/advice			
Market research	HR/payroll processing		
Answering services	Data processing		
Prospecting	IT outsourcing		
Information services	Logistics processing		
Customer relationship management	Quality assurance		
	Supplier invoices		

Source: Adapted from UNCTAD (2005), page 159

as international commitments grow in intricacy and coverage, national governments have to learn to think beyond their national borders, and to take advantage of opportunities to better serve their citizens in the process. Outsourcing, first to the national private sector and then across national borders, is hence becoming a growing part of the governmental equation worldwide. As a result, the public sector, both in developed and developing economies, could become a major source of demand for global sourcing, in particular in the field of back-office e-government services.

New conflicts looming

However, as governments become more aware of the combination of opportunities represented by the ICT revolution on one hand and the advent of global sourcing on the other, new conflicts are looming. Such conflicts are likely to enhance even more the visibility of governments on the outsourcing scene in the years ahead.

Governments' interests are likely to diverge when it comes to defining some of the pre-conditions and safety nets mentioned above; they will also likely clash about the definition of quality of services, as well as about their modalities of delivery. Such divergences will manifest themselves on the international scene (e.g., in WTO), but will be exacerbated by conflicts of a different order among various stakeholders such as trade unions, consumers.

Governments will hence be called to take higher profiles about outsourcing issues. Specific instruments will need to be designed and accepted at home and globally regarding (1) international negotiations/agreements (e.g., WTO), (2) analytical and statistical tools (e.g., to define quality of service, fiscal bases, or employment and welfare effects of outsourcing), and (3) governance issues private and public. Whether as sources of demand or as central players in shaping the global regulatory environment necessary to keep the momentum of the outsourcing wave, governments will play an increasingly important role in shaping the future of outsourcing. Because governments themselves are in a position to gather significant benefits from outsourcing some of their own activities, in particular in the area of e-government, they are likely to develop new attitudes and positions, both at home and internationally. Opportunities for dialogue and cooperation between the private sector and the public sector will grow accordingly. Hopefully, this is an opportunity that neither side will want to miss.

References

1   Dutta, S. and Lopez-Claros, A., The Global Information Technology Report 2004-2005 - Efficiency in an Increasingly Connected World, INSEAD, World Economic Forum, Palgrave Macmillan, 2005.

2   Friedman, T., The World Is Flat - A Brief History of the Twenty-First Century, Farrar, Straus and Giroux, New-York, 2005.

3   The eGovernment Handbook for Developing Countries, infoDev/CDT (2003), http://www.infodev.org/files/841_file_eGovernment_Handbook.pdf (last visited 29 August 2005).

4   Lanvin, B., "Leaders and Facilitators-The New Roles of Governments," Global Information Technology Report 2002-2003, Geneva: World Economic Forum, infoDev and INSEAD, 2003.

5   Melford, M., Wright, M., and Sengupta, S. "Next Generation IT Outsourcing: Profits or Perils?," Dutta and Lopez-Claros, GITR 2004-2005.

6   Osterhammel, J. and Petersson, N.P. Globalization - A Short History, Princeton University Press, 2005.

7   World Investment Report 2004 - The Shift Towards Services, United Nations, UNCTAD, 2005.

EXPERT VOICE

Shashi Tharoor
Under-Secretary-General
for Communications and Public Information
United Nations
New York, New York

The Theory of "Flatness" Confronted

Question: *What is your position on "flatness" and how would you describe the current state of the world?*

Tharoor: The theory of flatness, as proposed by Thomas Friedman, overlooks a number of inconvenient hills on the surface of that flat world. My first concern is that in many countries the weakness of the state is a bigger problem, paradoxically, than the celebration of the disappearance of the state boundaries. In a great number of cases states do not provide the basic essentials that enable people to participate in the global market.

Second, I worry about the tendency to generalize from specific examples. You have oases in many countries. In my own country, India, you go to Bangalore and celebrate companies like Infosys, but when you leave Infosys, you go into a society that is still very much a developing country with genuine worries about electricity, water, and infrastructure.

A third problem I have with the notion of flatness and the irresistible success of globalization is the persistence of the digital divide. We live in a world with colossal differences in the ability of people to partake of benefits of the information revolution, which offers a lot of liberty, some fraternity and no equality. And there are the 3 billion people who live on less than $2 a day—far away from being able to celebrate the triumph of globalization.

Question: *How do you think the boom in IT outsourcing is changing India's economy?*

Tharoor: The money coming from the IT sector is having a ripple effect across the society. It is benefiting a lot more people in a literal sense; for example, Infosys made millionaires out of waiters who have Infosys shares. But its benefits are reaching in a more general metaphorical sense in that prosperity has spilled out into shops, restaurants, clothing, automobiles and consumer lifestyles. There has been a conscious and a deliberate effort to take the benefits of IT to some degree into the rural area. In my lifetime I might not see a majority of the Indian population having access to IT, but I am expecting to see every Indian village being wired to IT with some sort of Internet equivalent of the STD booth where you can pay for five minutes of access or complete a particular transaction. And I hope the private sector will take that step forward. This is the way of the future.

Question: *What is the impact of entrepreneurship on economic development?*

Tharoor: It's terrific. The rise of Infosys and other Indian IT companies is an extraordinary example of entrepreneurship and its impact on economic development. India is now full of people who feel they can do the same. In addition, the non-residential Indians have done very well. In Silicon Valley—six out of every seven startups have Indians involved. The problem is India still has an oppressive regulatory framework. The IT sector got lucky because the government was slow to catch onto the reality of IT, and did not regulate it out of existence. Unfortunately, other areas have not been so lucky.

Question: *How would you compare China with India's state of economic development?*

Tharoor: In the '70s India and China were entirely comparable in terms of economic development. India might have been even slightly ahead because some Indian cities were probably better off than their equivalent Chinese cities. Today, that is simply no longer true. China pulled more people out of poverty. It's an absolute revelation for an Indian to go to Beijing or Shanghai today. They go expecting to see a slightly improved version of Delhi or Bombay only to realize that these cities are not in the same category. Beijing and Shanghai are first-world cities. There are very few sectors in

which India is ahead of China—for the vast majority of products and services, China is ahead. But India has done the right job in terms of its political system and its strongly established system of rule and law.

Question: *What should U.S. companies, U.S. workers and U.S. citizens do to remain competitive?*

Tharoor: So far, the U.S. has managed to enshrine the advantages of creativity, innovation and entrepreneurship in a way that has always kept it ahead of the world. Frankly, I see no major threat to the U.S. economy. I certainly see the U.S. heading more into the direction of a service economy. One advantage of services is they are more difficult to outsource. But things that can be done better in Bangalore should be done in Bangalore. The things that can be manufactured cheaper in China should be manufactured in China. I don't see any difficulty in the U.S. maintaining its lead provided it retains its adaptability, its creativity, its innovation. If the U.S. starts throwing up barriers, then I would start to worry. The world right now is a place where everyone has a stake in the success of everyone else. I genuinely believe that China's and India's success should not be a threat to anybody—including the U.S. The more people succeed the better. So prosperity is actually not a zero sum game, it is win-win game.

Question: *What about the threat of terrorism?*

Tharoor: Al-Qaeda is both a rejection of globalization and a product of globalization. It is inconceivable they could have accomplished what they did on 9/11 without globalization. It is ironic they conduct medieval barbaric practices on the Internet. These acts are rejections of modernity made possible by modernity. So I would argue that we have to live with that phenomenon, but I honestly think the phenomenon of extreme violent action is bound to burn itself out, as is true of every other past example of it. Terrorists would change their view if we were able to bring benefits of development and globalization to a large number of people. If we can bring better standards of life, greater freedom, greater respect for human rights, the rule of law, and personal dignity to large numbers of people, then the support for extremist behavior would melt away. We can triumph over terrorism if we work genuinely for a better world for all.

3.2

By **Dr. David Hee-Don Lee**
Vice Chairman
World Trade Centers Association
Washington, D.C.

Will Globalization Bring Stability?

"**P**eace through economic interdependence such as global and regional outsourcing" is the idea that stability can be obtained through the peaceful economic cooperation among a broad range of diverse countries. This is a belief that global and regional outsourcing among nations brings peace and stability, according to the International Monetary Fund (IMF) definition of globalization: "the growing economic interdependence of countries worldwide through increasing volume and variety of cross-border transactions in goods and services, freer international capital flows, and more rapid and widespread diffusion of technology."[1]

For a country, global and regional outsourcing has considerable non-economic benefits. It is clearly in the interest of the interacting countries to reward other countries for reducing their barriers to trade and investment. For example, some of the countries where U.S. firms have set up outsourcing operations—India, Poland, and the Philippines—also are vital allies in the war on terrorism. Just as the North American Free Trade Agreement (NAFTA) helped Mexico deepen its democratic transition and strengthen its rule of law, the United States gains considerably from the political reorientation spurred by economic growth and interdependence.[2]

Supposedly, in the trend of increasing global and regional outsourcing, a benefiting government would avoid violent conflict with others for fear of upsetting the economic benefits. Any disruption of an interconnected country's economy would feed back into one's own economy.

The stability model through global and regional outsourcing might be called the "my enemy is my friend" approach to world peace, whereby heightened levels of economic cooperation, i.e., interdependent global and regional outsourcing among otherwise hostile states, is intended to lead to some form of significant economic integration and interdependence.

In pursuit of peace, the world might well wish to promote economic development and security goals simultaneously. Those goals would be meant to strengthen ties between and among the various nations to such a degree that the strictly government-to-government ties become simply one part of a much broader pattern of interaction, rather than a particularly important part of such an interaction, for what yet seems to them to be peculiar historical circumstances.

It is, by nature, an economic security plan that has as a final goal to bring the hostile countries to negotiation and cooperation, balancing the heterogeneous groups of countries in the conflict. A country no longer aims to isolate the other country. Instead, it tries to bring the hostile country into the international community, because it worries that the country in dispute has placed itself into the wrong corner in case of a new war.

Economic interdependence among nations through global and regional outsourcing in the world has been realized more than other matters of world economy.[3] Economic interdependence among nations in the current decade has expanded at a much faster rate than in other periods.[4] In fact, the global economies connected with global and regional outsourcing are already well integrated, and there may be said to exist a de facto economic community.

As further global and regional outsourcing leads to higher levels of interdependence among the countries, a joint approach to security will become imperative.

Following are the security implications associated with global and regional outsourcing.

The cultivated security model

In this model there is a spillover, or "tie in," from economic coop-eration to security cooperation by conscious desire, i.e., cultivated spillover. The spillover effect of economic cooperation will serve to upgrade political interrelationships, since economic factors and political considerations can hardly be separated from each other. The commitment to security would be shared by all the commu-nity members and would come as a "package deal" when each joins the economic community. Then the community is formed with both economic and security measures in mind. Therefore, in the event that community members do face external aggression, there exists a ready apparatus for their defense.

However, before any traditional community structures can be developed, a shared set of norms, interests and goals must be pres-ent. For example, although the conciliatory atmosphere and eco-nomic interdependence between the centrally-planned economies such as communist and the free market economies have improved in recent years, the cultivated security model requires not only "mutual economic interest based on geographic term" but also "the compatibility of basic politico-economic value (ideology)" among member states before the establishment of an economic community can be enforced.[5] In other words, this model denies the capacity of the centrally planned economy and free market states, as examples of heterogeneous groups, to integrate.

The requirement for membership in this traditional economic community model makes clear to other non-members that they are perceived as a threat and are distrusted. In a region with deep political contradictions, this signal would only serve to heighten tensions.[6]

The mutual economic deterrence model

Different from the traditional economic community model, "peace through economic interdependence such as global and regional outsourcing" can be considered essentially as an open and functional membership model.

A functional web of interdependence can reduce international conflict by raising its net costs, creating a sense of community, and producing value changes that promote integrative solutions to conflict.

In fact, easing tensions may be considerably easier to attain in economic terms than in political terms, since its activities would essentially address the domestic issues, such as economic growth. These have tended to distract the attention of local governments away from political matters to economic matters.

A desire to achieve the gains from global and regional outsourcing creates incentives for interacting countries to maintain cooperative relations, and increased global and regional outsourcing is associated in this way with declining conflict.

If the countries already engaged in global and regional outsourcing are suddenly faced with the necessity of doing without it, then the gains from global and regional outsourcing become the losses resulting from the interruption of these interactions. Since both gain from global and regional outsourcing, both suffer losses; commonsense would therefore mandate that if they do not value the gains from global and regional outsourcing equally, then the one that values them more will be in the weaker bargaining position. The ability of one government to threaten to interrupt its global and regional outsourcing with another can be an effective weapon in the struggle for power, which is called the influence effect of global and regional outsourcing. Asymmetric economic interdependence provides a new form of power that can be used by less interdependent countries to gain concessions from others that are more interdependent. And the economic ties provide an opportunity to conduct war by other means. Vulnerabilities can be used like economic weapons, enabling countries that lack substantial military power or prefer not to use it to coerce their interaction partners.

Traditionally, in bilateral relations, deterrence involves manipulating an opponent's behavior by employing the threat of force as a response to its first use of force. For some opponents fear is the key element. For others it is a rational assessment of cost and gains. And for still others uncertainty and risk are important elements.

In the meantime, economic deterrence exercises fear of losing economic interest rather than fear of military retaliation. It includes sanctions, which can be used as a synonym for economic coercion, covert economic pressure, coercive uses of government aid, global and regional outsourcing curbs that affect two countries, boycotts and embargoes.[7]

In multilateral relations, if economic interdependence reaches high levels, the hostile states will give long and serious thought to the consequences of their actions before entering into conflict. Otherwise, they will lose the economic interest with the other states established through economic interdependence.

But the economic interdependence will act as a deterrent to dissuade not only the target country but also its allied countries from repeating the disputed action. This is because by making it possible for allied countries to exert such coercion, vulnerabilities can be a source of increased international conflict. The vulnerable countries would seek recovery through policies that produce tension with other countries.

A disadvantage to a dispute-initiating country is that economic coercion may irritate the initiator's allies, and then the initiator faces possible domestic costs. The cost to the economy is significant, because the economic coercion will force a shift from a disrupted lower cost supplier to a higher cost supplier. Furthermore, the economic coercion may diminish future global and regional outsourcing, as countries deem the initiator an unreliable supplier. Target countries will pursue diversification strategies and alternative sources of production.

As another disadvantage, the economic coercion may generate a political backlash against the initiator's leadership when it fails to modify the target's behavior.

In conclusion, if a broad number of countries are able to attain a significant level of economic interdependence, and each country recognizes its dependence on the economic cooperation through global and regional outsourcing, international stability is maintained. After intense economic interdependence becomes effective, no country would desire to disrupt the peace. Therefore, achieving this model rests on a high degree of economic integration and interdependence among countries.

In reality, hostile countries cannot accomplish their domestic priorities, for example, unless the other counterpart countries are doing well economically. To import technology, they must raise cash by borrowing more from the free market economy countries or by exporting more to them. Whether they rely on the free market economy countries' capital markets or export markets, they will benefit from a capitalist country's healthy economy. So a serious economic downturn could doom their modernization plans. This degree of economic interdependence is new. It gives the hostile countries an unprecedented stake in the free market economy countries' growth.

The hostile countries' reforms depend on a dramatic increase in domestic investment. But, as opposition to domestic reform grows internally (in bad circumstances), access to the free market economy countries' capital will become crucial.

Internal instability

For the developing countries the primary threat to security is internal instability, not external aggression. Authoritarianism and maldistribution of wealth have injected a strain of instability into the domestic politics of the developing countries.[8]

There is little, if anything, that external security ties can do to promote security when the threat is from within. Also, since the governments of the developing countries are preoccupied with maintaining internal stability and promoting economic growth, they are drawn away from regional and sub-regional affairs. This preoccupation with national interests exacerbates the lack of cohesion among governments.[9]

Global and regional outsourcing has assisted many regions of the world in overcoming age-old suspicions and distrust—and in realizing that healthy communication and commerce can bring not only prosperity but improved relations among all nations.

The vision and strategy of promoting peace and stability through global and regional outsourcing offers one of the best hopes available to improve and expand cooperation among peoples everywhere. The global and regional outsourcing process has advanced the concept that:[10]

1. poverty is a breeding ground for conflict;
2. prosperity is an antidote for conflict;
3. poverty can be overcome and prosperity attained through growth in business and employment;
4. business success for any region in today's world means success in world business;
5. success in world business requires effective training, global contacts and support services, and

6. global and regional outsourcing can supply the services and facilities needed to help regions and individuals prosper and relate peacefully with the rest of the world.

As a security system, the Mutual Economic Deterrence Model would not stand in contradistinction to the rest of Asia, Africa, Latin America and East and West Europe, because this model gives emphasis to the security function in itself. If this model could function idealistically, there should not exist external opponents throughout the "my enemy is my friend" approach. Thus, if internal stability is maintained and external threats are eliminated, security in the international arena can be achieved through economic interdependence such as global and regional outsourcing.

Therefore, the Mutual Economic Deterrence model equates security with economic development but does not ignore the value of deterrence. This model advocates peace through economic cooperation, such as global and regional outsourcing. Furthermore, it acknowledges that global and regional security is best served through economic development.

Economic interdependence through global and regional outsourcing, in general, equals peace. It might also mean universal prosperity.[11]

References

1 Out·sourc·ing: The procuring of services or products, such as the parts used in manufacturing a motor vehicle, from an outside supplier or manufacturer in order to cut costs. v. to send out (work, for example) to an outside provider or manufacturer in order to cut costs, *The American Heritage Dictionary of the English Language*, Fourth Edition, Houghton Mifflin Company, 2000.

2 World Economic Outlook, IMF, May, 1997.

3 Drezner, Daniel W., "The Outsourcing Bogeyman," *Foreign Affairs*, May/June 2004.

4 G-Index-Globalization Measured, Section 6. Analysis, World Markets Research Center, August 2001.

5 Sixth Annual Outsourcing Index Survey, 2003, the Outsourcing Institute and Dun & Bradstreet, 2003.

6 Lee, David H., *The Pacific Economic Cooperation and Strategy for Collective Security, California Journal*, April, 1997.

7 Lee, David H., "Collective Security and Regional Economic Cooperation: Pacific Region," California State Univ. Press, 1999.

8 Lee, David H., "Collective Security and Regional Economic Cooperation: Pacific Region," *Economic Deterrence*, 2nd edition, David H. Lee, California State Univ. Press, 2000.

9 Payne, Richard J. and Nassar, Jamal R., Politics and Culture in the Developing World: The Impact of Globalization, 2005.

10 The Least Developed Countries 2005 Report, United Nations Publications, 2005.

11 WTCA Mission Statement, WTC-Corps., World Trade Centers Association, 2005.

Martin Wolf
Associate Editor and
Chief Economics Commentator
Financial Times
London, England

Why Globalization Works

Question: *How is outsourcing being perceived in the developed world?*

Wolf: People have begun to realize that technological changes have made areas of the economy tradable, which until relatively recently people assumed were non-tradable, and therefore parts of the economy and jobs are subject to competition from other parts of the world. Naturally that has increased anxiety. And because this is new and anything new is always frightening, it is quite inevitable that there will be some sort of panic. I think back 30 years ago when people realized for the first time that developing countries could have a real competitive advantage in their export of labor-intensive manufactures. If you remember prior to that time, the industrial countries effectively had a complete monopoly on manufacturing and the exports of manufacturers—they exported manufactures and developing countries exported commodities, and that seem the normal pattern. Then suddenly Japan rose as a low-wage producer, and they were followed by Hong Kong, Singapore, Korea, Taiwan and then of course on through China.

Now we've gotten used to this idea, and we've come to realize that we can't keep these things and have had to adjust to that change. So now we are experiencing a new wave as we realized that there are important areas, particularly in the service sector, where the same form of unbundling of processes across borders and the location of processes in countries that have the right resources to do them is going to occur. It is another development of the international division of labor.

Question: *If you were to advise a European head of state on the impact of outsourcing, what would be your advice?*

Wolf: The big problem in some core European countries like Germany, France and Italy is that the labor markets have on the whole been working badly for a very, very long time and have failed to generate jobs overall. This is partly, I think, a function of labor market restrictions and regulations; it is partly a function of product market restrictions, particularly the difficulty in starting up businesses; it is partly about tax and benefits systems that make it more profitable for many relatively low-skilled people not to work, and it is partly the underlying weakness of demand growth, the dynamic of demand. If you look at Germany, the problem is international competitiveness. Germany, of course, is the world's largest exporter. It exports more than the United States; it has an enormous current account surplus. The problem is extreme weakness in the generation of demand growth within the economy over a long period. These, I think, are the consequences of the range of predominantly domestic factors as I indicated. Obviously when the domestic economy does not work very well and jobs aren't being generated, then hysteria about job losses increases to high levels. Europe has to reduce bureaucracy to spur economic growth, combined with a non-protectionist view on trade. Otherwise, Europe will continue to lose out in terms of competitiveness.

Question: *If you look at the regions around the world, where do you see the high growth areas for global outsourcing?*

Wolf: We should not exaggerate the power of technology to overcome distance and that is particularly true, obviously, if you need very intensive supervision from headquarters or if you are actually moving the physical goods as part of the activity. So countries with relatively low costs that are close to the countries that are large markets and have large productive systems are very well situated. That seems to me to be true for Central and Eastern Europe, and it ought to be true, at least for some of countries in Central and Southern America, vis-à-vis the United States. I think it is truer for Central and Eastern Europe because in addition to being extremely close to

major producing centers in Western Europe, they also have relatively high skills. In fact, one of the striking characteristics of Central and Eastern Europe is how cheap the countries are in relationship to the skill base. That is a well-known phenomenon of Central and Eastern Europe. So it seems to me that because of the advantages of proximity, relatively low cost and availability of skills, these countries are extremely well positioned to make big successes in this sort of activity.

Question: *How do you think globalization will impact the growth of outsourcing into the future?*

Wolf: The broader point is how well the developed countries will cope with challenges they confront—can they keep growing and innovating? Because if they don't, what they produce will turn into commodities and their terms of trade will collapse, and they will become significantly poorer than they would like, because nobody will pay as much as they now pay for the things they are generating. I don't want to exaggerate this, but there are genuine questions about the ability of both the U.S. and Europe to maintain anything like their present relative positions in the world.

Historically, if you look at it as a big picture in terms of centuries not decades, the position that the Europeans and then what were essentially European offshoots—the U.S. in particular—the position of absolute dominance and innovative capacity of the world economy they acquired over the last two centuries is not sustainable. It will be fantastically difficult to sustain it, and they are going to come under huge challenge from these gigantic reservoirs of very talented and hard working people in Eastern and Southern Asia, which contain four times as many people than developed countries. Europe and North America will find that adapting to that sort of world where they simply don't have the power, the economic dominance, the unquestioned sway that they have had for so long, will be very, very painful. But my own view is that it is inevitable. It is just so anomalous that so huge a proportion of the world economy and so huge a proportion of the world's technology are generated by and developed in such a tiny proportion of the world's population. There is a real adjustment there, but will it lead to conflict? As I said I am moderately optimistic we can avoid it.

Question: *Would you agree with the Goldman Sachs BRICS report (Brazil, Russia, India and China) that by the year 2050, China will be the number one economy? Will these four economies really be the stars of the future?*

Wolf: I don't think there is a serious chance that either Brazil or Russia will be stars of the future. Russia obviously has one huge asset—its natural resources. But Russia has such a severe demographic problem. So even if Russia does quite well and catches up on Europe to a reasonable degree, it will not be a giant economy of the future, it is simply too small. Brazil has a sizable population. But its economy has consistently disappointed. It seems to me to have a huge range of really deep structural problems, which will make it very difficult to grow. Brazil also has a pretty poor educational system, a very low savings rate, huge inequalities and an incompetent public sector. Given all these things and

given that it doesn't have a gigantic population, or extraordinary human resources, I don't expect Brazil to be a really big player. If you look at China or India, you get something utterly different because of the sheer size of these places. With a population well over a billion, India will be most populous country in the world probably in about 20 years. You have to be very, very, very pessimistic about the capacity in China and India to run their economies without reaching the conclusion they are going to be the biggest economies in the world. If China generates a GDP per head relative to the United States, much the same as Portugal today is relative to the United States, it will have the biggest economy in the world. This is a tyranny of numbers. Provided they are able to use their human resources even quite inefficiently, but not as inefficiently as today, it does seem to me fantastically plausible that they will be two of the biggest economies in the world by 2050. China will certainly be there before India, in my view, and will be equivalent with the U.S. I think the BRIC forecasts for India and China are pretty moderate; they don't imply very fast growth. And after all, it is worth noting that China is already the world's third largest trading entity and if China's trade continues to go anything like its recent rate, it will be the biggest trading entity in the world within another five to ten years.

Question: *What will multinational corporations look like in the future?*

Wolf: First, assuming away catastrophe, assuming the world remains on its present trajectory and that of course is a big assumption, I would expect businesses to become multinational. So purely national companies, in most businesses, will disappear and I think that it is very striking. It is very interesting point to ask yourself which economic areas of business are still dominated by companies that are predominantly national? Even in those areas where transport costs are very high, like cement or brewing, or where historically the businesses have been national, like steel, we are seeing very rapid growth of the multinational, multi-product, multi-plant business. That is a superior organizational form because, to put it very bluntly, it can take advantage of more opportunities than purely national firms can do with their market base contracting.

To go back to the theory of this, there are a lot of activities in the modern market economy where relatively hierarchical structures work better than arms length markets, and that is why multinationals exist. I expect that to continue to be the case. Second, I expect those businesses to continue as if they were half a trace of the country from which they originated, and I expect that trace to become increasingly diluted. There are a number of multinational companies that everybody would think of as American companies that operate multinationally: GE, IBM, Microsoft. Increasingly we will think of companies, which, while they clearly have a national base and there is a certain national culture, it will be quite difficult to locate them nationally. I would expect a large proportion of their business to be in China, for example, and I would expect a large proportion of their staff to be hired in China, which means much of their innovation will be done in China and probably so

much of their equity will be owned by Chinese that in fifty years we will not think of them as American companies. We will think of them as truly global. It is a very important development that companies are really becoming genuinely transnational.

3.3

By *Umesh Ramakrishnan*
Vice Chairman
Christian & Timbers
New York, New York

U.S. Leadership Complacency

Globalization is no longer about finding cheaper labor overseas. For years now, the American media has been filled with articles and television segments examining, and, for the most part, decrying the growing trend among American companies of shifting some of their operations overseas. Politicians threaten to pass legislation to prevent the loss of American jobs, labor unions are in a state of panic, and the American public, understandably, is uneasy about what this means for their future. I would submit, however, that the focus of all this attention has been in the wrong area.

Ask most people about the issue of offshoring, and they will tell you that the jobs being shifted overseas are the low paying jobs associated with call centers, technical support offices and the like. And they assume that the only reason that these jobs are being moved overseas is that the workers in places like China, India and Korea are willing to work for wages that are a fraction of what their American counterparts make. Until recently, these people would have been right. According to a recent report by McKinsey & Company, the salaries of professionals such as engineers in India and China are currently between 12 percent and 19 percent of comparable U.S. salaries.[1]

Today, however, they are dead wrong. The American public must wake up to the fact that the offshoring of jobs is no longer merely an attempt by corporations to find cheaper sources of labor for the backroom, mundane tasks of U.S. businesses. For one thing, wages and salaries are rising even in developing countries like India and China.[2] More importantly, however, the jobs that are moving offshore today include higher level, creative and strategically important positions in the areas of information technology, customer analytics, research and development, and strategy formulation. In a recent study, *BusinessWeek* magazine identified the following upscale jobs as already shifting overseas: basic research, chip design, engineering and financial analysis.[3] The higher the level of the position moving overseas, however, the less American companies save. So if cost savings are not driving this shift, what is?

The painful truth is that today jobs are moving overseas to places like India and China because those countries offer a highly educated workforce that is by and large better prepared to meet the needs of U.S. businesses—particularly technology businesses—than our own graduates. Both India and China have an enormous and fast growing class of young adults. Approximately 53 percent of the Indian population, or 590 million people, is below the age of 25. In China, reflecting the government policies favoring low birth rates, the percentage is somewhat lower—41 percent of the population is under the age of 25.[4] In contrast, only 35 percent of the American population is under the age of 25. The disparity in the number of college graduates per year among the three countries is also striking: 3.1 million for India, 2.8 million for China, and 1.3 million for the United States.[5] Nor can one assume that these young adults are graduating from mediocre schools. "The Higher Education Supplement" of the *Times of London* ranks the Indian Institutes of Technology as the third-best institute for engineering and IT in the world.[6]

Finally, the growth rate of young professionals also differs dramatically. According to the McKinsey study, the stock of suitable, young professional talent in emerging countries like India and China (defined as engineers, finance and accounting professionals, analysts, life science researchers and professional generalists with less than seven years experience), is growing at 5.5 percent annually. By contrast, the number of the same young professionals in developed countries, including the United States, is growing just one percent annually.[7] More importantly, new graduates of universities in India and China surpass their American counterparts in terms of innovation, creativity and drive. These young people in India and China are the equivalent of the new immigrants in the United States of 100 years ago. For most of them, the opportunities presented by the technology industry are life changing. They mean the end of an era in which these young adults would have looked forward to a life of poverty, isolated from the outside world in small towns and villages. Today, they are seizing the chance to earn significant salaries, to live in growing, modernizing cities and to connect to the world in ways that their parents never dreamed possible. For example, the two most prestigious university systems in India, the Indian Institute of Technology and the Indian Institute of Management, each admit classes of approximately 2000 students each year—from an applicant pool of more than one million. And while an Indian engineering graduate twenty years ago could expect to earn an annual salary of approximately $600, today the most prestigious graduates command salaries in the range of $100,000 per year. American college graduates, by contrast, have become complacent as they have grown up in an environment that did not require them to hone their survival instincts like their Asian counterparts. That is not to say that many of them are not hard working or determined to fashion a better life for themselves. But as a demographic group, they are far removed from their Asian counterparts.

Americans of the post-World War II generations have been raised to believe that we cannot be beat at anything. The truth, however, is that we are already being beat in many of the most important areas of innovation, productivity and implementation of new technologies. Silicon Valley will always have a role to play in the global technology industry, but unfortunately the power base will shift to countries that support innovation more than we do. American business leaders, politicians and the general public must all acknowledge this new reality and start implementing the changes that will be required if we are to have any hope of preserving our supremacy.

Below are changes American business leaders must make *now*:

Train global leaders. Training of business leaders must include significant exposure to global issues and must reach down past the upper levels of management to the younger, junior managers as well. All of these people must be given global exposure early and often in their careers. This includes such things as overseas postings, foreign language training, education in cross-cultural issues and exposure to customers, strategic partners and colleagues working in foreign countries. In assessing the success of these types of initiatives, U.S. companies must move to a cost-benefit analysis that is based on global criteria, not merely U.S. criteria.

U.S. corporations should also rethink how they develop overseas assignments for their emerging leaders. Traditionally, American companies have hired young managers, trained them stateside for several years until they were a "proven commodity" and then sent them overseas for a year to two. I would suggest that this process is backwards. Young people assimilate to different cultures more quickly than older people do—they learn the language more quickly, they adapt to the lifestyles, cuisines and cultural differences more easily, and they do a better job of integrating this new knowledge into their work. The financial services industry, led by General Electric, is the only industry that seems to understand this need. They are aggressively using foreign assignments to help their youngest hires develop global experience and perspective.

On the flip side, U.S. businesses generally send some of the most junior of their local employees from their overseas operations to the United States for training. This too should be reversed. Instead of bringing junior managers to the United States to learn management skills, companies should be sending their most senior foreign executives here for training so that they can return to their homes overseas and train their younger counterparts to become new leaders.

Advocate for new government policies. The federal and state governments are engaged at the moment in a push-me/pull-you dynamic: they want to support the ability of American businesses to compete globally, but they have difficulty breaking free of protectionist impulses. Policies that are based on trying to keep global competitors out of American markets will not protect American jobs in the long run. They will only ensure that we lose our economic dominance more quickly.

One of the most ill advised economic policies of the federal government involves the subsidies that are offered to (or denied to) various industries. These subsidies take the form of direct payments, tax breaks for U.S. companies in certain industries, and tariffs imposed upon goods produced by foreign companies, which artificially raises their prices in comparison to U.S. manufactured goods. Currently, we provide significant support to the agriculture and steel industries, but we do not offer similar support to the technology or life science industries. As Craig Barrett, former CEO of Intel, has suggested, we must stop subsidizing the industries of the 19th century and begin subsidizing the industries of the 21st century.[8] I am not suggesting that the government end its support for the steel industry or agriculture. Both continue to play an important role in our national and the global economy. However, it is time to put similar resources into the technology and life sciences industry—while simultaneously avoiding building barriers between U.S. corporations and overseas companies.

The government must act quickly to more actively support more and better scientific research. No matter what your beliefs are about stem cell research, or other issues that cultural conservatives oppose, it is indisputable that we are not devoting the resources we need to retain our supremacy in the areas of technology and life science. Yet, rather than increasing resources in these areas, the Bush administration just cut them. In the 2005-2006 Federal Budget, the White House cut the National Science Foundation budget by $100 million and it has proposed shrinking the 2006 Department of Energy science programs and basic applied research in the Department of Defense. Stated bluntly, these are not the kinds of policies that encourage innovation. Yet, at the same time, incredible advances in technology and life sciences are being made in almost every country in Asia, as well as in Israel and throughout Europe.

Insist on improvements in American education. American businesses cannot train effective global executives if our schools are producing graduates who are unprepared to work in a global economy. Corporate leaders must be out in front of educational reform efforts. Their voices are among the most powerful and effective in making the American public understand that our schools are failing all of us unless they produce the best-trained students in math, science and engineering. To do this, however, we must address the disparity between affluent and poor school districts, increase funding for teachers' professional development in the areas of math and science, hold schools and teachers accountable for their students' performances and reward those that succeed. Consider this statistic: in 2004, 65,000 American high school students competed in the Intel Science and Engineering Fair, one of the world's most prestigious and challenging competitions. In China, 6,000,000 students participated. The difference is chilling. Math education also is critically important. Mathematics is the "language" of the technology industry, and thus the language of the modern, global economy. It must be the language of anyone who wants to succeed in the new world. Science and engineering are also two areas in which the United States lags far behind other nations, particularly Asian nations.

And speaking of foreign languages, this is another area where educational reform is needed desperately. Only a small number of American middle schools and high schools offer classes in Asian languages. Most schools' foreign language departments remain firmly Eurocentric. As *Newsweek* pointed out in a recent issue, however, today 1 million American students study French—a language spoken by only 75 million people worldwide. By contrast, only 24,000 American students study Chinese—a language spoken by 1.3 billion people. In *Newsweek*'s words,[10] "The future does not speak French." While American schools may not recognize the need to revise their foreign language offerings, American business leaders do. In a recent study conducted by my executive search firm, Christian & Timbers, we asked senior executives which foreign language was the most important for a high school student to study. The choices were: Spanish, French, Chinese, Russian and German. Of the 234 responses, 43 percent answered Chinese. The full results were: Spanish (48 percent), Chinese (43 percent), French (4 percent), Japanese (5 percent) and Russian (0 percent).

Avoid protectionist actions that will only hurt us in the long run. Ironically, as the number one capitalist nation on the planet, the United States—through some of its legislative proposals—seems to have decided that we need to stop capitalist growth in other nations. For example, we place strict limits on the number of highly educated professionals whom we allow to work in our country, at the very time when we are not graduating enough students with the training that our businesses need. We must keep our doors open to welcoming the highly educated professionals of other countries. The federal government should increase the number of H1-b visas granted to highly educated, technically expert foreigners to work in the United States. The common objection made to raising the H1-b visa limit—that these people are taking jobs that should go to Americans—is nonsense. American businesses need the expertise of these people. Those who advocate limiting the number of H1-b visas are effectively saying to the world, "We don't want your smart people to come here."

I strongly believe that the more smart, highly educated, motivated, creative and hard working people we welcome to our country, the more Americans will be forced to do the necessary work to compete. When highly educated foreign workers don't come here, they stay in their countries of origin and add to the momentum of change there, which in the end makes us even less competitive globally. It is a classic double whammy: we lose their contributions here and suffer from their contributions over there.

Similarly, we need to revise our view of jobs that American companies send overseas. While it is understandable that many people view offshoring as a "theft" of American jobs, it is not at all clear that offshoring has been a significant factor in mass layoffs of U.S. workers. McKinsey's study indicates that mass layoff numbers—which continue even in good economic times—are much higher than trade-related or predicted offshoring-related layoffs.[11] Moreover, the Bureau of Labor Statistics predicts the creation of 22 million new jobs in the U.S. economy between 2000 and 2010, while simultaneously predicting that approximately 200,000 jobs will be lost due to offshoring.[12] A more positive view of the entire offshoring issue is to focus on profits, rather than jobs. Rather than protesting that companies that offshore some of their operations are depriving Americans of jobs, we should be working to insist that the profits of those companies—whether earned stateside or overseas—remain in the United States. In this way, it will be possible to maintain U.S. business leadership and fuel growth here at home. And growth will result in the creation of more jobs—here as well as abroad.

Until we are successful in re-educating American voters about the offshoring issue, however, it is not likely that the American Congress will end its efforts at imposing protectionist regulations on our businesses. As long as their constituents view offshoring as a theft of American jobs, it will be difficult for American legislators—who worry first and foremost about getting re-elected—to support proposals for cross-border training programs, for example. Witness the recent address to a joint session of Congress by the Indian Prime Minister, Dr. Manmohan Singh. He enjoyed an enthusiastic, warm reception from the Congress—until he raised the issue of outsourcing. The change in the mood of his audience was startling. Loud applause changed immediately to stony silence.[13] American political and business leaders can no longer remain complacent about the economic superiority that we have enjoyed for the last century. As a result of the phenomenal—and ongoing—rise of Asian economies and Asian technological capacity, we stand at a crossroads, and we are facing difficult choices. We can continue to make the same choices that served us well for much of the past century, such as tolerating mediocre education for our youth, not adequately supporting innovation in technology and life sciences, and attempting to protect our economy with protectionist measures that only hurt us in the long run. Or we can try a different path—one that embraces cross-border collaborations, demands and supports the development of new and innovative technologies—even at the cost of some of our traditional industries—and sets educational standards that will prepare our youth for success in a globally interconnected future. The choices are ours to make. But we also must know what is at risk if we make the wrong choices. That can be summed up in one word: everything.

References

1   "The Emerging Global Labor Market," McKinsey & Company, June 2005, p. 45.

2   Ibid.

3   Engardio, Pete, Bernstein, Aaron and Kripalani, Manjeet, with Balfour, Frederik, Grow, Brian, and Greene, Jay, "The New Global Job Shift," *BusinessWeek*, February 3, 2003.

4   O'Sullivan, Katie and Durfee, Don, "Offshoring by the Numbers," CFO *Magazine*, June 1, 2004.

5   Ibid.

6   "World University Rankings," *Times of London Higher Education Supplement*, October 28, 2005.

7   McKinsey.

8   La Monica, Paul R., "Intel: U.S. Could Lose Tech Edge," CNNMoney, October 3, 2003.

9   Friedman, Thomas L., "C.E.O.'s M.I.A," *New York Times*, May 25, 2005.

10 Adams, William, "The Future Doesn't Speak French," *Newsweek*, May 9, 2005.

11 McKinsey, Exhibit 7.

12 McKinsey, Exhibit 8.

13 Padmanabhan, Anil and Chengappa, Raj, with Shukla, Saurabh, "Big Step Forward," *India Today*, August 1, 2005.

EXPERT VOICE

Hubertus Hoffman
Founder and President
World Security Network Foundation
New York, New York

The Globalization of Foreign Policy

Question: *What is your view on the current state of the world?*

Hoffmann: In days gone by, a diplomat would stop his coach at the doors of the royal residence of a European king, remove his top hat and speak to His Royal Highness for an hour in French, discussing history, the latest gossip from his own city, politely share a few humorous anecdotes and end with a diplomatically formulated wish from his own king to peacefully resolve a potential border conflict. The approach was considered quite distinguished and diplomatic—with veils and charm at the highest level. But it was, for the most part, fruitless and futile. For more than 500 years before the 20th century, wars erupted in Europe every five, ten, or twenty years. Or WWI, the premier example of diplomatic inability that completely laid waste to Europe and planted seeds for WWII, which cost the lives of more than 50 million people. The result of classical, traditional diplomacy was quite sobering. The world today practices an entirely different foreign policy. In the age of 21st century globalization, the new foreign policy must be international, extending across the entire globe. It must develop new thought and convey a believable moral strategy designed to shape a better world, and it must focus on actions to promote these goals.

Question: *Who are the real movers and shakers in the new globalized world?*

Hoffmann: *The Research Institutes and the Famous Foundations:* There are outstanding institutes that stimulate motivation in global foreign policy—the IISS in London, the American Enterprise Institute in Washington, or CAP in Munich. However, most research institutes and famous foundations are occupied with themselves. As a result, their output and influence on foreign policy is in reality quite small. Why? It's because they are afraid to take a position. They should spend less time analyzing and more time shaping action proposals. They are more comfortable reacting rather than acting. They publish analyses years after a war, and they love conferences with big names that focus more on ego stroking than actively shaping a secure world. The majority of the money they raise is devoted to operating their own administrations.

Governments and Parliaments: Most politicians involved in foreign and security policy in parliaments and governments have the freedom to do almost everything, except one thing—take a position. They are prohibited from talking about things as they are and stating their stand on issues, because if they did, they would amount to nothing. And what professional politician wants that? Government representatives and parliamentarians react only then when the public makes a demand—usually when the media presents enough news about a war and it becomes intolerable.

Fritz Kraemer, a refugee from Nazi Germany who tutored generations of America's leading generals in historical and geopolitical thinking once said, "The very successful politician will lose his aggressiveness and part of his soul on every rung of the ladder leading him to the top during his long career of compromising and sailing with the wind. The harsh school of upward struggle may, in fact, have made him a master tactician, but the Holy Fire, the inner passion, the vision has gone, had to go.

Western foreign policy is, for the most part, reactionary. It does not take a proactive stance in shaping a better world. Almost no one stands out with creative concepts and plans by which we can design today's world more peaceably and safely in the coming decades. Foreign policy is for the most part a mix of lifeless bureaucracy and fear, almost always reactive and never preventive.

Military Force: The armed forces also are a very important stabilizing factor of foreign policy, regardless of the side they take. All over the world,

rational generals have prevented more wars than the average person wants to believe. In 1937 when Hitler asked his General Chief of Staff whether Germany ought to attack its neighbors, he said, "No!" and was removed from his position. And as we all know, Hitler was not rational.

Question: What are the new methods and actors for globalizing foreign policy?

Hoffmann: Under critical consideration of the actors in foreign policy we see there is a lot of room for the globalization of foreign policy. At the core, one has to identify just who is putting forth the topics and proposals for actions. It is a question of power, attention, and the genuine creation of peace. In my opinion, an excellent example of the globalization of foreign policy is al-Qaeda. With the implications of their mission notwithstanding, this is an international network of intelligent, highly motivated young people with decentralized leadership, who are willing to sacrifice their own lives for a simple mission attached to a global belief and a clear picture of the enemy. They have global sources of financing and are allied with other terror organizations all over the world. International terrorism creates a maximum effect with minimum expenditures. It is an active global network of true believers.

Question: What can—and should— we learn?

Hoffmann: From centuries of historical experiences, what we already know of the 21st Century and its direction, there is something very important for which we should be prepared: The new foreign policy in the age of globalization must be international—extending across and including the entire globe—and its actions must be focused to promote its goals. Sorry neo-cons in the U.S., your concept that, "We make America strong first and thumb our noses at Europe," is simply too provincial. That philosophy is no longer state-of-the-art, and in fact, it is less effective than the stripped down model of your enemies. A new and successful foreign policy in this age of globalization needs active comrades-in-arms on all seven continents and cannot remain organized on a national level only. The nationally centered foreign policy of the 19th Century has, in the 21st Century, been replaced by a never-before-seen globalized power of influences, organizations, media, and personal contacts. Never before have so many people maintained as many international contacts worldwide as they have today. Never before was the world such a village of global information and opinion. Never before have events at a distance of several a thousand miles had such an effect on us. And never before have so many committed people been involved politically in foreign policy as today. This real globalization is a fact—not a mirage. It has an enormous impact on the way in which nations interact with each other today. And yet, this new global interdependence is a question not determined by decisiveness, but rather by the positive goals pursued and by whom.

Question: *Could you give some examples?*

Hoffmann: Everyone wants less poverty and war, and more prosperity and peace on earth. But how? Even today the powers of totalitarianism put the ideology and power of the state before the freedom of the human being, with the advanced powers of freedom and human rights. Who, however, will win in the end and capture the opportunities of globalization to use for good or evil? It will be a decisive battle over who can win the commitment of subsequent generations—al-Qaeda or democrats. It is important for us to find courageous young talents who will work for the ideas of freedom and prosperity in the 198 states of the world, and take over responsibility. In my opinion, it will take a pool of only 500,000 young talents committed to excellence to create the new global elite. Great historical events, whether the October Revolution in Russia, 9/11, the Declaration of Independence of the United States of America or the Human Rights Charter—all were realized by a very few elites who, in a dark or bright moment of world history, used their moment of opportunity with courage and determination to their advantage. The gifted talent scout Fritz Kraemer once said, "Look for men and women of excellence! Guide, help, assist, encourage them!" In the business world in particular, more talent coming out of your companies should be groomed for and directed into foreign policy, thereby building up a new elite. Fritz Kramer rightly said, "Even large talents require a talent scout to discover and support them." We need different networks of mentors, who help guide young people over years in the taking on of responsibility.

A moral mission is indispensable. The only option is increased freedom in the world and the promotion of free, open and tolerant societies throughout our globe. We need a responsible elite that does not demand privileges for itself, but takes on responsibility for others. In this respect, we must once again attend to values more strongly and reduce the excesses of materialism. In particular, the new elite in the Western world needs spiritual orientation—a challenge for the Christian Church in particular. Moral relativism is our greatest danger in globalization.

Part 4

Into the Future

Innovation begets opportunities for organizations. But what promotes innovation? Education. Freedom. Research. Capital. Certainly these inspire those who innovate, but as globalization becomes a more common term in the business community, there is a rising element of fear.

The increasing impact of global competitive forces is causing companies to re-evaluate their customer propositions in search of higher value-add through innovation and business process re-design. As technological innovation causes barriers to entry to fall in most markets, the largest and even the smallest of companies are vulnerable to new and non-traditional competition. Traditional industries with relatively large back-office costs such as financial services, the media and transportation are under threat. Their rivals are willing to outsource their operations and increasingly offshore their work through distant third parties. Even the mighty pharmaceutical companies, who are renowned for their tightly controlled production processes, are now looking for ways to extract even more cost efficiencies through outsourcing to contract manufacturers.

Outsourcing has become an option not for just large corporations but an accepted resource for medium-sized companies. The result is an increase in the number of outsourcing service providers in the market.

Outsourcing is not just a one-way street. By analyzing their true core competencies, companies recognize they too can offer outsourcing services where others lack the will or the means to deliver for themselves. While many claim huge cost savings from straight outsourcing deals, others can point to the protection of jobs and increased revenues by also joining the market. The growth of outsourcing management associations offering conferences and forum exchanges, dedicated consultancies and new trade publications all indicate the potential mega-opportunities in this industry.

And yet, outsourcing has been with us for decades. Looking into the future, by 2050 what will companies look like? Increased personalization? A higher level of variety and diversity of products and service levels? What role will geography play 50 years from now? What will future corporate executives be taught in the universities about global outsourcing? Is McWorld waiting for us around the corner? As Ted Levitt wrote in *The Economist* at the end of the '90s, the civilization you belong to matters less than you might think.

The future of outsourcing has yet to be fully played out. Its rapid growth and increasing maturity is set to radically alter where work is done, how and by whom. Its impact will cause us all to work smarter and harder to meet, and exceed, the standards set in other parts of the world. Its effects will allow almost every global citizen to source any product from anywhere at similar prices and for wage costs to become comparable around much of globe in the long run. This must be a benefit to everyone.

4.1

By **Huib Wursten**
Managing Partner
ITIM International
Amsterdam, The Netherlands

Is McWorld in the Wings?

A t the end of the 1990s a lead article in *The Economist*[1] was dedicated to culture as an explanation for behavior. The author's conclusion, after reviewing a number of recent books on the influence of culture by authors such as Fukuyama (*Trust: The Social Virtues and the Creation of Prosperity*); Harrison (*Who Prospers? How Cultural Values Shape Economic and Political Success*); and Huntington (*The Clash of Civilizations and the Remaking of World Order*), was extremely cautious. His subtitle was, "Which civilization you belong to matters less than you might think."

In the marketing world one can see that authors, especially those from the United States, have a strong feeling that economic development, having access to the same information and being in contact via the Internet would lead to:

"Converging needs and tastes of consumers, which would in turn facilitate standardization of marketing and advertising. Economies of scale in production would lead to low price/high quality ratios, which consumers were supposed to prefer over the products/brands they were used to."[2]

Influential marketing gurus like Harvard professor Ted Levitt[3] were convinced that: "The world's needs and desires have irrevocably homogenized . . . Everywhere everything gets more and more like everything else as the world's preference structure is relentlessly homogenized . . . Ancient differences in national tastes or modes of doing business disappear."

The strange thing is that people like Levitt, as well as *The Economist* author, have strong opinions on the matter at hand, but are ignoring empirical evidence. The people being quoted in *The Economist* all have different basic premises (historical, philosophical and religious), which they link to views about the world. No wonder that *The Economist* author's conclusions are so inconclusive. It is, however, worth considering what he would have found had he included some empirical approaches.

Looking at the research findings of people like Professor Geert Hofstede[4] it is clear that it is possible to make verifiable statements on culture based upon comparative empirical research.

Following are a few observations around the question of whether values are converging as a result of globalization, or are more consistent then some people think.

1. Culture consists of different layers

Some of the layers are superficial and subject to change. Others are more fundamental and consistent over time.

Culture is like an onion. It has different layers.

On the most outer layer, the superficial layer of culture, symbolic behavior, one can see worldwide trends. Everywhere one can find brands like NIKE, Coca-Cola, Marlboro and McDonald's. Even in a tea-drinking nation like Japan one can find the American coffee chain Starbucks. This has led some to the observation that the world is Americanizing. This effect cannot be denied. But the Americanization of the world is at a superficial level of behavior. There is an all-too-human tendency to imitate success, and it is certainly true that the United States has been very successful the last fifteen years in terms of economic power. As a result people everywhere try to imitate this success on a symbolic level. But if one scratches at the surface other preferences are found.

Interestingly enough identification on this level is changing every 15 years or so. Around 1985 the United States was not the most notable economic power; Japan was. Around the world people were trying to imitate the Japanese. All organizations, including American, were trying to introduce quality circles to improve what they were doing. Around that time the CEO of Philips said in a worldwide address to his personnel: "We have to be more like the Japanese if we want to survive in the international competition."

If one goes back a little more in time, to the late 1950s, Germany had that position. Because of the "economic miracle" in Germany, everybody was trying to introduce the so-called DIN (German Industry Norm) in his or her own society.

The second layer, heroes and anti-heroes, is a little bit less superficial. This is a level where identification models are used to show how to be successful and how never to be.

In the advertising world the agencies learned it the hard way. Promoting products and services in, for instance, Germany, where people's interest is attracted by using expert information, should be done in a different way than in the U.K., where humor is the way to catch the viewer, or France, where style and elegance are the key focus points, or the Netherlands, where advertisements should stress the anti-heroes.

Regarding reward systems, in the United States it is very effective to reward individual performance with a portrait on the wall: being "employee of the month" makes you a hero. In a country like Denmark, being appointed "employee of the month" is the biggest punishment one can get. It makes this person the bait of biting sarcastic jokes from colleagues forever.

The third layer of culture, rituals, is even more consistent. An example of a ritual we all know is meetings. People all over the world have meetings. But what one expects a meeting to be is different from culture to culture. In some cultures a meeting is a place to discuss; in other cultures it is a platform for the boss to communicate decisions to the others. The effects can be very strange if people from different cultures have meetings together without being aware of these differences.

The deepest layer of culture is values. Professor Hofstede carried out fundamental research into the dominant values of countries and the way in which they influence behavior in organizations. Original data were based on an extensive IBM database for which 116,000 questionnaires were collected from 72 countries and in 20 languages between 1967 and 1973.

Analyzing his data, Hofstede found that five value clusters were the most fundamental in understanding the differences in answers to single questions. The results were validated against about 40 cross-cultural studies from a variety of disciplines. Hofstede gave scores for 56 countries on these 5 dimensions. Later research has extended this to 85 countries. The combined scores for each country explain variations in:

- Behavior of people and organizations.
- Differences between cultures.
- Five dimensions of national culture: power distance (PDI), individualism/collectivism (IDV), masculinity/femininity (MAS), uncertainty avoidance (UAI) and long-term pragmatism (LTP).

The five dimensions

Power distance is the extent to which less powerful members of a society accept that power is distributed unequally. In large power-distance cultures everybody has his/her rightful place in society, there is respect for old age, and status reflects power. In small power-distance cultures, people try to look younger, and powerful people try to look less powerful. It is my opinion that this dimension creates about 80 percent of the problems in international organizations that are trying to operate with multicultural teams.

People in countries like the United States, Canada, and the U.K. score low on the power-distance index and are more likely to accept ideas like empowerment, matrix management and flat organizations. Business schools around the world tend to base their teachings on low power-distance values. Yet, most countries in the world have a high power-distance index.

In individualistic cultures people look after themselves and their immediate families only; in collectivist cultures people belong to in-groups that look after them in exchange for loyalty. In individualist cultures, values are in the person. In collectivist cultures, identity is based on the social network to which one belongs. In individualist cultures there is more explicit, verbal communication; in collectivist cultures communication is more implicit.

In masculine cultures the dominant values are achievement and success. The dominant values in feminine cultures are caring for others and quality of life. In masculine cultures performance is important. Status is important to show success. Feminine cultures have a people orientation, small is beautiful, and status is not so important.

Uncertainty avoidance is the extent to which people feel threatened by uncertainty and ambiguity and try to avoid these situations. In cultures of strong uncertainty avoidance, there is a need for rules and formality to structure life. Competence is a strong value, resulting in a belief in experts, as opposed to weak uncertainty-avoidance cultures which believe in practitioners. In weak uncertainty-avoidance cultures, people tend to be more innovative and entrepreneurial.

The last element of culture is the long-term pragmatic index, which is the extent to which a society exhibits a pragmatic future-orientated perspective rather than a near term point of view. Low scoring countries are usually those under the influence of monotheistic religious systems, such as the Christian, Islamic or Jewish systems, and people in these countries believe there is an absolute truth. In high scoring countries, for example those practicing Buddhism, Shintoism, or Hinduism, people say truth depends on time and context.

The question is whether these values and the scores of countries are changing over time. It's good to look at the findings of other research replicating Hofstede's work:

A Danish scholar, M. Søndergaard[5], found 60 of these (sometimes small scale) replications. A meta analyses confirmed the five dimensions and the scores of countries.

A recent replication was carried out by including Hofstede's questions in the EMS, the European Media and Marketing Survey[2] of print media readership and TV audience levels within the upscale consumer group in Europe (E.U., Switzerland, and Norway), in 1996 and 1997. The country scores found in EMS were similar to those found 20 years earlier, and were particularly strong in explaining diversity in consumption and ownership of products as measured in EMS.

De Mooij in her analysis of the findings states: "Although there is evidence of convergence of economic systems, there is no evidence of convergence of peoples' value systems. On the contrary, there is evidence that with converging incomes, people's habits diverge. More discretionary income will give people more freedom to express themselves, and they will do that according to their own, specific values of national culture.

"National culture influences, for example, the volume of mineral water and soft drinks consumed, ownership of pets, of cars, the choice of car type, ownership of insurance, possession of private gardens, readership of newspapers and books, TV viewing, ownership of consumer electronics and computers, usage of the Internet, sales of video-cassettes, usage of cosmetics, toiletries, deodorants and hair care products, consumption of fresh fruit, ice cream and frozen food, usage of toothpaste and numerous other products and services, fast moving consumer goods and durables. These differences are stable or become stronger over time. Persistent cultural values are stable and with converging incomes they will become more manifest."

2. Culture is consistent but not static

The problem is that a great many people don't recognize these 'gross group' descriptions as having an influence and being consistent over time. On average people tend to feel: "I am very different from my parents and my grandparents are very different from my parents." The reason for this "true" observation is that usually the visible aspects of culture are compared. In so doing, it appears to be easy to establish that the clearly visible behavior of the present generation is different from the behavior of past generations.

Saying that culture is consistent does not imply that the behavior is consistent. Our parents and grandparents behaved differently because they lived in totally different conditions. Who had to deal with issues such as globalization, the European Union, Internet, mobile telephones 50 years ago?

The world is changing rapidly and we are being forced to adjust to these changes and to develop new behavior. But the development of this new behavior is constantly influenced by the set of collective preferences that we have designated as mind sets.

If people become aware of themselves in relation to their environment, they are able to make new choices. But when examining history, we find that the choices people make are by no means random. We recognize regularities, "scripts," which can be traced back to deeply rooted values that give direction to their actions.

Hofstede[4,5] defines culture as the collective, mental programming that distinguishes one group or category of people from another. This programming, or mind set, influences patterns of thinking, which are reflected in the meaning people give to the different aspects of their lives, and therefore help shape the institutions of a society.

This does not mean that everyone in a particular society is programmed in exactly the same way. There are considerable individual differences. But when fundamental values of various societies are compared, majority preferences are found to exist, which recur again and again as a result of the way children are brought up by their parents and the educational system. And when we examine how societies organize themselves, these majority preferences turn out to have a modifying influence at both micro and macro levels. They appear to have an influence on the ways in which good leadership is defined; on how the decision making process is structured, as well as on the way people monitor how policies are implemented. In short, everything that has to do with organizational behavior.

3. Culture is not the same as identity

Almost everybody feels emotional attachment to one group or another. Sometimes it's a nation or a region. Sometimes it's a football club. It's a known fact that a club like Manchester United has fan clubs all over the world, wearing the Manchester shirts and identifying with the team. Sometimes these feelings of identification are quite strong, leading to the infamous fights between supporters of the different clubs.

Don't confuse this with culture. In the words of Hofstede[6]: "Identities consist of people's answers to the question: where do I belong? They are based on mutual images and stereotypes and on emotions linked to the outer layers of the onion. Populations that fight each other on the basis of their different 'felt' identities may very well share the same values. Examples are the linguistic regions in Belgium, the religions in Northern Ireland, and tribal groups in Africa."

Sometimes people willingly try to create identities different from their environment in spite of sharing the same values, and this can be confusing. Two possible reasons:

The sour grapes
This label is related to the fox in Aesop's fable that tried to seize an attractive bunch of grapes, failed, and then announced that he had not really wanted them in the first place because they were sour. Like the fox, many of us decide that what we cannot have we didn't really want in the first place. This is what is happening with some minority groups in different countries. If people discover that they will never be able to compete with the majority culture because of lack of skills or opportunities, they sometimes create identity by claiming they are focusing on different (better) goals in first place.

The narcissism of the small difference
One way people define themselves is by comparing themselves with others in their environment. Sometimes people create difference where there is none to create their own self-definition. This can lead to the "narcissism of the small difference." This is a concept introduced by Freud. Especially people that are very much alike have a tendency to emphasize the small differences. Mostly it is a matter of style, musical preference, cooking and dressing. This is of course very superficial and can sometimes even lead to style surfing.

4. Grammar, style and dialect

A repetitive remark made by participants in my seminars is: I recognize what you are saying about my country. But, the people in the North of my country are different from the people in the South. The people in the South are different from the people in the East.

This is clearly evident for people born and raised in such a country. Belgians are convinced that people from West Flanders are different from the people in East Flanders. The Dutch are convinced that Rotterdammers are different from Amsterdammers. Americans are sure that Americans from the East coast are different from compatriots from the West coast.

A nice test is to ask the opinion of outsiders. Then the surprising reaction is mostly: well you are a local so you know best about these differences. But what I see is the same behavior all over the country.

How to explain this? Comparisons are always dangerous. But the best way is to compare the basic values of culture with the grammar of a language system.

Nobody will deny that the basic grammar systems of English, Chinese, Russian and Sanskrit are different. Still people sharing one basic grammar system can be different in style and dialect. Take the Scottish and the English. They share the same basic grammar system. Still the Scottish are so different in style and dialect that even the English have difficulty in understanding what they say. This is the way to understand most of the regional differences in culture. In almost all countries in the world people share a homogeneous (majority) culture. But styles and other elements of the superficial layers of the onion can be different.

5. Imagined and true realities: the problem of MBA programs

If one compares official organizational charts of organizations worldwide they look very much the same everywhere. The same is true about all other relevant issues for global business players: strategies; HRM systems, including reward techniques; management approaches like MBO; appraisal instruments like 360 degree feedback systems.

Seemingly the organizations are run in the same way. In MBA programs everywhere the same theories are taught and the general feeling is seemingly that organizational behavior is culture neutral.

An analysis of these theories finds that most of the handbooks of management, marketing and economy come from Anglo-Saxon countries: the United States, Canada, and the U.K. The students from MBA programs assume that what they are reading about is just the latest development, the latest description of best practices. After graduating they try then to implement these best practices in organizations of their own countries. If after a time they discover it's not successful they blame the failure on the people involved, accusing them of being resistant, backward, stubborn and ignorant. What they don't realize is that the promoted theories are not wrong, but have a value context that fits the motivations of the Anglo Saxon culture group, but not necessarily the motivations of people in their own country. This is not to be blamed on management gurus. Frequently I hear a guru say: you tell me that this is not possible in your country. Tell me please about the theories and research from your culture. Then most of the time there is silence. The non Anglo-Saxon cultures should do much more in making the realities in their own cultures more explicit. They should be more aware that there is a difference between the "imagined reality" (assuming for instance that what is true or valid in the United States is also true and valid everywhere) and the "true reality."

This difference between "I reality" and "T reality" explains for instance why Philips Netherlands decided recently to drop performance pay. This is something that could motivate employees in masculine cultures, but performance pay is not a motivator in feminine cultures like The Netherlands.

6. Culture, globalization and change

What are the conclusions one can draw from this analysis?

One important element is that in discussions about this subject it is necessary to define culture and to have common agreement about the layer of culture being discussed.

In most cases it's about the superficial layers. Most tourists, if they are interested in culture, will focus on the symbols, heroes and rituals—in short, the things one can see in museums, during folkloristic festivals, in theme parks—and will not really be confronted with the real values of the culture they are visiting.

Even stronger: it's mostly the locals who will be confronted with the different kinds of expectations and behavior. It is certainly a must for the tourist industry to realize this and to develop skills for their personnel to cope with this diversity. It's simply a matter of good business to be customer oriented.

Secondly: It's a revolutionary finding in marketing that after a certain level of income choices diverge again, based upon the five value dimensions.

Thirdly: Sustainable tourist development can only be achieved if the approach fits the local value structure. One element of this is good governance. This is not a culture free subject. The issues of good governance in Mexico are different from the issues in the United States or Switzerland.

The United Nations is aware of this. In a recent paper it concluded: "Although economic aspects of development are often taking front stage, such as attracting investment, building infrastructure, etc., not enough attention is given to the need to establish appropriate governance mechanisms and systems to deal with it. Effective and transparent political institutions; an efficient and accountable administration; and mechanisms to foster participation of citizens in the decision-making process are essential factors in ensuring that the potential benefits of development are maximized and its drawbacks minimized."

This is something that in the "I reality" everybody can agree to. The problem is however that in the "T reality," the issues of what is called good governance are different relative to the cultural background of the countries involved.

In masculine and individualistic countries like the United States with short term thinking and a clear hero culture, corporate CEOs have to show successes to the shareholders constantly; otherwise, the shareholders go away and invest somewhere else. The danger will always be that these heroes will be tempted to manipulate the figures.

In feminine, low power distance cultures such as in Scandinavia, the problem will be that the consensus mentality can lead to an avoidance of free competition and the tendency to make secret agreements between the different so called competitors.

In high power distance cultures like France and Italy, all countries in Asia and all countries in Latin America and Africa, the problem will be that the controlling institutes in the "I reality" are considered to be independent but in the "T reality" can be subordinate to the power structure.

In collectivist cultures, as in most African countries, the problem can be that the ruling "in groups" will help and involve the people of their own tribe, ethnic group, region or religious group, but will have a tendency to exclude the others.[7]

All this is leading to one conclusion: in the world of sustainable development there should be an awareness that naïve concepts about globalization can actually do harm instead of help.

Typology of national cultures

Starting from the four dimensions introduced by Hofstede, we can cluster countries into relatively homogeneous clusters. Based on the experience of ITIM from consulting with global companies on cross-cultural conflicts and management, we came to six different culture types. Each type has a different composition of value preferences, leading to different mental images of how organizations should be managed. These differences are manifest in micro organizations (including multinationals) as well as macro organizations (the way a country is looking at its economic/political approach.)

1. The Contest Model

A mental image that is applicable to all Anglo-Saxon countries. The cultural context of this mental image is: low power distance, lower uncertainty avoidance and a high individuality. The central assumption of this mental image is: if you give people and organizations the freedom to compete with each other, something good will always come out of it. The characteristic of this organizational outline is that hierarchy is not seen as an existential difference between people, but something that is agreed between people to facilitate the work in organizations; they should be clear who is delegating to whom and who is reporting to whom.

In principle, employers and subordinates negotiate objectives, targets and the work content. Targets are very important because people experience them as a challenge. No one should fiddle with targets once they have been formulated, as they function as the central element of performance monitoring. The assessment with respect to the targets formulated beforehand is the foundation for work motivation. People are rewarded against the fixed targets. The reward is given in the form of bonuses or career moves.

Solutions to problems are reached by communicating with each other. Open competition is central in this model. In order to motivate people, they must be able to compete with others, but also with themselves. Important concepts in this model are achievement orientation, target setting, winners and losers, making it, career, bonus systems as reward for competition, and special career paths for "high potentials."

The trap in a globalizing world is that there is a tendency to give these theories and concepts a universal value. The management theories that are taught at universities and business schools mainly stem from Anglo Saxon scholars. The explanation for this is a general human one. The inclination exists to imitate the conduct of economically successful people. This is true all over the world with respect to the American culture. All over the world people drink Coca-Cola. There is even a McDonald's on the Square of Heavenly Peace in Peking. They constitute, as it were, symbols of progress and success. American management ideas are blindly adopted by managers everywhere.

Some well-known consequences for organizations: introducing things like flexible reward systems, career-oriented management development systems, the introduction of management by objectives, and special training courses for "high potentials."

Consequently, people partly adjust to the new rituals. It is a common human tendency to act according to what is expected by your environment. However, this does not mean that this corresponds with people's own inner motivations.

2. The Network Model

This model is a combination of low power distance, high individualism and femininity. In actual practice of working for international companies like IBM, ABN-Amro, Heineken, Shell and Philips, I discovered that there is a big difference between the Anglo-Saxon view on leadership, motivation and negotiations on the one hand and the Scandinavian-Dutch way on the other. For instance, in the latter countries practically everyone agrees with the proposition that the biggest punishment one could be given at work would be to be rewarded in the American way: a portrait on the wall as employee of the month.

The Scandinavian countries and the Netherlands share something that is described in sayings like: just act normal, that's mad enough, and if your head sticks out above the ground level, it will be chopped off. It is not appreciated if you try to profile yourself as the "winner." People who try to do this give other people the feeling that something is quite wrong with them. This is known as the "Jante law" in Sweden, Denmark and Norway: don't think you are better than any other person in your environment. This is of course regarded as strange behavior in contest countries. Moreover, the entire theory development around organizations, management, motivation and leadership proceeds from the concepts described above in the cultural sense as feminine. These theories don't fit expected behavior in masculine countries.

Indeed a fundamental difference between the network model and the competition model is the feminine character of the cultures concerned. Competition, career and external material rewards are not central issues.

Other elements are important for work motivation in the network: having autonomy in your work field, the work content, quality of the relations network, cooperation, the work environment and the feeling of mutual independence and the harmonization of interests between heterogeneous groups. Decisions are normally made by involving all the relevant stakeholders and trying to develop consensus among them. The countless meetings that take place in organizations are the consequence of this.

The most important characteristic of these meetings is that the objective is to find "support," i.e., consensus between the main stakeholders on what should be done. A criterion for good policy is stakeholder satisfaction with respect to the manner in which their interests are covered by the decisions taken. That is why it is allowed to retract decisions that have already been reached. In principle, if a stakeholder after a meeting has second thoughts, it is not regarded as strange to allow him of her to return to the organization and say to a colleague: I've been giving it a lot of thought and have decided that it is not a good idea. Can't we do it in another way? In a country like the Netherlands, this means that decisions that have been taken tend to be open for further development the following day. This takes place on a macro-level in politics and in micro-organizations.

3. The Pyramid of People

The third image is that of organizations as pyramids of people. The main dimensions of culture are power distance, uncertainty avoidance and collectivism. In principle, this is the system in the majority of countries in the world. Some Asian countries, all Latin American countries, all Arab countries and Europe countries like Portugal, Greece, Poland and Russia have this in common. The decision-making process is top-down. Hierarchy is important and essentially acknowledged and accepted by everyone. There is a strong need for centralization by both governments and organizations.

A frequent reference point for legitimating actions is the "general interest," as formulated by the top people. There is a strong need to formalize communication between the various levels in the organization, and there is need to formalize the relationships between colleagues. In such countries, the way to evaluate policy is to inspect in a direct way whether the people lower in the hierarchy have implemented the decisions taken at a higher hierarchy level in an effective and efficient manner.

4. Solar System

This is the culture of countries like France, Belgium, the North of Italy and Spain.

The features are high power distance, high individualism and high uncertainty avoidance. The main difference of these cultures with the pyramid system is the tension between high acceptance of hierarchy and a high degree of individualism. This leads to a tendency never to contradict power holders in their presence, but to "draw your own plan," outside their reach. Because of the individualistic element, leadership not so much "father of the family," but being a highly visible intellectual technocrat. Delegation and control are the same as in the pyramid system.

5. The Organization as a Family

This is the dominant image in some countries in Asia, especially the Chinese-dominated cultures, and in some of the Caribbean countries. This image is formed by a combination of high power distance, collectivism and a low score for uncertainty avoidance.

Characteristics: there is a strong acceptance of hierarchy. In general, this is linked to old age or seniority. Old age is usually synonymous with wisdom. As in the pyramid model, there is a "moral" relation between employers and subordinates. In exchange for loyalty from employees, the employer will ensure their well being. This means that in a way he acts like a father of a family. His employees can always go to him if they have personal wishes or problems. In principle, they can do this in or outside office hours. This can be about anything from money problems to family problems. Any boss who backs out if this care is a bad boss.

In a deviation from the pyramid model, the communication between managers and their subordinates is not well-formalized. In principle, it is easy to get access to the boss if one has a good idea or a problem. This system is very flexible. The boss decides everything.

6. The Well-Oiled Machine

A fifth image fits countries like Germany, Austria, the German-speaking part of Switzerland and Hungary; it has a low score on power distance and a high score on uncertainty avoidance.

In principle, people in these countries feel autonomous and want to perform tasks independently. A condition is that all obscurities around expectations with respect to task completion and task description are reduced. Clarity in the structure, planning and explicit procedures form the core of the internal discussions about the organizations. Decentralization within clear, "unshakeable" agreements is the natural form of leadership and management.

Leadership is completely related to the "expert" profile of the people concerned. People get to top positions because of the "depth" of their subject knowledge. That's why academic titles are so important. The reference point for evaluation is: have all the parties involved observed the previously formalized planning?

References

1   *The Economist*, Feb. 8, 1997.

2   De Mooij, M., "The future is predictable for international marketers: converging incomes lead to diverging consumer behavior," *International Marketing Review*, Vol. 17 No. 2, 2000, pp. 103-113 (University Press)

3   Levitt, T. (1983). "The Globalization of Markets." *Harvard Business Review*, 61(3), 92-102

4   Hofstede, G. (1980a) *Culture's Consequences: International Differences in Work Related Values*, Sage Publications.

5   Søndergaard, M. (1994) "Hofstede's Consequences: A Study of Reviews, Citations and Replications. *Organization Studies*, 15, 447-456

6   Hofstede, G. (2001) *Culture's Consequences. Comparing Values, Behaviors, Institutions and Organizations Across Nations*, Sage Publications.

7   ITIM International made comparisons between six culture clusters. Good governance is one of the elements being compared. 8. Report of the International Colloquium on Regional Governance and Sustainable Development in Tourism-driven Economies. United Nations 2002.

Jim Clifton
CEO
Gallup Organization
Washington, D.C.

Polling the World

Question: *How can countries increase their gross national product (GNP)?*

Clifton: The creation of GNP is closely related to "brain gain"—those are inventors and entrepreneurs in a given city. So if all three of us start with an equal city, what we contend is whoever can attract and hold the most inventors and entrepreneurs will have GNP momentum in ten years. It is very important to attract "super mentors." It might be professors, CEOs, coaches or ministers, but they have a disproportionate number of stars that they somehow touch, light up. It is also important to attract rare individual achievers … musicians and artists. If you get one big famous conductor or even athlete, they can change the image or character of a city. Of course, what you want then is to hold the ones that you have and make sure you don't have brain drain. To keep this from happening, the local leadership must create conditions so that a positive tornado might occur in their town. I noticed in our global database whatever is going on in Moscow is not good, people hate their bosses there, and that is not good for the future of

Moscow. We've built what we call the "Gallup Path," which is a new Maslow's hierarchy of ten steps that create gross national product. Of course outsourcing is a huge driving force in all this. Let's say you run Omaha City, and you have a big shopping center to be built there. Now, let's say you got a new big set of movie theaters, big new ones, really nice. The only problem with that is you're just spinning around the same money, you'll draw in a little new, but what you really need is your new businesses to come in because that is new currency. So there really are two kinds of businesses: one is just spinning your own dollars faster, but the other is getting new business. We recommended to the state of Pueblo in Mexico that they create the best call center in Latin America so almost everybody can outsource all of that type of work and their state can become famous for that. That really works.

Question: *How can cities, regions and whole countries outperform?*

Clifton: The two things we have definitely found with a huge global sample size, and this was very surprising to me: perception of visual attractiveness and openness of the city, and diversity. We found the perception of diversity and openness, and I suppose that gets into the question of cause and effect in my business of survey research, but that is one of the predictors. If you have perception of openness and diversity, the third one we are still working on I call "the Nashville effect," but birds of the feather do some flocking together. So as an inventor, you need to go other places where you can have high collaboration to finish the invention.

Question: *Will established clusters of excellence lose out in a world where almost everything can be outsourced?*

Clifton: I think I disagree 100 percent with Thomas Friedman's thesis of a "flat world." I say that because he makes it sound like you can have world-class collaboration anywhere in the world. I just don't think so at all. I think nearness, proximity, propinquity, whatever the words would be, it looks to me like people are trying to get closer together—creativity is more likely to manifest itself when people are in relationship with each other. They don't have to be best friends, the whole deal about weak links, you learn more from weak links than from the strong links. That is why I think there will be clusters. And again I go back to my Nashville example, if you want to be in movies you need to go to Mumbai or Hollywood. Cities will have identities, and not unlike companies, that will be seen as products. Futurist used to say that now with laptops people can do their jobs from anywhere. I disagree. Technology has just insanely advanced mankind. But I think we will still get our best ideas in

relationships with other people. If Michael Dell took his business to San Antonio, Austin would be a different city. I've heard that with Nokia in Finland, the market cap of that company is half of the market cap of the whole stock market. If you think about migration, you want flow, but just a couple of stars can really change your city. I did a poll a few years ago and you know, CNN is not a big company, but Ted Turner became a real symbol of entrepreneurship for Atlanta. So my interviewer would say the name of the city and the interviewee would say what first came to his mind. So when you hear New York, they say Wall Street. But when you say Atlanta, they'd say Ted Turner. Ted did not put much money into Atlanta, but he really added a lot to the image of the city. I think that migration and outsourcing patterns are the biggest things leadership has to manage now.

Question: *What about the migration of corporate headquarters? Many companies might be enticed to move their headquarters or to merge with other companies. So, whole economies might lose their stars.*

Clifton: I was born and raised in Lincoln, Nebraska. We had two big banks downtown, so when people got out of college they went to work for those banks. One bank got bought by Wells Fargo and the other by Bank of America. The banks said, well, we are still here; we're just under new ownership. But they took out all the leadership jobs, because all the marketing, computers, information systems and advertising decisions are made out of San Francisco for Wells Fargo, which turns them all into franchises. The other thing is, they have very limited budgets for the community, but it is not just the money; they just don't have the engagement. It takes a piece of soul out of every city or country when headquarters move and it's not just money, it something very human that happens. Countries had better be giving all they've got to hold them.

Question: *What is your view of the emerging economies, especially China? Will China be the next superpower?*

Clifton: There is a big question I don't see people talking about and that is about profitability. Let's just look at China. China is going to have a GNP bigger than the United States in 2030 or 2050. But what is the quality of those earnings? Would you rather own Wal-Mart or would you rather own Toyota? Remember Wal-Mart is much bigger than Toyota. Of course Toyota's market cap is significantly higher. Maybe Brazil or China's GNPs can grow higher, but that is kind of like a company CEO saying, "Well I got my sales to grow but my profit keeps going down."

Question: *Who will be the next generation political leaders?*

Clifton: Qualities of the next generation of leadership will be extreme openness to all kinds of variations of talents. It looks to me like creativity will become the next highest demand talent, skill and product. You've got to have diversity and openness because you are going to have Jews and Muslims and blacks and whites and women and whatever else. But if you don't have that openness, you will have a group of people that you never can actually maximize for creativity and innovation.

PART 3

4.2

By **Dr. Michael Jackson**
Chairman
Shaping Tomorrow
Sussex, England

Managing the Outsourcing Future

The increasing impact of global competitive forces is causing companies to re-evaluate their customer propositions in search of higher value-add through innovation and business process redesign. As technological innovation causes barriers to entry to fall in most markets, the largest and even the smallest of companies are vulnerable to new and non-traditional competition. Traditional industries with relatively large back-office costs such as financial services, media and transportation are under threat. Their rivals are willing to outsource their operations and, increasingly, offshore their work through distant third parties. Even the mighty pharmaceutical companies, who are renowned for their tightly controlled production processes, are now looking for ways to extract even more cost efficiencies through outsourcing to contract manufacturers. Outsourcing has become an option not only for large corporations but an accepted resource for medium size companies. In turn, this has resulted in an increase in the number of outsourcing service providers in the market.

Outsourcing has been with us for decades. Its benefits are regularly cited as:

• Using third party knowledge and economies of scale to obtain greater cost savings.

• Streamlining outsourced systems.

• Innovating to achieve optimized value creation.

- Allowing executives to focus more on strategy and less on day-to-day operations.

Facilities management and bureau services were the first embryonic steps in what has become an outsourcing industry. Shared payroll services, printing and supplies, and vehicle management soon followed. Very few worried or were seriously affected. And, at the same time, Indian operations began offering overnight typing services to faraway businesses, thus creating the weak signal for future global offshoring services. Multinational corporations too have moved work around amongst their global outposts for many years, often centralizing in a low wage cost country. Very few noticed or were seriously affected. Only in the past five years has the wholesale outsourcing of call centers and other operations sparked interest as people complained to the media about poor service experiences and the fear of losing local jobs.

These negative incidents are more the fault of poor strategic thinking and analysis, vendor choice, contractual arrangements and execution on behalf of the buyer and supplier than an indictment of the whole outsourcing industry. The same issues are, of course, found in many companies that provide in-sourced services, and they too often command media attention. The issues will likely decline with better standards as will the resulting media reporting. Offshoring will therefore likely follow outsourcing in being a business as usual activity within a decade.

New horizons

The learning from early experiments developed and proved the outsourcing concept, and we have subsequently witnessed the high growth curve that usually follows a successful emerging trend. This previously unproven but lucrative market, estimated to be currently worth $300 billion[1], is now a key driver of improved stakeholder value. But will this now maturing industry slow down any time soon, will outsourcing prove illusory and the concept move into decline, or is the phenomenon here to stay?

For the answer we need to look deeper at the reasons why outsourcing and related offshoring is commanding such attention right now.

The landscape of competition is fast changing. The Internet is having profound worldwide effects through fast, accurate, low-cost delivery of products and services that were previously only delivered face to face, over the telephone or by snail mail.

Improving technological capabilities are making it possible for businesses to redesign their processes, take out waste end to end, and add functionality to improve customer service. The ubiquitous mobile phone is perhaps the best example of an innovative product that is now going way beyond its original function. Mobile phones already provide reliable text messaging, basic photography, audio and video recording, and access to the Internet and e-mail through just one, seemingly simple, device. New technologies mean that even the smallest companies can gain maximum leverage from global economies of scale, threatening more traditional industries. A case in point here is the media industry, in which blogs, wikis, RSS and podcasts threaten the traditional delivery of news media.

Complexity through increased regulation, broader services, and customer demands means organizations are stripping away their non-core competencies to focus on what they do well and where they can differentiate themselves. As a result the growth of both internal and local shared services is on the rise as businesses are becoming more knowledgeable and confident that other people and companies with lower unit costs can provide even better value for stakeholders. Concerns over information security and reputation are fast receding locally with the pioneers proving that these same issues can be addressed even in an offshored outsourcing arrangement.

The arrival of co-opetition means those embracing this philosophy of simultaneously collaborating and competing with rivals have the potential to offer broader, deeper and cheaper services against those who stand alone. A company can now simultaneously be a customer, competitor and supplier of another as the global supply chain becomes ever more integrated. Industry boundaries are blurring as holding companies move to own and maximize the synergy between businesses, none more so perhaps than empires recently created through the merger of communications, computing, leisure and entertainment industries.

Most of these underlying trends will surely run and run as more value innovation is sought throughout business worldwide. Outsourcing, it seems, will remain a key competitive weapon for many in the medium term. A decline in outsourcing business looks very unlikely for the foreseeable future; on the contrary the market is likely to continue to expand but with lower margins for the sellers in many service arenas.

Industry maturation

The end of the growth phase probably occurred around the turn of the century. Now new entrant organizations are forcing rates down. Market rates are also being pushed down by new providing countries entering the market. Brazil, China, Hungary, Russia, Ukraine and Vietnam are newly arriving outsourcing destinations. Use of online bidding auctions is also likely to reduce pricing.

That means the buyer is in the driving seat. Buyers can now insist on service excellence and value innovation from the outsourcers, thus raising standards and outcomes and further increasing the gap between self-delivered versus third party offerings. That is, unless similar efficiencies and innovations can be obtained by keeping the service in-house.

And outsourcing is not just a one-way street. Through analyzing their true core competencies, companies are recognizing that they too can offer outsourcing services where others lack the will or the means to deliver for themselves. While many claim huge cost savings from straight outsourcing deals, others are able to point to the protection of jobs and increased revenues by also joining the market as providers. The growth of outsourcing management associations offering conferences and forum exchanges, dedicated consultancies and new trade publications all indicate the potential mega-opportunities in this industry.

A changing scene

Maturation has brought all the classic signs of industry players making moves to own slices of the market.

Long-standing players are now looking to segment their market in favor of the existing high earning, high-end processes. But surely, these too will be a target for those successful in building larger businesses at the low end. This market perhaps has few hiding places in the long run.

At the same time outsourcers are buying niche players to gain entry into new vertical markets. They both gain expertise and a customer base that gives them credibility with new clients. Customer references are seen as key for an outsourcer to gain a toehold in a new vertical. This could signal the end of the long-tail niche market as the larger players strengthen their hand by offering wider and deeper services. Shared service centers now exist across all business functions from sales to operations and from full HR outsourcing to IT. It now seems that outsourcing has the potential to serve every market, every industry and every business worldwide.

The buyers, too, are learning how to multi-vendor outsource in this segmented world and, through earlier experiences, are now able to choose the right vendor for each of their needs.

Buyers will recognize both the opportunity loss and the threat of doing nothing, but a number of existing barriers may lower the supply of services and their appetite. The prime reason is suitability of the candidate providers, which includes their ability to offer the right language capabilities, communication and practical skills, education levels and above all trust in their ethics. Competition for skills within the country where tax benefits for local companies drain off the best talent and produce a lack of middle managers may well reduce growth in offshore services. And finding the right skill base may not be restricted to the big outsourcing countries since smaller ones may well have better competencies in niche areas. While India and China currently dominate the outsourcing markets, we are likely to see the multi-national corporations carve out large chunks of this business. Their existing broad representation in and knowledge of suitable outsourcing countries and industries, their ability to spread risk (particularly catastrophic risk) and pare unit costs will give them significant competitive advantage. Since America has the largest agglomeration of multinational corporations in the world, expect the United States to challenge the leading players in the decades ahead[2].

This suggests that far from seeing an enormous job drain to lower cost countries any time soon, we will witness a general reordering of who does what, with old roles being transferred and new and more roles being created both locally and abroad. Hiring trends are certainly on the way up in shared service companies and Asian offshorers, but there is little concrete evidence that thus far local markets are witnessing one-way seismic job losses.

Managing change

Service and information jobs are certainly being lost, causing fear among staff. However, responsible and imaginative employers will act early to up-skill, multi-skill and re-skill their people to create more knowledge workers for increased innovative and productive contributions. They will also work to help displaced people into new external roles and place as many as possible with the shared service provider, often on the same benefit package. Professional businesses know that communicating constantly, fully and widely to their remaining people will minimize the corrosive impact of the rumor mill on productivity levels and service. Town meetings, truthful progress updates, executive clinics, regular staff surveys with feedback and action all help to ensure the business minimizes brand damage and maximizes its image as a caring employer. The alternative is eventual gut-wrenching change, large redundancy costs, the best people leaving and financially damaging reputation issues or, worse, oblivion for the laggards.

While some processes are more easily redesigned, all will likely fall under the spotlight. Therefore, it makes sense for companies to take a strategic look at their entire business before embarking on a piecemeal approach. The CEO's and his board's involvement in setting and monitoring outsourcing's strategic fit in the business mix is therefore key. Allowing a few well-intentioned middle managers to make isolated decisions without the context of an overall policy framework may well damage rather than enhance a company's performance.

Getting the right people

The CEO will need to rely on his CIO to lead technology outsourcing efforts; this is a skill that the latter may well not have obtained. Yet the new CIO will have to display far greater business rather than technical expertise to deliver. In the past he was responsible for running systems and developing software, but now the CIO must understand the business, its vision, strategies, goals and its value propositions far more. He must be a strategist and change master, helping to define the business' value proposition, determining the best way to organize technology both internally and externally and managing all the components in an optimum manner.

He must therefore have the acumen and knowledge to find and work with an entirely different set of partners, often with entirely different mind-sets and cultures and in a world of managing service level agreements. The problem of refocusing the CIO is compounded by the fact that a traditional IT function is one of the obvious candidates for outsourcing. But, since businesses and people use the number of people managed as a simple benchmark to describe a role's power, influence and most times reward, getting a CIO to relinquish the old and embrace the new may prove problematical. The likelihood is that many current CIOs will find themselves side-lined or red-lined in favor of more business oriented and lesser technical people if they fail to see and adopt the new realities.

We can use the past to do better in the future by studying the experiences of both those who succeeded and failed.

Whether the CIO is the program leader or not, the CEO, as champion, will be well advised to ensure that a dedicated relationship manager is named for both his own organization and that of the shared servicer. Without regular communication and understanding between the change teams, progress updates, decisions on next steps and using learning to date, the program will be doomed to failure.

Doing up-front homework

While an outsourcing program is both complex to manage and tricky to get right, the successful companies always seem to have done much homework up-front before deciding to take the plunge or step back from the brink. Analyzing existing processes and taking out costs pre-contract not only yields solid analysis on determining likely future cost, people and management issues, but also puts the buyer in a stronger negotiating position with the vendor.

And the successful companies generally use proven and detailed tendering processes to extract maximum understanding of the opportunities and risks associated with a decision before proceeding to contract.

Most companies appear to initiate their forays into outsourcing by choosing low risk, high cost saving, non-core competency work. After having gained sufficient knowledge they move on to tackle more lucrative, riskier projects that combine elements of greater innovation particularly in improved customer service. They learn from their early experiences just how much cost saving, speed to market improvement and quality of service they can expect from future forays. Many also adopt a more strategic approach to working out their core competencies before giving away their crown jewels inadvertently.

Truly discovering an organization's core competencies and discarding often long delivered products, channels, functions, resources and even customers is simultaneously exciting, frightening and challenging. Fundamental beliefs, biases and previously protected assumptions are put under the spotlight to discover the true essence of the organization's past, present and future, leading to the creation and agreement of a new recipe for success. In the author's experience, just involving the top team in this exercise is fraught with difficulty. As with refocusing the CIO, most of the other executive members will display fear, uncertainty and doubt as their organizations come under the spotlight and a potential knife. It is far better to involve teams of open-minded and intelligent people from across the business to create the redesign using the executive team as coaches, reviewers, and approvers of the recommendations.

Generally, a well defined set of high level design principles is used to gauge which parts of the organizations should remain, be downsized or externalized. The following is a simple but powerful example:

We outsource:
- when others can do it better
- when we need specialist services never provided by ourselves
- when we can gain competitive advantage
- when activities become too complex too manage

- to focus on our core competencies and business
- to reduce our cost base
- to improve productivity and responsiveness

So that:
- we increase stakeholder value.

Using similar design principles, businesses then determine to retain their core competencies in-house while deciding the fate of the remainder. Usually the fate comes down to exiting entirely, redesigning the non-core competence to minimize resource use while delivering an acceptable level of service, or buying a shared service. The results, if done well, lead to reduced complexity, better customer service and lower costs and risks simultaneously.

And in many cases, these companies used outsourcing to clear processing headaches such as backlogs or conduct across the board account reviews of their entire customer base where they were light on human resources. Whichever way their businesses entered and for whatever reason, a larger and larger cadre of experienced set-up managers is being created that will help sustain and grow the international market.

Pitfalls and handholds

But for the many successes there have also been many burned fingers. In the latter cases most can be put down to a combination of the following factors:

- The executive team/board did not champion the process or monitor progress.
- The vendor was never treated as a partner or was distrusted.
- Contract negotiations were weak from the outset and service level agreements under-defined.
- Performance standards and internal controls were weak and not set against a background of key strategic metrics agreed by both executive teams.
- Key processes were badly managed.
- IPR and confidential information protection was poorly handled.

- The existing business suffered disruption during the setup process.
- Pricing competitiveness declined over time and hidden costs appeared.
- Innovation declined or ceased after the initial setup.
- Local regulations were not adequately considered in the design phase.
- Politics got in the way, and dialogue was poor between all the interested parties including management and its staff.

Almost all organizations have outsourcing arrangements and shared services on the periphery of their businesses. The insourcers may well have powerful reasons to restrict shared services to the periphery (especially those in personal services), but it is surely good practice to explore the possibilities of outsourcing rather than out-right rejecting the concept. Exploration pre-contract and through a robust tender process almost always generates ideas for improvement and highlights weaknesses against best practice that more than pay the costs of the exercise. The saying "keep your friends close and your enemies even closer" is particularly relevant since outsourcers are the new competition. The key questions for all to ask is, "Can we deliver better value innovation at equivalent or better risk levels than outsourcers can achieve, in the long-term, in all parts of our business?" And, "Can we manage and respond nimbly to future business and customer intelligence better than the outsourcers?" If the answers are no, then organizations face real competitive disadvantage that must be made up elsewhere. In this case their shareholders would surely be unhappy to learn about the capital waste.

Perhaps the wildcards for outsourcing are the effects that artificial intelligence and increases in computing power and bandwidth, at near zero cost, will have on the industry. In the not too distant future we will see more and more avatars, interactive voice response, expert and predictive systems and robots, full electronic language translation, new automated production methods, more sophisticated supply chain management, new virtual business models, intuitive self managing networks and improved Internet services. These technologies may potentially deliver the same zero cost benefit to the customer as Skype, and soon Google, do in the telecommunications markets thoroughly disrupting the traditional incumbents' pricing models. While both insourcers and out-sourcers will have access to these technologies, we may well see a day soon when resource use is so minimized or virtually networked in many processes, call centers being a prime example, that the shared service operators profit turn and overhead comes under scrutiny as an unnecessary expense. If that happened then a truly declining shared service market would have arrived with wafer thin margins, multiple and mega-mergers of the suppliers and per-haps buy-back of these organizations from those who funded them in the first place.

Taking the plunge

The future of outsourcing has yet to be fully played out. Its rapid growth and increasing maturity is set to radically alter where work is done, how and by whom.

Its impact will cause us all to work smarter and harder to meet, and exceed, the standards set in other parts of the world. Its effects will be to allow almost every global citizen to source any product from anywhere at similar prices and for wage costs to become comparable around much of globe in the long run. This must be a benefit to everyone.

Industry captains accept the phenomenon or rail against it. But, in the latter case they will surely not be immune to the eco-nomic advantage of those who embrace the concept and learn to use it well. Even those who work hard at reducing costs through automation, innovation and improved working practices will still have a cost disadvantage to those whose residual costs are lower. Companies with the will to rethink their entire process architec-ture will likely flourish.

For the professional, strategically managed company with great execution skills and a need to drive up innovation and service while reducing complexity and cost, the water's warm! Why not get your feet wet, do a few lengths and then decide if a long-dis-tance swim makes good business sense? You have nothing to lose by testing the temperature, but nothing will be gained by standing poolside watching your competitors make informed decisions on outsourcing.

References

1 "It's a Buyer's Market," Vales Consulting Group, March 8, 2005.

2 Minevich, M. and Richter, F., "The CIO Insight Whiteboard: Opportunities, Costs and Risks," CIO Insight, March 2005.

Dr. Soumitra Dutta
Dean of Executive Education
INSEAD
Paris, France

The Global Mindset

Question: *How do you think outsourcing today is affecting economic dynamics worldwide?*

Dutta: Technology has essentially destroyed national boundaries and made it possible to delocalize business processes. The delocalization of business processes, across time and geography, has had tremendous implications in terms of opportunities for doing things differently. Western corporations are forced to question their core strategies. At the same time, looking at corporations from emerging economies, outsourcing has provided a wealth of opportunities for new business creation. Some of this new business creation is happening because of offshore centers being set up by Western corporations. But along with that, there is a whole native set of entrepreneurs who are starting up their own businesses. Of course, this process is more advanced in some economies, like India and China, but it is happening across the board—even in places like Egypt and Morocco.

Question: *What is your view on the Indian IT outsourcing industry?*

Dutta: I am very optimistic about the Indian IT sector. India built up its outsourcing job sector through fairly low-level software programming work, but it is increasingly attracting far more sophisticated work. Indian IT companies are just doing the right thing as they invest in talent management and training. Indian companies mostly consider employees to be critical because most innovation comes from employees. And they have built quite close contacts with leading Western corporations.

Question: *What role does IT outsourcing play in innovation?*

Dutta: Technology, in general, is an enabler for the whole explosion in offshoring and outsourcing. Without technology, one would not have telecom bandwidth. The IT outsourcing sector has, to some degree, shown the way for the BPO sector to develop itself. It has shown that it is possible to do complex knowledge-intensive tasks in a remote, delocalized fashion. One can identify three kinds of BPOs. One is the BPO associated with simple call centers. The second is transaction processing, where providers are executing calls and some remote business processing. The third is R&D in remote locations. There will be an enormous wave of innovation linked to this third type happening in the next five to ten years. And we will experience the global integration across various BPO locations—the emergence of globally integrated BPO capabilities.

Question: *How will outsourcing affect the developed economies of North America and Western Europe?*

Dutta: American and European corporations will not suffer, simply because there is so much potential to innovate. The potential to innovate is almost limitless. Today most companies are severely resource constrained in innovation and R&D. This allows companies to invest more resources in the emerging economies and to become more effective in innovation as they leverage cheaper resources in countries like India and China.

Question: *Will corporations finally "outsource themselves" as they can move almost everything to service providers in India or China?*

Dutta: Multinational corporations are looking at developing global capabilities as they diversify across multiple locations. However, I do not predict the wholly virtual corporation, as firms still have to execute the core business processes themselves. There are very few industries that can operate virtually on a permanent basis. In most industries there is a value in domain knowledge. Domain knowledge is knowledge about the product, knowledge about the customer, knowledge about branding. It is not that easy to replicate domain knowledge.

Question: *Outsourcing is often described as a make or break decision. How should companies handle the risks associated with outsourcing?*

Dutta: Corporations have to assess the perceived risk. A lot of Western corporations still perceive a fairly high level of risk with outsourcing to these emerging economies. I believe that risks associated with outsourcing—corruption in the host country, geographical distance, cultural differences, etc.—will be manageable as business processes become more mature. And as more role models of other companies who do it emerge, corporations will have no choice but to follow. Similar to what is currently happening with Wal-Mart. Wal-Mart is sourcing in China so extensively that competitors have no other choice but to follow and do what Wal-Mart is doing if they want to remain competitive.

Question: *How will the corporation of the future be different from today's mainstream corporation?*

Dutta: Management will need to have a much more global mindset, because even today managers still have a very high perception of risk associated with emerging economies. And for good reason. Troubles in emerging economies have left people feeling burned. So the perception of risk and the mindset will change, and that will lead to a change in terms of how companies are structured; it will lead to a way in which the product and information flows are configured.

Question: *What will companies look like in 2050?*

Dutta: We will see increased personalization of everything. Because the customers will take more control of the buying process, they will make big demands—not just for your computer, but also for medication, for treatment, for service. So companies will have to offer much greater variety and diversity in terms of product and service levels they give to the marketplace. It won't be possible to just offer mass commoditized products and processes any longer.

Question: *What role does geography play?*

Dutta: Most major corporations will have massive operations in China and India. Because the world will be much more global, management teams will be much more global. Because of demographics and human competitiveness, there will be more employees from Asia, more employees in Asia, and more work being driven from Asia. This Asia angle will change the way companies are structured in 2050.

Question: *What do university students need to be taught early on in terms of global outsourcing?*

Dutta: Students studying to be corporate executives will have learned how to make the right outsourcing decisions. Other students might be interested in becoming entrepreneurs and outsourcing represents a tremendous growth opportunity for them. Besides the usual challenges associated with the creation of a business, they need to learn how offshore operations create value for corporations. Outsourcing will be at the core of entrepreneurship.

4.3

Agenda for the Future

Throughout this book we have shown that globalization is the single biggest challenge facing corporations, whether they are American, European or Asian. The businessmen and women who contributed to this book all agree that globalization is here to stay, and that simple measures are not sufficient to succeed in the global economy. So how do we all prepare for the coming changes? New rules are needed to reign in the unrestrained use of economic forces. These rules must be written by the civil society at large—not solely by the traditional world powers.

In the United States, the educational system must be improved so that it can graduate students who are prepared to deal in a global world. In Europe, more fundamental structural change is necessary. At the Lisbon Agenda for structural reform, held in 2000, E.U. leaders essentially agreed to liberalize their labor markets. Five years later, that has not yet happened, mostly due to opposition from trade unions and others who cling to the notion of job security rather than employment security—which means the ability to find a new job. Europe's seemingly endless struggle to define its priorities only heightens the stakes—and the risk. Globalization is real, and the competition is here.

And yet, there is no deep understanding of what globalization and global outsourcing mean for our businesses and economies. The United States and Europe must act now, or face a diminished global leadership, and the talent pool required to support our high-tech economy will evaporate. This is not just a question of economic progress. Not only do our economies and qualities of life depend critically on a vibrant R&D enterprise, but so too does our national and homeland security, as pointed out by the Rudman Commission on National Security in 2001.

We call on politicians, economists and entrepreneurs to conceptualize the future world economic paradigm—of a world filled with knowledge clusters, innovation and global outsourcing! American national leadership must understand these deficiencies as threats to its national security. If we do not invest heavily, wisely rebuild our core strengths and invest in homeshoring, America will be incapable of maintaining its global position well into the 21st Century.

U.S. policy makers will have to determine whether structural changes are needed to allow American businesses to better compete against foreign manufacturers and services providers that don't have to shoulder extensive employee benefits, such as health care or pensions, on their own. The government of Japan handles most health costs, while developing nations do not offer any equivalent Western type benefits. America's safety net, which for the past half-century has effectively been shared by employers and government, needs to be addressed. Investors should press companies to use global outsourcing not just as a cost-cutting tool but also as a way to transform their businesses so as to maintain more stable long term employment levels back home.

Americans "write the script" of their lives and can easily "pave their own paths" and "be whatever they want to be." Americans have control over their destiny. Immigrants from India, China and Russia move to the United States for two reasons: greater opportunity for education and vastly greater pay.

The United States has always been the leader of globalization. Ever since the U.S. rise to global eminence in the 19th Century, the country has influenced trade, economic growth, and life-styles in a major way. People in other countries want to move towards an American way of life or they want to preserve their way of life against it. The United States is rich in technologies, economic might and innovative ideas that developed into major change agents in a new economy driven by globalization. Since the inventions of the radio, light bulbs and Franklin stove, Americans have identified themselves as the fountainhead of innovation and invention around the world. America's people have been very flexible and creative. America is the country in this world that people don't want to leave. We have a head start in outsourcing and innovation. Change has always happened in the world, and often it happened in America first.

America might be over for those who don't see the future, but for many Americans—next generation idealists, entrepreneurs, innovators, to name a few—and for those immigrants and their children arriving at the airports, it is still the land of opportunity. The world still travels here to create its ultimate dreams. It's the mysterious culture of America that pulls one along and which ultimately creates dreams and aspirations.

We must develop better strategies to compensate the Western workers who lose in the global trade game—and crucially, boost education and training efforts so they acquire the "skill premium" they'll need to get or stay ahead. Given the speed with which globalization is unfolding, there's little time to lose. "The premium on having an effective policy response is greater than it's ever been before, and nobody seems to be paying attention to it," according to Catherine Mann, an economist with the International Institute of Economics in Washington.

Research, education, the technical workforce, scientific discovery, innovation, and economic growth are intertwined. To remain competitive on the global stage, we must ensure that each remains vigorous and healthy. That requires sustained investments and informed policies.

Early adopters, whether outsourcing IT or the miniskirt, get significant benefits either in profits or popularity. As others follow suit, the competitive advantage erodes and people who frankly shouldn't have been seen dead in that style start appearing on the street. And then the world moves on.

As outsourcing becomes more widespread and matures, and as the competitive landscape changes, some bad or disappointing experiences will happen, and some services will come back in-house. The best outsourcing contracts now explicitly recognize this fact. We should expect more sophisticated models—shared services, for example, is making a major comeback—as companies try to get the best of both worlds.

Many companies are still multinationals—traditional companies with distinct operations in different countries, rather than a single company operating globally as a seamless entity—which is the preferred business model of the future. We recommend they take the necessary move to become global companies. We must transform global industries by reshaping our management for the next generation and aligning business and technology to produce innovation.

We will see homeshoring take off during the next few years. Easier access to broadband, online collaboration tools, VoIP, etc., will help create virtual IT teams regardless of location. And the current global economic and political order indicates that rural U.S. workers may complement the offshore workers in the knowledge-based service economy in the coming years.

For long-term sustainable advantages involving regions and people—not just bottom lines—companies might complement in-shore, home-based urban or rural workers with their offshore counterparts to provide the needed software and information technology services.

A robust educational system to support and train the best U.S. scientists and engineers and to attract outstanding students from other nations is essential for producing a world-class workforce and enabling the R&D enterprise it underpins.

The United States still leads the world in research and discovery, yet its advantage is eroding rapidly as other countries commit significant resources to enhance their own innovative capabilities. America needs more sweat equity, more time back at the drawing board, more quality-driven testing, and core research. It needs more attention to its real future—its children and their education. We know there will be a future. We know that global outsourcing is here to stay. But we don't know what it looks like. What we do know is that it will happen in the United States. The challenge now is how best to manage it.

There are six billion minds on this planet, all with their own beliefs about how to make the world work, and most of their beliefs are different, so there is bound to be conflict. In fact, conflict is inevitable. Yet, the greatest resource of all is people, and that's why a population increase is to be celebrated, not lamented. Six billion people on the face of the earth? They are also six billion minds capable of discovering the new knowledge economy with billions of resources and twelve billion hands to extract and refine them. The vast majority of people contribute far more to the world than they ever take away—and that's just in material terms. In a world with over six billion minds (and climbing), sustainable globalization is a miracle.

Mark Minevich
Frank-Jürgen Richter
and
Ratings Contributors

2006 Global Outsourcing Report

ndia is the most competitive and popular IT-outsourcing destination in the world and tops the ranking of The 2006 Global Outsourcing Report. China is in second position, followed by Costa Rica and the Czech Republic. The report examines the risk and costs profile of the world's leading outsourcing destinations by proposing two different metrics—the Global Outsourcing Index (GOI), which describes the current competitiveness of doing outsourcing work in the top 20 countries, and the Future Outsourcing Rank, which assesses the long-term (10 year) competitiveness of the top 30 future outsourcing destinations. China takes the lead in the Future Outsourcing Rank, followed by India, the United States, Brazil and Russia. In the future, the authors believe that China will most likely become the largest and most competitive outsourcing destination, assuming China makes significant progress in geopolitical and legal arenas and demonstrates reasonable results in all categories outlined in this report. Outsourcing of manufacturing to China has become a standard practice and caused a $200 billion trade deficit with the United States in 2005.

The Global Outsourcing Index offers the business community a baseline. It is the first milestone in a process that should give the corporations a road map to the right outsourcing decisions. The report offers all relevant information about specific countries, their relative advantages, and their specific resource capabilities.

The Future Outsourcing Rank forecasts the competitiveness of outsourcing destinations for 2015. The index is determined by GDP growth, population growth, labor pool and extrapolated analysis from the results of an executive opinion survey of 50 leading entrepreneurs, economists, and other thought leaders. Future assessments include the interpretations, predictions and expert review of language risk, internal political risks, global image risk, changes in global competitiveness, and change in origin of the work or service to be outsourced or offshored. Furthermore, the global strategic enterprise demography is likely to change dramatically by 2020. This report offers standardization in reducing outsourcing risk analytically and holistically.

Competitiveness has been measured along seven dimensions of risk: geopolitical, legal, cultural, economic, IT infrastructure, human capital, and IT competency. An added dimension is the cost of outsourcing in the respective countries. Finally, this report measures the market opportunity according to market, expert opinion, global competitiveness, and third-party sources. The report contains a country profile for most of the 20 economies featured in the study, providing a comprehensive summary of the overall opportunities, costs and risks, as well as a guide to what are considered to be the most prominent competitive advantages and competitive disadvantages of each.

Table 1 Detailed View of Country Risk and Overall Global Outsourcing Rank

Rank	Country	Geo-Political Risk	Human Capital Risk	IT Competency Risk	Economic Risk	Legal Risk	Cultural Risk	IT Infrastructure Risk	Overall Risk Rating	IT Outsourcing Market	Global Competitiveness Index	Business External Index	Expert Opinion Index	Market Opportunity Index	Cost	Global Outsourcing Index
1	India	3	1	2	1	3	1	4	2.1	1	3	1	1	1.8	2	2.02
2	China	3	1	4	1	5	4	3	2.9	1	3	1	1	1.8	1	2.16
3	Costa Rica	2	2	3	2	3	2	2	2.3	2	3	3	2	2.5	2	2.24
4	Czech Republic	1	2	2	3	2	2	2	1.9	3	2	1	2	2.0	3	2.26
5	Hungary	1	2	2	3	2	2	2	1.9	3	2	2	2	2.1	3	2.28
6	Canada	1	1	1	2	1	1	1	1.1	4	1	2	2	1.9	5	2.40
7	Latvia	2	2	2	3	2	2	2	2.1	3	2	3	2	2.3	3	2.40
8	Russia	3	1	2	2	5	3	2	2.4	3	4	3	2	3.0	2	2.40
9	Chile	2	3	3	2	2	2	2	2.4	1	1	2	2	1.5	3	2.42
10	Romania	2	2	2	3	5	2	3	2.6	2	4	4	2	3.0	2	2.46
11	Ireland	1	2	1	2	1	1	1	1.3	2	1	4	2	1.9	5	2.50
12	Singapore	1	2	1	3	1	1	1	1.4	2	1	1	2	1.5	5	2.50
13	The Philippines	3	1	4	3	4	1	3	2.7	2	4	2	3	3.1	2	2.56
14	Poland	2	2	2	3	3	2	2	2.2	3	4	2	2	2.9	3	2.56
15	Armenia	3	3	3	2	4	2	4	3.0	4	5	5	3	4.1	1	2.58
16	Brazil	2	2	2	2	4	3	3	2.4	1	3	2	2	2.3	3	2.58
17	Ukraine	3	2	3	2	5	3	2	2.8	3	5	4	3	3.9	2	2.74
18	Israel	3	2	1	3	1	1	1	1.8	2	1	4	2	1.9	5	2.76
19	Mexico	2	3	5	3	3	2	3	3.1	2	3	3	4	3.3	2	2.78
20	South Africa	3	3	2	2	2	1	3	2.4	1	2	3	3	2.4	4	2.86

Table 2   Macro View of Global Outsourcing Index and Future Rank

Rank	Country	Global Outsourcing Index	Future Outsourcing Rank 2015	
			Rank	Country
1	India	2.02	1	China
2	China	2.16	2	India
3	Costa Rica	2.24	3	USA
4	Czech Republic	2.26	4	Brazil
5	Hungary	2.28	5	Russia
6	Canada	2.40	6	Ukraine
7	Latvia	2.40	7	Romania
8	Russia	2.40	8	Belarus
9	Chile	2.42	9	Philippines
10	Romania	2.46	10	Canada
11	Ireland	2.50	11	Ireland
12	Singapore	2.50	12	Malaysia
13	The Philippines	2.56	13	Armenia
14	Poland	2.56	14	Chile
15	Armenia	2.58	15	South Africa
16	Brazil	2.58	16	Thailand
17	Ukraine	2.74	17	Vietnam
18	Israel	2.76	18	Moldova
19	Mexico	2.78	19	Mexico
20	South Africa	2.86	20	Poland
			21	Bulgaria
			22	Israel
			23	Pakistan
			24	Kazakhstan
			25	Albania
			26	Hungary
			27	Czech Republic
			28	Latvia
			29	Singapore
			30	Costa Rica

Methodology:
Global Outsourcing Index

Twenty countries are featured in the Global Outsourcing Index, while thirty countries are featured in the Future Outsourcing Rank.

The twenty countries in the Global Outsourcing Index (GOI) are ranked according to their competitiveness as outsourcing destinations. The index comprises three main factors:

Cost: Few companies would outsource at all if doing so didn't save them money. The cost factor, which includes compensation and wages, infrastructure cost, and tax and regulatory costs, makes up 30 percent of the GOI.

Risk: Every country possesses its own strengths and weaknesses, risks and rewards. The Overall Risk Rating, which makes up 54 percent of the GOI, aggregates a variety of risks every potential outsourcer must take into account:

- Geopolitical risk (10 percent of GOI) includes stability of government, corruption, geopolitics, security.

- Human capital risk (10 percent) includes quality of educational system, labor pool, number of new IT graduates.

- IT competency risk (10 percent) includes project management skills, high-end skills and competence (custom code writing, system writing, R&D, business process experience).

- Economic risk (6 percent) includes currency volatility, GDP growth.

- Legal risk (6 percent) includes overall legislation, tax, intellectual property.

- Cultural risk (6 percent) includes language compatibility, cultural affinities, innovation, adaptability.

- IT infrastructure risk (6 percent) includes IT expenditure, quality of key access infrastructure.

Market Opportunity Rating: This number, which makes up 16 percent of the GOI, includes expert third-party analysis of each country, its global competitiveness, and its IT market share. The rating serves as a check on any imbalances elsewhere in the report. Cost, risk and market opportunity are rated on a scale of 1 to 5, where 1 is the least risk and 5 is the greatest.

Future Outsourcing Rank

The Future Outsourcing Rank compares each country by its competitive position in the overall outsourcing market as it will look in ten years, based on such factors as population growth, GDP growth, labor supply, and IT expertise. In the Future Rank, China will rise to No. 1, while India will drop to No. 2. The United States will enter the list at No. 3, thanks to competitively priced high-value offerings. Countries such as Israel and Singapore will become much less competitive because they won't be able to slow rising costs, while others, such as Costa Rica, will struggle to remain competitive because they'll be unable to maintain the population growth and skilled workforces necessary to remain attractive. India's 60% share of outsourcing business will likely decline due to a growing wages threat. China leads the pack in the future due to its large human resources and success in attracting manufacturing work. Countries like Russia, Israel and South Africa are ready to step in and could account for $30 billion in outsourced services in two years.

The Global Outsourcing Report only ranks countries active in outsourcing now and likely to be in the future. Among the major trends over the next ten years, however, is the growth of multinational outsourcers—large corporations with the capacity to go anywhere in the world for the skills their clients need. In ten years, they will actually become the second most attractive outsourcing option, after China, not just because of their wide-ranging outsourcing options, but because they will be better able to spread the costs and risks of outsourcing, relieving many corporations of the need to make country-by-country decisions.

United States of America

The United States remains the world's most powerful nation. The economy is marked by steady growth, low unemployment and inflation, and rapid advances in technology. The United States is a dominant global influence in economic, political, military, scientific, technological and cultural affairs. Because of its influence, the United States is considered a superpower.

The United States has the largest single-country economy in the world, with an annual gross domestic product of $41,747 trillion. In this market-oriented economy, private individuals and business firms make most of the decisions, and the federal and state governments buy needed goods and services predominantly in the private marketplace. This is financed through taxes and borrowings in the money market. Federal borrowings are subject to borrowing caps to theoretically prevent fiscal irresponsibilty. The cap as of 2004 stands at $8.2 trillion.

The largest industry in the United States is now services, which employs roughly three quarters of the work force. The United States has many natural resources, including oil and gas, metals, and such minerals as gold, soda ash, and zinc. Economic activity varies greatly from one part of the country to another, with many industries being concentrated in certain cities or regions. For example, New York City is the center of the American financial, publishing, broadcasting, and advertising industries. Silicon Valley is the country's largest high technology hub, while Los Angeles is the most important center for film production. The Midwest is known for its reliance on manufacturing and heavy industry, with Detroit, Michigan, serving as the center of the American automotive industry. The Great Plains are known as the "breadbasket" of America for their tremendous agricultural output; the intermountain region serves as a mining hub and natural gas resource; the Pacific Northwest for fish and timber, while Texas is largely associated with the oil industry; and the Southeast is a major hub for both medical research and the textiles industry.

Several countries continue to link their currency to the dollar or even use it as currency. Many markets are also quoted in dollars, such as those of oil and gold. The dollar is also the predominant reserve currency in the world, and more than half of global reserves are in dollars.

The largest trading partner of the United States is Canada (19 percent), followed by China (12 percent), Mexico (11 percent), and Japan (8 percent). More than 50 percent of total trade is with these four countries.

U.S. popular culture has a significant influence on the rest of the world, especially the Western world.

According to the CIA database, the United States has the largest and most technologically powerful economy in the world, with a per capita GDP of $40,100. U.S. business firms enjoy considerably greater flexibility than their counterparts in Western Europe and Japan in decisions to expand capital plant, to lay off surplus workers, and to develop new products. At the same time, they face higher barriers to entry in their rivals' home markets than the barriers to entry of foreign firms in U.S. markets. U.S. firms are at or near the forefront in technological advances, especially in computers and in medical, aerospace, and military equipment. The onrush of technology largely explains the gradual development of a "two-tier labor market" in which those at the bottom lack the education and the professional/technical skills of those at the top and, more and more, fail to get comparable pay raises, health insurance coverage, and other benefits. Since 1975, practically all the gains in household income have gone to the top 20 percent of households. The response to the terrorist attacks of September 11, 2001, showed the remarkable resilience of the economy. The war in March/April 2003 between a U.S.-led coalition and Iraq, and the subsequent occupation of Iraq, required major shifts in national resources to the military. The rise in GDP in 2004 was undergirded by substantial gains in labor productivity. The economy suffered from a sharp increase in energy prices in the second half of 2004. Long-term problems include inadequate investment in economic infrastructure, rapidly rising medical and pension costs of an aging population, sizable trade and budget deficits, and stagnation of family income in the lower economic groups.

Think America's position as a global big power is secure? It's not. All around the world, other countries have their eye on the United States' championship belt. America is coming out fighting with homeshoring.

The United States has to become a super-contender in the outsourcing provider ranks. This counter-intuitive foresight is evidenced by the latest offshoring evolution taking current form in the nearshoring movement with an evolving shift to "homeshoring" outsourced services back to the United States. In its "World Investment Report 2004," the United Nations Commission on Trade and Development argued that offshoring of corporate service functions could become "the next global shift." The United States, in particular, should be the biggest winner in meeting the need that the shift for service employees is creating globally. Secondly, also contributing to the prediction is a leveling of the outsourcing playing field. The costs of supplying services are anticipated to eventually level off. The price of fuel, professional personnel shortages, customer dissatisfaction and demands, and upward creeping costs of labor are major factors will that propel and disrupt the balance. Rural America and urban zones, combined with transitional professional management expertise from executive management community groups and opportunistic U.S. entrepreneurs, can reap the benefits if they prepare. Individuals in the United States who are focusing on the technology, finance, human resources, and business processing professions will begin to re-tool their skill base to include the fundamentals of outsourcing processes. Hence, we have identified a U.S. trend to move non-critical functions offshore while per-forming critical projects with nearshore or homeshore resources. This model has proven to be successful for many companies because it allows them to operate in almost the same mode they have been accustomed to for years. We next expect to see forward-thinking companies moving their offshored operations to U.S. regional pockets of higher than average unemployment.

Existing threats

1. China: Economic, political, military. China believes its destiny is to rule the globe in the 21st Century, and America's destiny is to like it. "China is almost certainly going to represent a serious challenge to American interests region-ally and globally," according to Robert Hathaway, director of the Asian Program at the Woodrow Wilson International Center for Scholars. China is eager to shake hands with any country that can help level the American-dom-inated playing field.

2. Iran: Ideological. Possible nuclear empowerment could disrupt President Bush's Middle East master plan. "Iran wants to dominate the world arena, and if they have the bomb—and there's a good chance they do—then they will," said Al J. Venter of Jane's International Defense Review. Iran has 10 percent of the world's oil reserves; 940 trillion cubic feet of natural gas; and is a devoted customer of China.

3. European Union: A strong Euro and weak dollar is the reason most Americans can't afford to do business or enjoy vacationing in the E.U. "With GDP the size of the U.S., and 450 million people, there is a lot of room for growth," says Robert Niblett, director of the Europe Program at the Center for Strategic and International Studies. The E.U. was invented to counter American economic hegemony. The meteoric rise of the euro—between 2002 and 2004, the dol-lar lost about 30 percent of its value against what some see as the global reserve currency of the future—indicates ruthless monetary efficiency to come. If OPEC decides to use euros instead of dollars to price oil, watch how fast these two dozen or so countries roll out the red carpet for China.

4. North Korea: Worldwide concern about the possibility of a rogue, cash starved dictatorship with nothing to lose pawning WMDs to terrorist organizations. Fueled by worthless currency, a $400 million trade deficit, a starving rural pop-ulation that can barely grow grass, and a manufacturing sector producing noth-

ing in particular, the isolated economy produces weapons. Its nuclear missiles could potentially hit Tokyo and Guam.

5. Russia: "Big challenges are advancing interest in democracy and human rights, cleaning up Russia's 600 tons of unsecured nuclear material, and stopping its support of rogue regimes," says Mark Brzezinski, former director for Russian Euro-Asian Affairs for the National Security Council.

6. India: India's army of tech experts is busy programming Silicon Valley computers. Comparing India's economy today to where it was even as recently as the early '90s, you can see how far they have come.

7. Pakistan: Instability with insurgency. The nuclear situation is causing some tension. For years, Pakistan's nuclear program, led by sacked national hero, Abdul Khan, ran the "Home Depot" of black market nuclear weapons technology. Money spent on a single nuke might supply the whole country with phones.

8. Brazil: The only country capable of helping U.S. enemies displace American influence in Latin America. Today, Brazil is one of the countries that is part of BRICK, and could be larger than the G6 in U.S. dollar terms.

9. Mexico: Six million immigrants crossing into the U.S. illegally. Texas, now part of a wider trend, is the third state where Hispanics represent the largest population group.

Major Players: Of all countries, the United States has the largest set of companies—BPOs, IT solutions providers, service providers, consultants and vendors—involved in offshoring and outsourcing, from the largest (IBM, EDS, KPMG), to the smallest boutique. Certain MNC consulting firms like Cognizant are also based in United States.

India

RISK DIMENSIONS

Political Risk: The world's largest democracy; high political risk and ongoing dispute with Pakistan over Kashmir, rivalry with China, not clear if newly elected government will stick to open-door policies; corruption is a big issue, religious diversity, natural disasters, disease, some violence, political and social instability, government is supportive of IT programs, massive overpopulation, extensive poverty, and ethnic and religious strife, environmental degradation. Kashmir is the world's most heavily militarized territorial conflict—a bitter struggle between India, Pakistan, and local Kashmiris.

Legal Risk: Overloaded legislation, intellectual property rights: situation is improving, especially with respect to the potential bid to become a member of the WTO; good legal system due to the nature of India's democracy and contract enforcement; a lot of red tape; favorable tax policies and tax exemption based on English common law; limited judicial review of legislative acts; accepts compulsory international jurisdiction; IPR weak, but improving; piracy is a problem; weak data protection regulations.

Cultural Risk: English is the most important language for national, political and commercial communication; English language is a major asset, proficiency in all major key areas; disadvantages such as accent; language neutralization is a must; Indian culture is geared up for innovation; high ability to understand Western practices; high people skills; good work ethic and productivity; some areas/regions are not exposed to Western culture; focusing on culture training. According to Joel Plaut, SendWordNow vice president of program management, "More subtly, it includes divisions/conflict between internal castes, mutual professional respect between the sexes and ability to contribute ideas across reporting lines. These issues frequently interfere with project success by impacting the individual knowledge workers."

Economic Risk:
Purchasing power parity: $3.003 trillion. GDP Growth: 8 percent.
Investors' confidence rising as FDI continues to grow. Financial structure is high and developed; there is no major currency risk (as rupee is not fully convertible). India's economy encompasses traditional village farming, modern agriculture, handicrafts, a wide range of modern industries, and a multitude of IT and support services. Government controls have been reduced on foreign trade and investment, and privatization of domestic output has proceeded slowly. The economy has posted an excellent average growth rate of 6 to 8 percent since 1990. Our expert, Pichappan Pethachi, associate partner with IBM Business Consulting Services for the Communication Sector, says, "The currency exchange rate difference is reducing; India rate was 46 rupees to a dollar, but now it is 43, and the salaries of the employees are going up." Furthermore, Joel Plaut adds, "Increase in rupee and a decrease in the dollar has had a significant impact already on the benefit of outsourcing."

After posting an average 5.6 percent growth per year since 1990, India is Asia's third largest economy, home of the world's software development, and riding the job outsourcing wave with $18 billion U.S. trade partnership. India booked $22 billion in business in 2005, answering calls, managing computer networks, processing invoices, and writing customer software for multinational corporations.

IT Infrastructure Risk:

Telephones: 48.917 million

Internet users: 18.481 million

Good IT infrastructure, but needs improvement; key cities and states (Bangalore, Hyderabad) invest heavily in IT. Depends on the region. Risk: power shortages, public utilities not dependable. Telecom infrastructure is improving, and telecom bandwidth issues have been addressed; private ISPs entered the market and telecom costs have dropped dramatically in recent years. Special IT-developed zones offer independent telecom/power infrastructure, high-speed digital communication. Recent deregulation and liberalization of telecommunications laws and policies have prompted rapid change; local and long distance service provided throughout all regions of the country, with services primarily concentrated in the urban areas; telephone density remains low at about 7 for each 100 persons nationwide, but only 1 per 100 persons in rural areas and a national waiting list of over 1.7 million; fastest growth is in cellular service with modest growth in fixed lines.

IT Competency Risk:

IT CMM level 5 certification = 48; quality project management; BPO specialties in application maintenance, enterprise application, developing call centers

Custom Code Writing (body shopping): Strong

System Writing Project R&D: (CMM Level): Average to poor.

Another expert, Derek Stephens, director of global business transformation outsourcing at IBM Corp., says he "found success moving testing to India, but not core applications, given core application architects on EST time."

Human Capital Risk: Population of 1 billion people. More than 2 million IT graduates per year. Large pool; very good education system (Indian Institutes of Technology, etc); many good universities and institutes. Cons: increasing attrition rates for service providers; labor force is familiar with Western expectations and requirements; availability of human resources is very high; IT pool is expected to touch 2 million over next 10 years. India created 1.3 million jobs in outsourcing during the last 10 years.

Labor force: 472 million

Cost: Favorable cost structure, but driving up labor costs as India prepares to become a superpower; low-cost telecom and infrastructure services; employee cost is $5,880 per annum on average.

MARKET OPPORTUNITY

Market:
2005: 35 percent
2006: 32 percent
2007: 38 percent compounded growth
2005-2009: 27 percent (Source: Forrester Research)
India's IT software and services export market will grow from nearly $10 billion in 2002 to $60 billion by 2008.
Population growth: 1.44 percent a year
Market size: $6,200 million

Global Competitiveness: Average

Overall Assessment: Most popular outsourcing location worldwide, early mover advantage; experienced, as it has been an offshore destination for more than a decade; ahead in the BPO curve; excellent education; huge experienced labor, acquiring management expertise; familiarity with global customers; government supportive. Low wages, favorable tax rates, quality of IT training and education, English language skills. Political and economic risk, poor infrastructure.

Major Players: Largest—Cognizant, Infosys, Polaris, Satyam, Tata Consultancy, Wipro. Others—Ajuba Solutions, Polaris Software Labs Limited, Arambh Newtork, Birlasoft, Daksh (IBM), Data Infosys Ltd, DataMatics, Earnest John Technologies, eData Infotechp Ltd, eFunds Corporation, Epicenter, Espire InfoLabs Inc, Fortune Infotech, Gateway TechnoLabs, GENPACT, HCL BPO, Hinduja TMT Ltd, Hughes BPO Services, ICICI OneSource, I-Flex Solutions, iGATE, India Life Capital, Infosys Technologies Limited, Infosys- Progeon BPO Division, ISeva, Larsen & Toubro Infotech, Machindra- British Telecomm (MBT), Mastek, Motif, MphasiS, NIIT SmartServe, Olive Optimized - EBusiness Solutions, Tata(TCS), Satyam, Par Computer Sciences, Patni Computer Systems, Process Mind, Redix Web Solutions, Sand Martin, Sirei Technologies Pvt Ltd, Sundaram Finance Group, TATA Infotech Ltd, Technovate eSolutions, ThinkSoft Global Solutions, Trinity Partners, Wipro, WNS Global Services, Zenta Technologies.

HP has 10,000 people in India doing everything from writing software code to managing other companies' IT needs.

FUTURE

Multi-location strategy companies are moving and expanding in parts around the world, Hungary for EE Canada, etc.; losing cost advantage; trying to compete for multinational corporation status.

China

RISK DIMENSIONS

Political Risk: Communist government; tight political control. Relatively stable government. Potential risk: conflict with Taiwan; strong government support to develop outsourcing industry; corruption is rampant, especially in provinces far away from Beijing. The Chinese Congress unanimously voted in spring 2005 to use force if Taiwan declares independence. According to our expert, Joel Plaut, "Political tension with Taiwan is probably higher than is realized, due to lack of an actual recent military incident." According to our expert, William Sanford, Principal, Columbia Strategy Group, "There is a fear of instability and many companies will not make investments for core/R&D operations in China due to the U.S. government advising against or denying such operations and the fear that the Chinese government may seize their business." Worst case scenario could include crushing foreign markets with cheap goods, unleashing 130 million unemployed peasants on the world, and skirmish with Taiwan.

Legal Risk: This is China's weak point; bad IPR protection, lack of enforcement, copycat mentality. Taxes are relatively low, but tax grace periods for investors are expiring; there are special economic zones; regulations, censorships; decision-making is improving and becoming quicker; state enforces the law (pushed by the WTO); continuing efforts are being made to improve civil, administrative, criminal and commercial law; lack of transparency; poor trademark protection.

Cultural Risk: Chinese culture is relatively difficult for Westerners to understand; management is based on guanxi (connections); English language proficiency is still an issue; young IT graduates, however, speak English well. Language skills/understanding of Western culture are good thanks to aggressive programs. Other Asian nations with similar cultures (especially nearby Japan) are using China as a major outsourcing center. People skills are average; bureaucracy levels; isolation; and censorship. According to expert Tsvi Gal, there is a possibility that, "Japan may revolt as the deficit continues to grow and may turn to 'anywhere but China' policy." Furthermore, Gal says, "It is not only the language. Chinese culture is much further from Western culture than India." According to Cyrill Eltschinger, CEO, IT United, "The government, overseas investments, the Olympics, and the society in general all contribute to this massive English push."

Economic Risk:

GDP-purchasing power parity: $6.449 trillion
GDP growth: 9.1 percent
China has the world's most dynamic economy, in terms of overall GDP growth. About $6 trillion-huge economy; huge domestic base. Economic prospects are good. China will be the world's new growth engine. Chinese renminbi (RMB) is still pegged to the U.S. dollar; we expect that to remain that way for the next two years. Even after the start of a more liberal currency policy, we do not expect a major currency risk as the RMB will not freely float. Financial structures are solid and growing; China entered the WTO; services sector is growing.

The result has been a quadrupling of GDP since 1978. Measured on a purchasing power parity (PPP) basis, China stands as the second-largest economy in the world after the United States, although in per capita terms the country is still poor. Economic influence of non-state organizations and individual citizens has been rising steadily. Increase of the authority of local officials and plant managers in industry has permitted the start up of a variety of small-scale services and light manufacturing enterprises and opened the economy to more foreign trade and investment.

$50 billion per year of foreign investment, $70 a month labor force cranking out 40,000 DVD players per minute, and an average of 9 percent GDP growth for 25 years, all under state controlled pseudocapitalism. China's favorite borrower is the U.S., in the red for $242 billion.

Infrastructure Risk:

Telephones: 263 million
Internet users: 74 million
In major cities there's good infrastructure and it's improving; national software and technology parks/incubators. Cons: There are power ruptures in big cities due to China's ever-rising energy demand; many R&D facilities set up by Western companies. Domestic and international telephone services are increasingly avail-

able for private use; unevenly distributed domestic system serves principal cities, industrial centers and many towns.

IT Competency Risk: Quality project management lacking; lack of technical and business management experience
Custom Code Writing (body shopping): Strong
BPO: Poor to average
System Writing Project R&D: Average. Core competencies: basic functionality, applications development, application maintenance; embedded systems; data processing service.

Human Capital Risk: Population of 1.3 billion people. Universities graduate very competent people; large pool of IT workers, 50,000 new IT graduates per year, and more than 200,000 work in IT.

The population under age eighteen in China is larger than the combined total population of the United States and U.K. In other words, it has an unlimited supply of people.
Labor force: 778 million

Cost: Low salaries, but higher in bigger cities; outsourcing centers move westward to benefit from lower costs; labor costs are low; lowest real estate; lowest power cost.

MARKET OPPORTUNITY

Market:
2005: 30 percent
2006: 29 percent
2007: 26 percent
Compounded growth 2005-2009: 25 percent
(Source: Forrester Research)
-Population growth: 0.57 percent
-Market size: According to McKinsey, annual revenues in software and IT services have risen 42 percent on average since 1997, reaching $6.8 billion in 2003

Global Competitiveness: Average

Overall Assessment: China is still aligned to hardware manufacturing and development. Software/offshoring services still in their infancy. Indian companies (Infosys, Wipro) have started software development centers in China to gain a cost edge and take advantage of the local Chinese market. China's labor pool, government support, and low cost put it in second place. It currently lags behind India in experience, country risk, experience, project management. China offers incredible market opportunities. Low wages, good education system. Intellectual property, privacy, bureaucratic red tape, English language skills are issues.

Major Players: Asiainfo, Datacraft, Digital China, Eastcom Group, Electronics Global Services, Huawei, I.T. United, NeuSoft, Sichuan Yinhai, ZTE Corp, CS&S, Ufida, Kingdee, Neusoft, Genersoft, Datang, Amid New & Grand, Anyi, QAD, Fourth Shift, Symix, Censoft, Doublebridge, Objectiva, Red Flag Digitalchina, Neusoft, CS&S, CVIC Engineering, Tshinghua Tong Fang, Oriental United Software, Beyongdsoft, Achievo, isoftstone, Shanda, Sina, Sohu, Netease, Ctrip, Flashempire, The9, Baidu (search engine), Alibaba (B2B), eBay Eachnet, Huicong.

IBM opened a new IT/BPO data center. Accenture has 1,000-person software development unit in the northeastern city of Dalian.

FUTURE

Destination for Asian economies, such as Japan for offshoring; will become attractive over the next 5 to 10 years in IT; will become India's major competitor for outsourcing services. China will spur new growth and investment. Its market opportunities will continue to grow.

China will continue to expand R&D and focus on high-end offshoring.

Costa Rica

RISK DIMENSIONS

Political Risk: Political stability; relatively stable government; called the "Switzerland of Central America;" corruption has been an issue recently (three former presidents are under investigation). Costa Rica is a Central American success story.

Legal Risk: The government is investing in the IT industry; digital agenda strategy by government; "punto.com" initiative with free Internet at post offices;

Banco Nacional computer financing for IT computer loans. Inability to enforce IP laws, lack of venture financing; based on Spanish civil law system; steps to advance intellectual property protection through a government strategy for improving the enforcement of intellectual property rights.

Cultural Risk: Good English skills; primary language is Spanish; geographic and cultural proximity to the U.S.

Economic Risk:

GDP-purchasing power parity: $35.34 billion

GDP growth: 5.6 percent

Difficult to continue the success story of the past, competition from India and China; good economic freedom; expanded its economy to include strong technology; the standard of living is relatively high; Costa Rica's basically stable economy depends on tourism, agriculture and electronics exports. Poverty has been substantially reduced over the past fifteen years. The government continues to grapple with its large deficit and massive internal debt.

IT Infrastructure Risk:

Telephones: 1.132 million

Internet users: 800,000

Good to fair infrastructure and telecommunication industry; over-reliance on hydroelectric energy production; good domestic telephone service.

IT Competency Risk: Some skilled project management. Custom code writing (body shopping): Very good mainframe

BPO: Average

System Writing project R&D: Poor

Human Capital Risk: Well-educated workforce, but small labor supply; country of 4 million people; MNCs are setting base operations in Costa Rica.

Labor force: 1.758 million

Cost: Low cost, wage structure lower than India.

MARKET OPPORTUNITY

MARKET:
2005: 33 percent
2006: 31 percent
2007: 27 percent
Compounded growth 2005-2009: 26 percent
(Source: Forrester Research)
-Population growth: 1.52 percent

Global Competitiveness: Average

Overall Assessment: Ideal for outsourcing from the U.S.; low-cost, good infrastructure; it has geographic and cultural proximity to the U.S.; only few hours flying time; government supports technology offshoring.

FUTURE
Costa Rica will remain a major outsourcing center. Further growth, however, will be restricted due to size of its economy/labor supply; some companies may be acquired by bigger players in the U.S. and South America.

Czech Republic

RISK DIMENSIONS

Political Risk: Stable government; least corruption in Eastern Europe; part of E.U.; one of the most stable and prosperous of the post-Communist states.

Legal Risk: Strong government support; excellent tax incentives; intellectual property getting better; major base of intellectual property.

Cultural Risk: Proximity to European companies allows for constant interaction; cultural affinity with Western Europe, good relationship with the U.S. Skills improving, good German skills; English-language proficiency growing; high productivity; multilingual workforce; similar cultural background.

Economic Risk:
GDP-purchasing power parity: $161.1 billion
GDP growth: 2.9 percent
Modest economic growth, stable economy (mainly profiting from E.U. enlargement); economy slowing down a bit. Financial structures are becoming more stable and growing; government is promoting IT services; excellent support for investments, technology-driven economy. Czech Republic is one of the most developed economies in Eastern Europe. High current account deficits, which have averaged around 5 percent of GDP in the past several years, could be a persistent problem.

IT Infrastructure Risk: Modernization of the Czech telecommunication system is advancing steadily; good telecom system; good real estate; well-developed and stable infrastructure; infrastructure cost are competitive.
Internet users: 2.7 million
Telephones: 3.626 million

IT Competency Risk: Some skilled project management; solid technical skills; strong base of programmers; skilled cost-effective workforce
Custom Code Writing (body shopping): Good
BPO: Average to good
System Writing project R&D: Excellent

Human Capital Risk: Population: 10 million. Highly educated engineers and IT specialists and growing; many R&D centers; strong, fully developed education system; high availability of talent, but small country. Czech universities have a history of turning out highly skilled technical graduates, a legacy of the Communist era.
Labor force: 5.25 million

Cost: Costs are low now, but they will rapidly go up; not as low as in Asia; wages are getting to be high; rising property prices, with monthly rents for businesses on the upswing; on a par with any other Western city.

MARKET OPPORTUNITY

Market:
2005: 20 percent
2006: 24 percent
2007: 23 percent

Compounded growth 2005-2009: 21 percent
(Source: Forrester Research)
-Offshore services market is growing at greater than 10 percent annually
-Population growth: 0.05 percent
-Market size: 26 million in Czech Republic 2003

Global Competitiveness: Very good

Overall Assessment: Ideal for MNCs from continental Europe and E.U., well positioned for nearshoring from E.U.; wages are getting higher with E.U.; cultural compatibility; stable political system and a competitive infrastructure; English proficiency; limited labor pool. Competitive infrastructure costs, good education system, stable business environment, higher labor costs relative to Asian countries, small population limits market size.

Major Players: AXA Assistance, Fractal, ICON Communication Center, Internet Info, Lion Tele Services, Logos, Telia Call and Unicorn and Systinet Brain Systems Accenture has IT and BPO operations; IBM and Sun have IT and business support centers; Dell has multilingual center for European customers.

FUTURE
Czech Republic is becoming a good solid outsourcing center, but a limited labor pool and rising costs might not make it a top 20 of future offshoring player; might lose wage advantage.

Hungary

RISK DIMENSIONS

Political Risk: Stable political environment and government; smooth transition from former Communist rule, government support of IT.

Legal Risk: A rule-based economy, good IP protection; data exclusivity protection.

Cultural Risk: Very friendly. Some English spoken; cultural affinity to Western Europe. Hungary is aligned to the German, Austrian, and Swiss markets.

Economic Risk:

GDP-purchasing power parity: $139.8 billion

GDP growth: 2.9 percent

Hungary has made the transition from a centrally planned economy to a market economy, with a per capita income one-half that of the Big Four European nations. Hungary continues to demonstrate strong economic growth and joined the European Union. The private sector accounts for more than 80 percent of GDP. Foreign ownership of and investment in Hungarian firms are widespread. Economy is flat; inflation declining; growing deficit, Euraccession might provide opportunities for growth.

IT Infrastructure Risk

Telephones: 3.7 million

Internet users: 1.6 million

The telephone system has been modernized and is capable of satisfying all requests for telecommunication service. Initiatives to augment the IT infrastructure, e-governance, Internet penetration, etc.; real estate structures are good; excellent conditions of telecom infrastructure.

According to our expert Steven Carlson, organizer of First Tuesday Budapest, "Hungary was the first in the region to privatize and begin rebuilding the national network." Furthermore, Carlson noted, "I know of two VOIP companies based here serving subscribers in North America and around the world. Even a home user can get an ADSL connection set up in as little as week to ten days. One cable company, UPC, now bundles cable TV, phone, and Internet service. In this respect, Hungary is still ahead of her neighbors."

IT Competency Risk: Good project management; highly skilled employees

Custom Code Writing (Body shopping): Good

BPO: Good

System Writing Project R&D: Good to excellent

Human Capital Risk: High level of education, but labor pool is limited; good university education.

Labor force: 4.164 million

Cost: Costs are low now, but they won't stay that way.

MARKET OPPORTUNITY

Market:
2005: 20 percent
2006 24 percent
2007: 23 percent
Compounded growth 2005-2009: 21 percent (Source: Forrester Research)
-Population growth: 0.25 percent
-Market size: $20 million in 2003

Global Competitiveness: Good

Overall Assessment: A good nearshoring destination in Europe. Very skillful and good base to other destinations in Western Europe. Excellent education and highly qualified IT workforce; proximity and access to E.U.; good infrastructure.

Future: A major destination for nearshoring in Eastern Europe and a central hub for offshoring in Europe.

Major Players: Eurotrend, FreeSoft, Graphisoft, ICON, Kurt Computers, Lursoft IT, Marketlink, Montana, Revelution Software, Synergon and Sysdata

FUTURE
Becoming a hub of U.S., Asian and Indian companies for Central and Western Europe. Low supply of resources and rising costs will continue to climb and may drop Hungary from the Future Growth Index.

Canada

RISK DIMENSIONS

Political Risk: Very stable democratic government; solid political system, one of the most efficient administrations worldwide; Quebec government referendum and a continuing constitutional impasse between English- and French-speaking areas have raised the specter of a split in the federation.

Legal Risk: Tax breaks for IT-related exports, and NAFTA enables a free-trade market in IT services; based on English common law, except in Quebec, where civil law system based on French law prevails. Strong IP protection and privacy rules; favorable laws. NAFTA provides for free trade market in IT services; the government grants favorable tax treatment for software development and maintenance companies.

Cultural Risk: Similar culture to the U.S.; English and French spoken; high level of customer satisfaction; proximity to U.S. and similar time zones; understands U.S. mentality and cultures are compatible; no culture training is necessary.

Economic Risk:
GDP-purchasing power parity: $958.7 billion
GDP growth: 1.7 percent
Stable economy with a favorable exchange rate; high-tech economy; high living standards and GDP growth. As an affluent, high-tech industrial society, Canada today closely resembles the U.S. in its market-oriented economic system, pattern of production and high living standards Given its great natural resources, skilled labor force, and modern capital plant, Canada enjoys solid economic prospects. A key strength of the country's economy is its substantial trade surplus.

IT Infrastructure Risk:
Telephones: 19.95 million
Internet users: 16.11 million
Excellent infrastructure and communications system; well developed; similar to or better than the U.S.; excellent service provided by modern technology.

IT Competency Risk: Good project management; highly skilled employees; good business skills; good technical talent; high-quality workers; technically skilled labor pool capable of handling high-end work; skill set comparable to that in U.S. and Europe
Custom Code Writing (body shopping): Average
BPO: Excellent
System Writing Project R&D: Very good to excellent

Human Capital Risk: Population: 32 Million
Superior education; actively promoting job creation; strong university and academia pool; flow of professionals lured south to the U.S. by higher pay, lower taxes and the immense high-tech infrastructure.

Turnover at CGI, one of Canada's largest call centers, is just 6 percent versus 25-50 percent turnover at most U.S. call centers
Labor force: 16 million to 17 million

Cost: High cost, lower cost than U.S., but still higher than in most other outsourcing centers. Labor costs work out to be quite high: $28,174; employees average $22 to $37 an hour.

MARKET OPPORTUNITY

Market:
2005: 12 percent
2006: 20 percent
2007: 21 percent
Compounded growth 2005-2009: 18 percent
(Source: Forrester Research)
-Population growth: 0.92 percent

Global Competitiveness: Excellent

Overall Assessment: Canada is a world leader in IT outsourcing, specializing in call centers, BPO and infrastructure. Low risk, high quality, similar time zones and compatible cultures. Considered to be a safe and stable nearshoring destination, mainly for U.S. firms. High cost. It is a good way to start offshoring processing in a safe manner and avoid major risks. High quality workers, high end infrastructure and language skills.

Major Players: AICOM Solutions, CGI, Fujitsu, IBM, Keane Canada, March Networks, OAO Technology Solutions and Unisys Canada, AMG Logistics, EDS which has more than 1,500 employees in Nova Scotia; services include a call center. GM moved a lot of white collar jobs to Canada.

Associations: Information Technology Association of Canada

FUTURE
Will remain a competitive player with specialized high-level services with competitive R&D and BPO. Excellent regional destination for Asian companies competing for business in the U.S., Canada will specialize in high-end services. Will have to work hard on lowering cost structures.

Latvia

RISK DIMENSIONS

Political Risk: Latvia has been able to engineer a smooth transition from Communist rule; stable government. Russian minority is a concern.

Legal Risk: One of the most efficient tax systems in Europe; rule-based economy; liberal economy modeled after Anglo-Saxon economies; IPR protection is still an issue, but Latvia has improved its intellectual property rights. Cultural risk: It is extremely hard for a Slav to get rid of Slavic accent when speaking English; however, it is rather easy for Latvians or Lithuanians, whose language is much more similar to English. Great affinity with Nordics.

Economic Risk:
GDP-purchasing power parity: $23.9 billion
GDP growth: 7.4 percent
Continuing economic growth; accession to the E.U. offers great opportunities. The majority of companies, banks, and real estate firms have been privatized, although the state still holds sizable stakes in a few large enterprises.

IT Infrastructure Risk:
Telephones: 653,900
Internet users: 936,000
Very good infrastructure; government is making more improvements with the help of Nordics and the E.U.; telecom is inadequate, but is being modernized to provide an international capability.

IT Competency Risk:
Good project management; excellent regarding software development
Custom Code Writing (body shopping): Average to good
BPO: Average to good
System Writing Project R&D: Excellent

Human Capital Risk: Much better educated workforce technically. There is a larger percentage of IT students and students of technical sciences in the Baltic States than in the rest of Eastern Europe, especially for software development; good universities; limited supply.
Labor force: 1.18 million

Cost: Costs are low now, but they won't stay that way. Proximity to Scandinavian companies. The average salary in Latvia and Lithuania is higher than other parts of Eastern Europe and Russia. To our knowledge, telecommunication costs from the ten new Eastern European E.U. member countries are the highest in Latvia.

MARKET OPPORTUNITY

Market:
2005: 20 percent
2006: 24 percent
2007: 23 percent
Compounded growth 2005-2009: 21 percent
(Source: Forrester Research)
-Population growth: 0.71 percent

Competitiveness: Very good

Overall Assessment: Excellent destination for outsourcing, proximity to Nordics and the E.U., good infrastructure and skills; limited labor pool and an aging population; wages and costs are getting higher due to E.U. integration.

Major Players: Exigen Group, Runway and Transcom Worldwide

FUTURE
Together with its neighbors Estonia and Lithuania, Latvia is a major outsourcing center for Northern/continental Europe.

It may lose its status as a top 20 player due to an aging population that's getting smaller as well; limited labor pool; costs would increase dramatically.

Russia

RISK DIMENSIONS

Political Risk: Highly censored and controlled; stable and "strong" government of President Vladimir Putin; corruption is an issue, mafia is still all-around but less of an issue in IT/software outsourcing. While some progress has been made on the economic front, recent years have seen a recentralization of power by President Putin and erosion in nascent democratic institutions. American support for breakaways such as Ukraine and Georgia could cause problems for Russia. Putin continues to sell arms to Iran and Syria. Worst case scenario is with 300 million disenchanted Muslims, the Russian southern borders could blow the war on terror beyond control.

Legal Risk: Old-fashioned tax/legal system, law not fully enforced and IPR not really respected. Weak protection of intellectual property rights; considerable progress in revising several of its intellectual property laws recently, however; progress toward alleviating red tape and bureaucracy; strict labor laws; government only recently supporting IT growth; piracy of works on optical media is a significant and growing problem.

Cultural Risk: European culture, but still early stage of capitalism; close to Nordics; cities like St. Petersburg are full of European culture; creative and innovative people; affinity toward Europe; limited understanding of foreign markets, customer service and culture; ability to work in undefined environment and succeed. English is being practiced at top levels and people are gaining proficiency, but most programmers still have difficulty with the English language. Russia is proving a convenient location for Nordic companies looking for inexpensive, highly skilled labor.

Economic Risk:
GDP-purchasing power parity: $1.282 trillion
GDP growth: 7.3 percent
Constant growth, averaging 6.5 percent annually; high oil prices and a relatively cheap ruble are important drivers of this economic rebound; high-growth perspectives, but high volatility as well; firm economic policy; high inflationary trends; tight currency controls.

Real fixed capital investments have averaged gains greater than 10 percent over the past four years, and real personal incomes have averaged increases of more than 12 percent. Russia has also improved its international financial position since the 1998 financial crisis, with its foreign debt declining from 90 percent of GDP to around 28 percent. Strong oil export earnings have allowed Russia to increase its foreign reserves to some $80 billion. These achievements, along with a renewed government effort to advance structural reforms, have raised business and investor confidence in Russia's economic prospects.

Problems include a weak banking system, a poor business climate that discourages both domestic and foreign investors, corruption, local and regional government intervention in the courts, and widespread lack of trust in institutions. President Putin is granting more influence to forces within his government that desire to reassert state control over the economy.

Putting most of its eggs in its enormous natural gas reserves (world's largest), coal reserves (second largest), and oil reserves (eight largest), Russia plans to double its energy export-dependent GDP in the next decade.

IT Infrastructure Risk:

Telephones: 35.5 million

Internet users: 6 million

Improving infrastructure, but still inexperienced in managing large scale offshore development centers; communication costs are getting higher in St. Petersburg and Moscow. Communication costs are even higher outside large cities. Many R&D labs and institutes; government is only starting to spend capital on improving connectivity and infrastructure; growth of specialized software companies; government is fostering programs such as Electronic Russia and others. Cost of bandwidth is expensive and infrastructure is poor in cities other than Moscow and St. Petersburg.

Telephone system underwent significant changes in the 1990s; there are more than 1,000 companies licensed to offer communication services; access to digital lines has improved, particularly in urban centers; Internet and e-mail services are getting better; Russia has made progress toward building the telecommunications infrastructure necessary for a market economy; a large demand for main line service, however, remains unsatisfied. In the beginning of 2005, President Putin announced the beginning a special program to set up, develop and support IT technoparks in four regions of Russia. Putin noted that technoparks, with new zones with special economic conditions, will be created to benefit information technologies companies. The benefits will include:

- Significantly reduced corporate and income taxes (up to 75 percent reduction);
- No more than one tax audit in a three-year period;

- Simplified custom conditions for the import of equipment and experts in software products; no custom duties;
- Construction of affordable housing for young programmers, kindergartens, etc.

IT Competency Risk: Quality project management; excellent technical and management experience lacking, but growing; highly skilled IT workers
Custom Code Writing (body shopping): Average
BPO: Average, but growing
System Writing Project R&D: Excellent
Preferred country for R&D and innovation expansion. R&D creative experience; growth of specialized software companies; excellent research; extremely skilled programming workforce; expertise in large complex engineering and algorithms; project management is lacking, but developing. Programming, software/hardware reengineering, telephony based solutions, wireless, radio technology, security, hardware technologies such as laser, substrate growing, molecular chemistry.

Human Capital Risk: Large pool of engineers, scientists, a lot of young talent; stable workforce; small group of MBAs and managers; Russia has more than 20,000 professional IT personnel and growing; most Russian programmers have a formal science degree and have worked in complex defense programs. Programming is a secondary skill; major expansion in deep Russia/Siberia; leading universities focus on technology, engineering and IT. With a significant R&D heritage, it is one of the world's best educational systems and the largest pool of highly qualified software engineers and researchers.

The World Bank estimates that Russia has the third-highest number of scientists and engineers per capita in the world
Labor force: 71.68 million

Cost: Labor costs are moderate but starting to grow in major cities; moderate costs; cost advantage in remote areas of Russia.

MARKET OPPORTUNITY

Outsourcing Market:
2005: 20 percent
2006: 24 percent
2007: 23 percent
Compounded growth 2005-2009: 21 percent
(Source: Forrester Research)

-Population growth: 0.45 percent

-Market Size: Region was expected to exceed US$1 billion in outsourcing revenue by 2005. In 2003 exported IT services totaled $475 million. According to Ernst & Young, the Russian IT and telecommunications sectors are experiencing an average growth of 45 percent and are expected to reach $20 billion in 2005. Russia is planning to increase the current US$500 million software exports market to US$1.3 billion by 2008.

Global Competitiveness: Average to poor

Overall Assessment: Focusing on niche software companies; Russian companies tend to focus on building personal relationships; pay close attention to small projects; flat organizations; highly skilled, creative talent; Russian IT offshoring is expanding; economy has been growing to assist IT offshoring, government has to be more committed for IT outsourcing and lessen bureaucracy and restrictions; poor enforcement of IP; needs to bolster management.

Independent Rating: Recently achieved investment grade status by independent Moody's Investment Services. Made the list of the world's ten most attractive countries for direct foreign investments.

Major Players: Auriga, DataArt, Diasoft, EPAM, Estyle, Exigen and IBS/Luxoft

FUTURE

Russia will become a major outsourcing center and the focus will be on creative solutions and R&D services; Russia has a large technical labor pool, but declining population growth; may become a center of intellectual growth and innovation.

Chile

RISK DIMENSIONS

Political Risk: Geopolitical risk is moderate and it may be the most stable country in South America; followed the advice of international organizations and opened up its economy and installed a fully democratic system in the post-Pinochet area. Chile has assumed more of a regional and international leadership role befitting its status as a stable, democratic nation. Its sound economic policies have contributed to steady growth and have helped secure the country's commitment to democratic and representative government.

Legal Risk: Rule-based economy, fair and simplified tax system; government is promoting IP and secrecy rights; U.S.-Chile Free Trade Agreement provides high levels of protection appropriate for the digital age, including U.S. software, music, text and motion pictures. Protections for U.S. patents, trademarks and undisclosed information exceed past trade agreements (e.g., NAFTA and the U.S.-Jordan FTA), and obligate Chile to make its IP laws and enforcement practices conform to the most advanced standards.

Cultural Risk: Affinity for Spanish outsourcing services; thousands of young IT people are being trained to speak English; geographic and time zone proximity to the U.S.; English proficiency, however, is poor. It is the most European community in South America. Chile might lack the entrepreneurial zeal it needs to become a real offshore player.

Economic Risk:
GDP-purchasing power parity: $154.7 billion
GDP growth: 3.3 percent
Chile has a market-oriented economy characterized by a high level of foreign trade and a solid business environment; free trade agreements with the U.S. and other countries; overall business ratings are high and consistent. Chile is developing into a preferred trading partners of Asia, especially Japan and China.
    Santiago is among the least expensive cities in the world.
    GDP growth is set to accelerate to more than 4 percent as copper prices rise, export earnings grow, and foreign direct investment picks up.

IT Infrastructure Risk:
Telephones: 3.467 million
Internet users: 3.575 million
Modern system based on extensive microwave radio relay facilities; growing infrastructure; robust connectivity and satellite services; infrastructure/communications are good. State-of-the art infrastructure, including network digitalization, fiber optics and satellite equipment.

IT Competence Risk: Good project management; highly skilled employees
Custom Code Writing (body shopping): Average to good
BPO (Spanish) Very good
System Writing Project R&D: Average

Human Capital Risk: The government is training for offshoring services; lacks top universities; scarcity of labor and educated workers; high level of education; small size;
Labor force: 6 million

Cost: Higher cost than other nations in Latin America; Chile is a little more expensive than Brazil, but relatively competitive in other ways.

MARKET OPPORTUNITY

Market:
2005: 33 percent
2006: 31 percent
2007: 27 percent
Compounded growth 2005-2009: 28 percent
(Source: Forrester Research)
-Population growth: 1.01 percent

Global Competitiveness: Excellent

Overall Assessment: Spanish-speaking offshoring services; ranks high in competitiveness; one of the least expensive cities; call centers are growing and MNCs are settling in South American centers. Pros include the high level of education, low costs, high-tech infrastructure and availability of great scientific minds. Good infrastructure, including telecom networks, good business environment, high level of education; small size. More costly than other Latin American countries; lack of bilingual technicians and intellectual property protection.

Major Players: Citigroup has a software development group and funds an advisory center.

Association: Information Technology Association of Chile

FUTURE
Good outsourcing location, but growth might be limited by scarcity of labor and rising costs; will continue to be a major player in the Future Outsourcing Rank of South America.

Romania

RISK DIMENSIONS

Political Risk: Rampant corruption; Hungary amended status law extending special social and cultural benefits to ethnic Hungarians in Romania, who had objected to the law. Romania has good relations with the former Soviet Union states (from the point of view of political doctrine and economic relations) and the Middle East (it has always had very good links to the countries from that region). Romania is in the privileged position in which it can serve as a bridge between the nations and companies from this area.

Legal Risk: Red tape hinders foreign investment; ongoing piracy issues; lack of IPR protection; lack of enforcement, but piracy rate has decreased more than 20 percent in the past few years. The government is committed to attracting and retaining IT talent by exempting IT professionals from income tax payment.

There's a lack of legislation, but the important laws are already being prepared for approval, including copyright, electronic signature, electronic commerce and a ruling concerning personal character data processing.

Cultural Risk: Attractive for European outsourcing; same time zone for E.U.; very little time overlap; understands Western European culture.

The business culture and Romanian attitude is European and a very high percentage of the workforce speaks English, French, German or Italian.

Economic Risk:
GDP-purchasing power parity: $155 billion
GDP growth: 4.9 percent
Romania has successfully concluded an IMF agreement; has to achieve a lot to enter the E.U. An effective public-private partnership in the IT sector will ensure a competitive and consistent rules-based business environment; inflows of foreign direct investment (FDI). Romania's future integration in the European Union, most likely in 2007, offers investors an established presence in the Common Market.

IT Infrastructure Risk:
Telephones: 4.3 million
Internet users: 4 million
Poor domestic telco infrastructure, but improving; ranks sixth in the world in the number of certified IT professionals. The government's IT "Vision for

Romania" is summed up in the following mission statement: "Romania should aspire to become the 'Internet hub' for the Black Sea region."

The Romanians have implemented almost all the international standards of mobile telecommunications, and the country has registered one of the largest growths of mobile communication in Europe during the last five years.

The extension of the e-procurement system to a national level has become a key component in the process of modernization of the government in Romania. With electronic procurement, the Romanian government can lower the cost and encourage the private sector to move to B2B. It also creates the premise for lowering corruption, reducing bureaucracy and ensuring transparency. Companies investing in R&D centers in Romania include IBM, Oracle, Siemens, Alvarion and Alcatel.

IT Competency Risk: Highly skilled workforce, focus on specialized software; excellent R&D and creative skills
Custom Code Writing (body shopping): Very good
BPO: Poor
System Writing Project R&D: Excellent

The Romanian IT industry will become a leading regional supplier of Internet-based services, specialized software and contract manufacturing by 2010 by leveraging national competitive advantages; Romania has a history of scientific achievement and technical expertise.

Human Capital Risk: It has an abundance of well-educated and highly skilled workers; 20,000 IT certifications; surpasses almost all Europe in its IT resource pool creation.
Labor force: 9.28 million

Cost: Wages are low. It will take seven to eight years for wages in Romania to catch up with the rest of the E.U.; IT costs are $2,360; very top MCSE annual cost is $12,000.

MARKET OPPORTUNITY

Market:
Annual rate of growth of the Romanian IT companies exceeded on average 25 percent for the last few years, and that of export 60 percent; IT spending is the lowest in the region.
-Population growth: 0.11 percent

Global Competitiveness: Poor

Overall Assessment: Romania has an abundance of well educated and highly skilled workers. Being located in the heart of Europe, Romania is the best choice when targeting both the massive E.U. market and the emerging CIS region with its unsurpassed labor costs and IT expertise. Highly-skilled, relatively cheap labor. A very high percentage of the work force speaks English, French, German or Italian

Major players: More than 5,000 software-producing companies are located in Romania, mainly at the great university centers in Brasov, Bucharest, Cluj, Lasi, and Timisoara.

Associations: ANIS (dealing mainly with software), ATIC (covering different IT sectors), ANISP (an association of Romanian Internet service providers), and ARIES (the largest and most active Romanian IT association with member companies from all areas).

FUTURE

Romania will be a promising player in the Future Outsourcing Rank with quality and abundant IT resources in Central Europe. Costs might rise a bit in the future, but on the whole it remains competitive.

Ireland

RISK DIMENSIONS

Political Risk: No risk. The only point could be conflicts from Northern Ireland spilling over. The Irish government has set up huge incentives to software companies to produce software in Ireland. Most companies use this to their advantage and have set up software production for distribution in Europe.

Legal Risk: European (high-class) standard; based on English common law; very promising tax incentive of 12.5 percent for companies and maximum taxation of about 40 percent.

Cultural Risk: English is national language.

Economic Risk:

GDP-purchasing power parity: $116.2 billion

GDP growth: 1.4 percent

Ireland is a small, modern, trade-dependent economy with growth averaging a robust 8 percent in 1995-2002. The global slowdown, especially in the information technology sector, pressed growth down to 2.1 percent in 2003. "Celtic tiger" enjoyed an influx of foreign investment throughout the '90s as a result of low corporate tax rates and a flexible workforce. Stellar economic performance; high growth will continue for a few years; Ireland's overall economic competitiveness has already surpassed Germany and France. Per capita GDP is 10 percent above that of the four big European economies. Over the past decade, the Irish government has implemented a series of national economic programs designed to curb inflation, reduce government spending, increase labor force skills and promote foreign investment. There's a positive attitude toward foreign investors and no specific conflict between labor and capital sources. As noted by Dr. Ami Eyal, CEO, Bio-Light, Life Science Investments, "The real income is similar to that of Switzerland, the U.S.A. and Norway, despite the fact that 30 years ago Ireland was the poorest country in the region."

IT Infrastructure Risk:

Telephones: 1.955 million

Internet users: 1.26 million

World-class infrastructure, infrastructure development was major endeavor of Irish government, private sector actively participated; private-public partnerships; large development centers for IBM, Microsoft and others.

IT Competency Risk: Quality project management; excellent technical and business management experience; highly skilled IT workers

Custom Code Writing (body shopping): Good software development

BPO: Excellent

System writing and R&D Project: Average

Human Capital Risk: Top educational system; Irish government recognized the need for a world-class education system. Universities attract students from around the world in big numbers. Programmers are very skilled in latest technologies; the number of new graduates is rather low, however, despite government initiatives.

Labor force: 1.871 million

Cost: Relatively high, ideal for nearshoring from continental Europe. Europe-based U.S. clients; cost will soon approach those of Europe's most expensive countries (France, Germany), challenging the long-term attractiveness of Ireland as an outsourcing destination; employee cost is $28,000.

MARKET OPPORTUNITY

Outsourcing Market:
2005: 26 percent
2006: 27 percent
2007: 25 percent
Compounded growth 2005-2009: 24 percent
(Source: Forrester Research)
-Population growth: 1.16 percent
-Market size: $6.7 billions

Global Competitiveness: Excellent

Overall Assessment: Dr. Ami Eyal summarizes that Ireland shows tremendous potential as an outsourcing destination, "despite the fact that it does not have a relative advantage in any field—no heavy financial background, relatively small community, no oil or other natural resources, no banking system." A high performer of IT experts today. Currently a top player. Excellent BPO and IT services capability. Excellent workforce and education. Has been able to keep costs under control for many years. A stable environment and very popular destination.

Major Players: Fyntel, Vision Consulting; other players are mainly subsidiaries of multinationals (IBM, EDS, etc.) Equitant, Meridian

FUTURE
Ireland will have difficulty surviving as major outsourcing center. In the future, it will continue to be in the top 20. With the recent rise of outsourcing to India, China, and EE, Ireland is emphasizing the intelligence of its workforce and their understanding of Western customer service in an attempt to remain an attractive outsourcing center.

Singapore

RISK DIMENSIONS

Political Risk: Politically stable. Singapore is a strong government, not a democracy in a Western sense, due to the quasi one-party rule. Low corruption listed in many international reports; administration is known for its efficiency; disputes with Malaysia over deliveries of fresh water to Singapore; one of the world's most prosperous countries with strong international trading links and a per capita GDP equal to that of the leading nations of Western Europe.

Legal Risk: Pro business tax and regulations; excellent IP and security protection.

Cultural Risk: English spoken; excellent language skills; Western values.

Economic Risk:
GDP-purchasing power parity: $109.4 billion
GDP growth: 1.1 percent
On a purchasing power parity, Singapore has the second highest income per capita in the world. Highly developed and successful free market economy; enjoys a remarkably open and corruption-free environment; stable prices and a high per capita GDP. The economy depends heavily on exports, particularly in electronics and manufacturing; economic stability; growth is modest and there's strong competition from China. Singapore is giving up more traditional sectors of industry and focusing on high-value added industries (especially biotech), helping to establish it as Southeast Asia's financial and high-tech hub. Fiscal stimulus, low interest rates, and global economic recovery should lead to much improved growth.

IT Infrastructure Risk:
Telephones: 1.9 million
Internet users: 2.31 million
Singapore's modern infrastructure is excellent. It has a number of high-profile technology and bio parks; high-quality telecommunications and available real estate.

IT Competency Risk:
IT CMM level 5 certification = 0; good project management; highly skilled employees; good business skills; good technical talent
Custom Code Writing (body shopping): Average

BPO: Very good
System Writing Project R&D: Average to very good

Human Capital Risk: population of 5 million; high-quality education; limited labor supply; small city country island, in terms of geography.
Labor force: 2.2 million, most from outside of Singapore

Cost: High and growing

MARKET OPPORTUNITY

Market:
2005: 29 percent
2006: 29 percent
2007: 26 percent
Compounded growth 2005-2009: 25 percent
(Source: Forrester Research)
-Population growth: 1.71 percent

Global Competitiveness: One of the best in the world.

Overall Assessment: Singapore is a high-end niche player and a major international and regional hub for international business in Southeast Asia; excellent infrastructure, good technical talent, excellent education; pro business; expensive. Education system, infrastructure, intellectual property protection, stable political environment, higher labor costs, small population

Major Players: Business Technovise Echnovise International, HoneyComb, Jayasoft Solutions, MNCs (IBM, Sun, Oracle, EDS, PWC) and Systech Software Consultant, ERP Outsourcing Asia Pte Ltd.,
HP has BPO center and Eli Lily has an R&D Center. Attracts U.S. companies as a place for regional headquarters and, increasingly, higher end technology and services.

FUTURE

Leading location for Asian offshoring headquarters, labor intensive IT development no longer favorable; will focus on global investments and specialized offshore outsourcing in micro-technology and biotechnology. The safety and legal systems will provide an edge in handling high security and business continuity services.

Malaysia

RISK DIMENSIONS

Political Risk: Unfriendly toward the U.S.; insurgency near borders with Thailand; disputes with Singapore; but there's been a recent reemphasis on "globalization" and free trade.

Legal Risk: IP piracy issues; favorable government investments. The Malaysian government intensified its efforts to eliminate the use, sale and production of pirated products over the past few years; lack of prosecution of IPR. Malaysia has even less bureaucratic red tape than Canada

Cultural Risk: English widely spoken; some fundamentalist movements; good global integration; former British colony.

Economic Risk:
GDP-purchasing power parity: $207.8 billion
GDP growth: 5.2 percent
The economy grew 4.9 percent in 2003, stable financial structures; attractive business environment; high level of global integration and linkages. Economic growth will continue in sync with its Asian neighbors.
   Malaysia's economy remains vulnerable to a more protracted slowdown in Japan and the U.S. The Malaysian ringgit is pegged to the U.S. dollar.

IT Infrastructure Risk:
Telephones: 4.5 million
Internet users: 8.7 million
Modern infrastructure system; international service; excellent government support for infrastructure; good connectivity. Development of cyber cities and CyberJava; many corporate regional centers in CyberJava and Putrajaya as "intelligent cities;" multimedia supercorridor project with MNCs; strong government support.

IT Competency Risk: Good project management; good business knowledge and understanding; lack of pool of programmers
Custom Code Writing (body shopping): Average to poor
BPO: Very good
System Writing Project R&D: Poor to average

Human Capital Risk: Population: 23 million. Relatively small labor pool; university system is average.
Labor force: 10.2 million

Cost: Low cost; low wage structure; employee cost is $7,200.

MARKET OPPORTUNITY

Market:
2005: 29 percent
2006: 29 percent
2007: 26 percent
Compounded growth 2005-2009: 25 percent
(Source: Forrester Research)
-Population growth: 1.83 percent

Global Competitiveness: Good

Overall Assessment: Excellent BPO capabilities in the region, proximity to Asia and South East Asia; lower cost and strong business environment; good infrastructure and investments from MNCs; good location for smaller operations. Low costs, high level of global integration, strong government support. Piracy, relatively small population will keep it from reaching India's scale.

Major Players: MayBan, SciCo and Vsource Asia
The government backed "intelligent city" of CyberJava has become home to regional offshore service centers for Motorola and IBM.

FUTURE
Remains a major player and its standing is improving, yet Malaysia is being challenged by outsourcing opportunities in China, mainly due to geographical proximity. The market will keep improving; MNCs will continue to set up their regional operations.

Philippines

RISK DIMENSIONS

Political Risk: Stable government. Under President Gloria Macapagal-Arroyo, the Philippine government faces threats from both Muslim separatist groups and Communist insurgents. Major reforms are under way, but there's frequent political insurgence. Corruption is still an issue; needs to improve image. The government has begun to explore and promote itself as an ideal outsourcing center, modeled after India.

Legal Risk: Good legal system, IPR protection increasing; designation of special economic zones; attractive tax policies and exemptions. Flexible labor rules, deregulated telecom policy are supported by the government. The Philippines has taken some steps to strengthen IPR legislation and enforcement, including providing patent protection to plant varieties, enhancing the ability of the Customs Bureau to stop IPR violations at ports of entry, and increasing the number of raids on suspected counterfeiters. Overall, it is still safe haven for piracy and counterfeiting.

Cultural Risk: English is widely spoken (de facto national language); third-largest English speaking nation in the world, former U.S. colony; friendly; customer service skills need improvement; great compatibility with Western culture.

Economic Risk:
GDP-purchasing power parity: $390.7 billion
GDP growth: 4.5 percent
Economic growth stable, but below Asian neighbors; divide between the poor and the rich. GDP growth of 4.5 percent is driven by services business; peso, the Filipino currency is unstable. Good financial structures.

GDP growth accelerated to 4.4 percent in 2002 and 4.2 percent in 2003, reflecting the continued resilience of the service sector, gains in industrial output and improved exports. Needs a good plan for higher, sustained growth path to make appreciable progress in alleviating poverty, especially given the Philippines' high annual population growth rate and unequal distribution of income. Reforms by the government help the Philippines match the pace of development in the newly industrialized countries of East Asia. The strategy includes improving the infrastructure, strengthening tax collection to bolster government revenues, furthering deregulation and privatization of the economy, enhancing the viability of the financial system, and increasing trade integration with the region.

IT Infrastructure Risk:
Telephones: 3.3 million
Internet users: 3.5 million
The Philippines has good infrastructure; U.S. military bases left behind a solid telecom infrastructure. Good international radio, telephone and submarine cable services; domestic and inter-island service is adequate.

IT Competency Risk: Low availability of skilled project management; deficiencies in project management; ideal for voice-based services, call centers, BPO, high-tech nursing services
Custom Code Writing (body shopping): Average to good
BPO: Excellent
System Writing Project R&D: Poor

Human Capital Risk: Population: 77 million; good educational system, ample human resources; more students enrolled in universities than in Europe; one of the highest number of graduation rates in the world; university system is quite good and more than 380,000 graduate each year, including more than 15,000 technology students-more than any other country except India, Russia, Brazil, China,
Labor force: 34.56 million

Cost: Low costs, relatively low-cost structure to perform a variety of business processes; lower travel costs from North America; IT cost is $6,500 per person.

MARKET OPPORTUNITY

Market:
2005: 29 percent
2006: 29 percent
2007: 26 percent
Compounded growth 2005-2009: 25 percent
(Source: Forrester Research)
-Population growth: 1.88 percent
-Market size: $1 billion

Global Competitiveness: Fair to poor

Overall Assessment: The Philippines offers strong education and low-risk off-shoring, strong BPO success and excellent language compatibility. English language skills, low costs, cultural affinity for U.S., overall business environment, political instability, infrastructure,

Major Players: AJK Consulting, AmberGrenis, SVI, Sykes, CCC, Converges, Headstrong, Radix Systems Services Corp., SPI, eTelecare, Convergys, Time Warner, Chevron- Texaco, Procter & Gamble all have call centers and BPO centers.

FUTURE
Future outsourcing attractiveness will grow with a focus on BPO and low cost. Will draw on long standing cultural ties and solid English skills to snare Anglophone call center work

Poland

RISK DIMENSIONS

Political Risk: Strong government is relatively stable, but corruption is an issue. There's growing support for the IT industry; continuing to work with foreign governments; political stability; E.U. member.

Legal Risk: An inferior and sometimes nonexistent IP and legal system; growing set of incentives, but not as high as other countries; mixture of continental (Napoleonic) civil law and holdover communist legal theory. Changes are gradually being introduced as part of a broader democratization process; limited judicial review of legislative acts; lack of political will by the Polish government to shut down the open air market for selling copyrighted materials, plus a lack of enforcement; lack of legislature to enforce; improvements are slowly made.

Cultural Risk: English not widely spoken, but gaining; German is the major foreign language, affinity and respect for the U.K., U.S. and Germany; lack of customer service.

Economic Risk:
GDP-purchasing power parity: $427.1 billion

GDP growth: 3.7 percent

Polish Agency for Information and Foreign Investment aims to get 25 percent of foreign investment flows targeted on advanced technologies.

Small and medium-size state-owned companies and a liberal law on establishing new firms have encouraged the development of the private business sector. Poland has steadfastly pursued a policy of economic liberalization throughout the 1990s and today stands out as a success story among CE/EE economies; strong economic growth during past year. Poland is now facing a rather flat growth. E.U.-membership may provide new impetus; strong foreign investment; fiscal problems; economic reforms under way; losing out at FDI inflows. Poland currently suffers low GDP growth and high unemployment.

IT Infrastructure Risk:
Telephones: 12.13 million

Internet users: 9 million

Good infrastructure, but some areas need improvement, liberalized telecom policy, strong telecom infrastructure; well developed public infrastructure; good transportation system.

IT Competency Risk:
Quality project management lacking; excellent technical experience; highly skilled IT workers

Custom Code Writing (body shopping): Average

BPO: Growing, but average

System Writing Project R&D: Excellent

Human Capital Risk: Population: 39 million; 40,000 graduates per year; biggest Eastern European country; larger labor pool than other EE countries; highest number of universities, excellent education system.

labor force: 16.92 million.

Cost: Still low, but growing. Wages are growing.

MARKET OPPORTUNITY

Market:
2005: 20 percent

2006: 24 percent
2007: 23 percent
Compounded growth 2005-2009: 21 percent
(Source: Forrester Research)
-Population growth: 0.02 percent
-Market size: $22 million in Poland in 2003

Global Competitiveness: Fair to average

Overall Assessment: Interesting for continental European countries especially. Good for nearshoring from continental Europe. Major outsourcing for Western defense manufacturers; excellent relationship with the U.K.; pool of educated IT workers; growth is slowing down; a player in EE/CE market; political stability; losing out on foreign investments; good telecom infrastructure; proximity to Western Europe. Good education skills, slightly lower cost than Czech Republic and Hungary; needs improvement in English language skills; infrastructure, business environment; IP Security inferior to Hungary and Czech Republic.

Major Players: ComputerLand, DRQ, Prokom, PolSoft, Spin and Winuel, U.S. companies outsourcing are IBM, GE, Motorola; all have BPO centers.

FUTURE
Poland's outsourcing industry will build on the enthusiasm with regard to the E.U.-accession; costs will get higher, but due to a larger pool of it workers, Poland will remain a future favorite destination; larger than the Czech Republic or Hungary.

Armenia

RISK DIMENSIONS

Political Risk: Corruption; geo instability in the areas of Azerbaijan and Georgia.

Legal Risk: Armenian government recognizes IT; excessive government interference; improving IP and copyrights, corruption are still an issue.

Cultural Risk: People in IT and scientific centers speak English; has developed alliances with Germany; English is improving; strong and supportive diaspora in the U.S.

Economic Risk:

GDP-purchasing power parity: $11.79 billion

GDP growth: 9.9 percent

Armenia had developed a modern industrial sector, supplying machine tools, textiles and other manufactured goods to sister republics in exchange for raw materials and energy. The country also has managed to slash inflation, stabilize the local currency (the dram) and privatize most small- and medium-size enterprises. Economic stability; will benefit from the general growth trends in Eastern Europe. Minimal impact of trade embargos and blockades; support by the World Bank. Future high-growth GDP.

Armenia's severe trade imbalance has been offset somewhat by international aid and foreign direct investment. Economic ties with Russia remain close, especially in the energy sector.

IT Infrastructure Risk:

Telephones: 562,600

Internet users: 150,000

Telco system is inadequate; now 90 percent privately owned and undergoing modernization and expansion; lack of international networking; expensive and poor infrastructure; low-speed, but improving.

IT Competency Risk: Poor project and IT management; excellent R&D and creative skills

Custom Code Writing (body shopping): Average

BPO: Poor

System Writing Project R&D: Excellent

Human Capital Risk: Includes a number of new IT graduates; quality of educational system. During the days of the former Soviet Union, Armenia was a hub of IT/software development. Educational institutions can support the need for IT training; Heavy investments in incubation centers; brain drain, many people emigrate from Armenia.

Labor force: 1.4 million

Cost: Low cost. A recent study concluded that Armenia represented the best value location in the world for IT products, with a quality-price ratio even better than India's.

MARKET OPPORTUNITY

Market:
-Population: 15,958,700

Global Competitiveness: Poor

Overall Assessment: Highly skilled IT workforce with scientific institutions; good affinity with the U.S. and E.U.; low cost; limited labor supply; focus on custom applications and R&D; high economic and IT growth.

Major Players: CIT, LANS, Manes Yev Vallex JS, MIGMA, MSHAK, Tire Ltd., and Unicomp

FUTURE

Armenia is one of the world's most promising future outsourcing centers; costs will continue to remain low; high IT talent; the challenges are declining; experiencing a slow population growth.

Brazil

RISK DIMENSIONS

Political Risk: President Luiz Inacio Lula da Silva's government proved to be relatively pro-business, but there's still a major divide between the rich and the poor; good national IT policy in place. Brazil is the largest and most populous country in South America; instability within its political system; some violence and kidnappings have been reported. Difficult climate. In retaliation against a U.S. programs, Brazil began requiring American visitors to be fingerprinted and photographed. Worst case scenario could be when Latin America unites, diverts oil reserves to China and India, funds terrorists, and spreads anti U.S. ideology.

Legal Risk: IPR still a big issue; overall government laws are fair; most cases of piracy in the world; largest losses by copyright industry; inadequate enforcement.

Cultural Risk: Modest English skills; very innovative society. Development of top innovation parks. Language is a major barrier, and English proficiency on the whole is poor. Close physically and time-wise to the U.S.

Economic Risk:

GDP-purchasing power parity: $1.375 trillion

GDP growth: 0.2 percent

Brazil is South America's leading economic power and a regional leader. Highly unequal income distribution remains a pressing problem. The country has large, well-developed agricultural, mining, manufacturing and service sectors. Its economy outweighs that of all other South American countries, and Brazil is expanding its presence in world markets.

Three areas of its economic program include a floating exchange rate, an inflation-targeting regime and a tight fiscal policy, all of which have been reinforced by a series of IMF programs. Brazil has been recovering recently, but there's still uncertainty about President Luiz Inacio Lula da Silva's future course; modest financial structures, but growing. Brazil's economy is expanding its presence in world markets partially due to outsourcing. The challenge is to maintain economic growth over a period of time to generate employment and make the government debt burden more manageable

Being Latin America's largest economy still does not make it a world player. Brazil's $1.6 billion trade partnership and strategic alliance with renegade Venezuela comprises relationship with United States.

IT Infrastructure Risk:

Telephones: 38.8 million

Internet users: 14 million

Major companies, including GE, Goodyear and Xerox, have partnered with Brazilian outsourcing companies.

IT Competency Risk:

Good project management; excellent technical and management experience; highly skilled IT workers; growing sophistication of expertise in software and new technologies

Custom Code Writing (body shopping): Application development and maintenance is the specialty of Brazilian IT programmers; very good.

BPO: Excellent

System Writing Project R&D: Average

Human Capital Risk: Population: 182 million; big country with high turnout of IT graduates; huge labor; overall education needs to be improved. The total workforce is estimated to be around 80 million; the availability of educated workers is

very high; international call center workforce is expected to grow to 5,000 from just 700 few years ago.
Labor force: 83 million.

Cost: Lower costs; strong cost advantage. The average IT programmer's salary in Brazil is higher only than that of workers in India and Russia, thus making it the "cheapest" country in the region.

MARKET OPPORTUNITY

-Population growth: 1.11 percent

Global Competitiveness: Average

Overall Assessment: Brazil has a huge labor pool, good people skills and availability; quality human capital; good player in offshore outsourcing in South America; the country must focus on controlling its overall economy. Low costs, large population, good business process outsourcing results; education and English language skills need improvement.

Major Players: CPM Systemas, G&P Projectos e Systemas, Proceda and Vetta Technologies
Fort Motor has a motor plant in the northeastern state of Bahia, and Flextronics International has a 172-acre campus in Sao Paulo state that makes cell phones and telecom infrastructure products.

Associations: The National IT organization is the Sociedade de Usuários de Informática e Telecomunicações

FUTURE
Brazil will become a major outsourcing center for U.S. industry, especially with the further integration of North and South America. Brazil has a larger IT-capable labor pool with a growing consumer market.

Ukraine

RISK DIMENSIONS

Political Risk: Recent elections have shown that the country is still very unstable. The new government gives hope that the country might at last attain true freedom and prosperity. Ukraine is a young state, possessing both the material resources and the political will to enter into the world market as a valuable emerging partner. Serhiy Loboyko, president, TECHINVEST, states there "is a great hope that Ukraine would adhere to democratic values and accelerate integration into the E.U."

Legal Risk: Mafia still dictates daily life; no rule of law; piracy, specifically identified USTR foreign IP protection; sanctions imposed; hidden costs of outsourcing. Expert Loboyko believes that the "new government will set the rule of law and fight with the 'shadow economy'."

Cultural Risk: English skills still not very advanced; affinity toward the U.S. and the E.U.; Ukraine is the largest neighbor of the E.U.

Economic Risk:
GDP-purchasing power parity: $260.4 billion
GDP growth: 9.4 percent 2003 and 12.4 in 2005
Ukraine has the highest economic growth in Europe. It has the largest economy, and credit rating is growing; country is hungry to catch up with its neighbors. Ukraine depends on imports of energy, especially natural gas, to meet some 85 percent of its energy requirements. Growth has been undergirded by strong domestic demand, low inflation, and solid consumer and investor confidence. Growth was a sturdy 8.2 percent in 2003. The middle class plays an important role in the economic and social life. A sufficiently large middle class (certain estimates claim more than 30 percent) is laying the foundations of social stability and economic development. This middle-class group is reported to include middle and lower-ranked management, skilled workers, craftspeople and people who run their own business. Lack of investments in the IT sector.

IT Infrastructure Risk:
Telephones: 11 million
Internet users: 900,000

Good IT infrastructure; however a lot of countrywide infrastructure under development; country improving telco trunks and mobile connections. A lack of investments hinders development of IT infrastructure. Ukraine has taken important steps in recent years to improve basic telecommunications infrastructure and to introduce modern operating standards. The best IT infrastructure is in largest cities, where large universities and IT resources are concentrated. The government has launched "Innovations Springboard," leveraging information and communications technologies for Ukraine's future. It is aimed at strengthening the process of balanced national development and alleviating poverty though the appropriate and innovative use of information and communications technologies. There are numerous scientific and technological institutes, universities and R&D companies. Expert Loboyko notes, "Ukraine has launched more satellites than NASA."

IT Competency Risk: No project management; many top programmers specialized in various areas
Custom Code Writing (body shopping): Average
BPO: Poor
System Writing Project R&D: Excellent
High technological level of development. The country is producing complex systems such as carrier rockets, satellites and space research equipment. Ukraine is a considerable producer of military equipment, including tanks, military transport aircrafts, SAM complexes and optical equipment.

Expert Loboyko notes: "The well-known Glushkov Cybernetics Institute in Kyiv produced many talented specialists. Ukrainian scientists have achieved world-class results in mathematics, physics, computer sciences, biology, electric welding, new materials and space sciences."

Loboyko adds, "Ukrainian software engineers have deep knowledge of mathematics, physics and applied sciences. They have the ability to analyze and understand large-scale, complex applications, using all available information. This makes it possible for them to add value to the outsourcing and provide solutions and to offer IT consulting services rather than pure outsourcing. Ukraine also has many experts in legacy application services, reengineering and renovation of IT technologies developed in 1960-1990s."

Human Capital Risk: Good pool of IT workers (legacy of the Soviet Union), with strong knowledge of mathematics and natural science; good education system (especially hard sciences); good technical universities. The country provided many top computer programmers to the former Soviet Union's space and military efforts, and much of that expertise has spilled over to the country's private sector.

Ukraine has approximately 1 percent of the world's population, but 6 percent of the world's physicists, chemists, mathematicians, biologists, computer programmers and other highly trained professionals.

Technical schools provide specialized education in many fields and higher education is gained at numerous universities, granting bachelor's, master's, and doctoral degrees.

Ukraine is considered a country with one of the highest levels of education in Eastern Europe. Expert Loboyko says there "are more students per 10,000 people in Ukraine than in Japan or the U.K. Educational institutions produce about 15,000 graduates in IT and related disciplines annually, but few of them work in the IT sector because of its small size. Ukraine continues to possess considerable intellectual potential, even though the educational system is now suffering from under-funding. Many of our IT specialists have advanced degrees in computer science, aviation, electronic engineering, physics and mathematics, including doctorate degrees."

Labor force: 21.29 million

Cost: Costs are low now, but they won't stay that way (especially when Ukraine starts negotiations to become a member of the E.U.). Serhiy Loboyko says, "The cost gap with new E.U. countries will grow and Ukraine will integrate into the E.U. in no sooner than 10 years." Rates charged for programming in Ukraine are more expensive than those in India, but they are 25 percent cheaper than in Russia.

MARKET OPPORTUNITY

Market:
2005: 20 percent
2406: 2 percent
2007: 23 percent
Compounded growth 2005-2009: 21 percent
(Source: Forrester Research)
-Population growth; 0.66 percent

The Ukrainian IT market has demonstrated a steady 30-40 percent annual growth for the past three years. Expert Loboyko explains: "According to the research completed by TEHINVEST and Market Visio, Ukrainian IT services and products export industry is growing very quickly. In 2004, the industry exceeded $100 million, and expected growth is 40-50 percent."

Competitiveness: Poor

Overall Assessment: Ukraine's big resource pool of qualified IT specialists and the low cost of labor make it a competitive location for offshore programming firms. Currently, popularity is low, but growing. The country is making a lot of progress to establish its position as a competitive location in Europe; costs will remain low compared with other countries.

Major Players: The largest players (more than 300 IT specialists), Miratech, Softline, SoftServe, USC (formerly Tessart)

Associations: The Ukrainian Association of Software Developers (UASWD) is an international nonprofit, non-government organization.

FUTURE
Good future. The new government is fighting favoritism and corruption and willing to transform the country into a rule-based economy; Ukraine has the potential to unleash even more capacity to become a vibrant player in the global economy due to a large, highly educated labor force. The challenge is political and economic risks.

Israel

RISK DIMENSIONS

Political Risk: Unstable; multiple party changing coalition government; both parties in the coalition and opposition support technology. Israel is a democratic country, however; peace road map to be implemented; regional turmoil.
Legal Risk: European standards; mixture of English common law and British mandate regulations.

Cultural Risk: English is widely spoken; culture embraces innovation.

Economic Risk:
GDP-purchasing power parity: $120.9 billion
GDP growth: 1.3 percent
Limited growth prospects are linked to the geopolitical risk; Israel has a technologically advanced market economy with substantial government participation. It

depends on imports of crude oil, grains, raw materials and military equipment. Despite limited natural resources, Israel has intensively developed its agricultural and industrial sectors over the past twenty years. There are difficulties in the construction and tourism sectors; fiscal austerity in the face of growing inflation led to small declines in GDP in 2001 and 2002. The economy grew at 1 percent in 2003. In 2004, rising business and consumer confidence, as well as higher demand for Israeli exports, boosted GDP by 2.7 percent.

IT Infrastructure Risk:
Telephones: 3.006 million
Internet users: 2 million
Very good, world-class infrastructure; excellent research facility; the country enjoys the patronage of large multinationals such as IBM, Microsoft, Motorola, Compaq, HP and Intel. Telco is the most highly developed system in the Middle East, although not the largest.

IT Competency Risk:
IT CMM level 5 certification = 0; quality project management; excellent technical and business management experience; highly skilled IT workers; shrink-wrapped software production; excellent research; extremely skilled programming
Workforce Custom Code Writing (body shopping): Average to good
BPO: Average
System Writing Project R&D: Excellent

Human Capital Risk: Highly qualified graduates, immigrants (scientists) from the former USSR; but limited labor pool. There are 2.61 million in the labor force.

Cost: High cost of labor; employee cost is ($25,000). According to Tsvi Gal, senior vice president and CIO of Warner Music Group, certain changes in cost structures are occurring "with the emergence of companies based on the recent Russian immigration, the costs are within range of Indian prices. In addition, Israeli and Jordanian companies are emerging with Israeli technology genius and Jordanian cheap labor (Jordan still fancies British-like culture)."

MARKET OPPORTUNITY

Market:
-Population growth: 1.29 percent
-Market size: $2.6 billion

Global Competitiveness: Excellent

Overall Assessment: Highly skilled in R&D and product outsourcing; cost is relatively high; excellent quality and reputation for innovation; currently a major player.

Major Players: Adgal, Logon, Matrix, MiddleTier, and Ness

FUTURE

With the ongoing peace process, Israel's attractiveness as an outsourcing center will rise, mainly as a developer of licensed intellectual property and with specific niche areas of telecommunications, security and life sciences; Israel may combine its offerings with Arab countries like Jordan and Egypt. Israel will continue to be an expensive destination.

Mexico

RISK DIMENSIONS

Political Risk: Lower geopolitical risk than some other offshoring destinations; corruption; no major threats of violence; stable government but there are clashes between the rich and the poor. The nation continues to make an impressive recovery. Six million illegal emigrants in U.S. and Texas.

Legal Risk: Laws are good, copyright piracy and trademark counterfeiting exist; lack of enforcement of trademark rights; weak government support for IT; only recently starting various IT related programs. President Vicente Fox is leading a software development initiative to strengthen capabilities and promote them abroad. The government needs to modernize the tax system and labor laws and provide incentives to invest in the energy sector, but progress has been slow.

Cultural Risk: Mexico's geographic proximity and similar time zones mean close commercial ties and links to the U.S.; language is Spanish. English spoken widely in IT locations and universities; English proficiency is poor.

Language barrier can also be a problem (though some companies send their programmers to English boot camps).

Economic Risk:

GDP-purchasing power parity: $941.2 billion

GDP growth: 1.3 percent

Ongoing economic and social concerns include low real wages, underemployment for a large segment of the population, inequitable income distribution, slow growth in economy. Real GDP growth has been weak; slowdown in the U.S. economy affected Mexico's economy. Mexico experienced economic growth rates of 3.4 percent in the late 1990s, mostly as a result of U.S. outsourcing raising the price of Mexican exports; strong competition from China (especially in the manufacturing sector, threatening the existence of the maciladoras). Mexico has a free market economy with a mixture of modern and outmoded industry and agriculture, increasingly dominated by the private sector. Recent administrations have expanded competition in seaports, railroads, telecommunications, electricity generation, natural gas distribution and airports. Per capita income is one-fourth that of the U.S.; income distribution remains highly unequal. Trade with the U.S. and Canada has tripled since the implementation of NAFTA in 1994.

Nearly 90 percent of exports go to the U.S., and more than $16 billion in earning are imported back annually from illegal aliens (Mexico's largest revenue source).

IT Infrastructure Risk:

Telephones: 16 million

Internet users: 10 million

Telecommunication system infrastructure dominated by TelMex monopoly; quality of telecommunication equipment is average to good; key cities and resort areas are in average shape. Infrastructure and communications are good and are strongest in the country's three technology parks. Mexico needs to upgrade infrastructure.

IT Competency Risk: Project management not developed; generalists; Mexican programmers are not focused on hard core engineering or R&D

Custom Code Writing (body shopping): Average

BPO: Very good

System Writing Project R&D: Poor

Human Capital Risk: Average labor pool; education system needs improvement.

Labor force: 34 million to 41 million

Cost: Wage structure is low; average IT programmer salary is $1,400 a year; costs are typically 25 to 45 percent less than in the U.S.

MARKET OPPORTUNITY

Market:
2005: 33 percent
2006: 31 percent
2007: 27 percent
Compounded growth 2005-2009: 26 percent
(Source: Forrester Research)
-Population growth: 1.18 percent

Global Competitiveness: Average

Overall Assessment: Strong nearshoring destination for the U.S., Mexico may be suitable for low-level, high-volume projects; Spanish BPO capability. Low wage manufacturing country

Associations: Asociación Mexicana de la Industria de Tecnologías de Información

Major Players: Expert Sistemas Computacionales, Grupo, Hildebrando, IDS Commercial, North American Software and Softek, Genpact

FUTURE

Mexico will continue to be a player in the Future Outsourcing Rank due to its proximity to the U.S. and Spanish BPO market; needs to focus on IT education and improving work competency.

South Africa

RISK DIMENSIONS

Political Risk: Smooth transition from apartheid regime, African National Congress and Nelson Mandela are recognized as major political powers; major risk: health/AIDS. Plus, there are still clashes between minorities; high crime rate.

Legal Risk: Presidential task force is reviewing how to improve IT. The government is taking an active role in promoting offshoring and IT services; corruption and favoritism of the new political class is a major issue; well-developed financial and legal systems.

Cultural Risk: English language native; excellent customer services, because South Africa offers a better cultural fit than India.

Economic Risk:
GDP-purchasing power parity: $456.7 billion
GDP growth: 1.9 percent
Stable economic growth, Africa's economic superpower and home of world-class companies. Well-developed communications, energy and transportation sectors; its stock exchange ranks among the ten largest in the world and a modern infrastructure supports an efficient distribution of goods to major urban centers throughout the region. Growth, however, has not been strong enough to lower South Africa's high unemployment rate, and daunting economic problems remain from the apartheid era. South African economic policy is fiscally conservative, but pragmatic and focuses on targeting inflation and liberalizing trade as means to increase job growth and household income.

IT Infrastructure Risk:
Telephones: 4.844 million
Internet users: 3.1 million
The system is the best developed and most modern in Africa with a 30-mile stretch between Johannesburg and Pretoria that is evolving into the country's first technology hub. Overall: good infrastructure.

IT Competency Risk: Good project management; highly skilled employees in specialized areas like security
Custom Code Writing (body shopping): Poor to average

BPO: Excellent
System Writing Project R&D: Poor to average

Human Capital Risk: Limited supply; education needs improvement in poorer cities; employee cost is $18,000.
Labor force: 16.35 million

Cost: Competitive wage structure.

MARKET OPPORTUNITY

Market:
2005: 36 percent
2006: 33 percent
2007: 29 percent
Compounded growth 2005-2009: 28 percent
(Source: Forrester Research)
-Population growth: 0.25 percent
South Africa is also an outsourcing destination to watch; its popularity is actually forecast to grow at a faster rate than India's over the next few years. Low level of outsourcing penetration.

Competitiveness: Very good

Overall Assessment: Excellent language compatibility; strong IT market; competitive wages that are rising; needs to improve education and IT experience and skills.

Major Players: mainly small and midsize firms, Dimension Data; serving mainly 500 call centers serving companies such as Lufthansa and GE

FUTURE
Low levels of offshoring, but growing. South Africa needs more IT graduates; offshoring market is increasing, may become a more aggressive player in the future. Focusing on providing call center support in English, Dutch and other languages.

Bulgaria

RISK DIMENSIONS

Political Risk: Bulgaria is the 15th largest country in Europe. Situated on the crossroads between Europe and Asia, it benefits from busy flow of transportation. Bulgaria's principal economic and foreign policy priority is to achieve the earliest feasible accession to the European Union. Political and economic stability; corruption; strategic geographic location and stable political and macroeconomic environment. Reforms and democratization keep Bulgaria on a path toward eventual integration into the E.U.

Legal Risk: Some major priorities are gradually lowering the corporate tax burden and reducing payroll taxes. IPR is an issue; complex legislation; recently allocated appropriate incentives for private sector investment and job creation.

Cultural Risk: Attractive for European outsourcing; same time zone for E.U.; very little time overlap; understands Western European culture. The business culture and attitude are European.

Economic Risk:
GDP-purchasing power parity: $57.13 billion
GDP growth: 4.3 percent
Bulgaria has GDP growth prospects of about 5 percent per year; experienced macroeconomic stability and strong growth; sizable foreign investments. Job creation and higher incomes and improvement of the trade balance are among the key priorities of the Bulgarian government. The country has had continual growth and stable development of the IT industry; government is committed to economic reform and responsible fiscal planning.

IT Infrastructure Risk:
Telephones: 2.86 million
Internet users: 630,000
Extensive, but antiquated; national infrastructure being developed; there are considerable scientific potential, R&D institutes and production facilities.

IT Competency Risk: No project and IT management. Excellent R&D and creative skills

Custom Code Writing (body shopping): Good
BPO: Poor
System Writing Project R&D: Excellent
The development of science-based technologies in communications and high technologies are at the forefront of the Bulgarian IT industry. Bulgaria's workforce is known for its high quality and competitive labor. There are many very talented programmers and developers; particular strengths include computer programming and electronics.

Human Capital Risk: Rather good education system. The advanced level of education ensured by science and technology facilities at Bulgarian universities has produced scientists with leading position worldwide Bulgaria ranks second in international IQ tests (MENSA International).

Young graduates in the Bulgarian workforce are intelligent and responsive. Their strengths, combined with the high standards of education and specialization they get, are a real treasure for the development of national IT business.

Many Bulgarian universities have R&D experience. They have created structures and favorable conditions for the development of scientific research, production and applied research implementation activities on contract basis with industry. Bulgaria ranks third in world for certified IT professionals per capita and eighth in the world in terms of absolute numbers of IT graduates.
Labor force: 3.333 million

MARKET OPPORTUNITY

Market:
-Population growth: 0.92 percent
-Stable market growth of around 30 percent per year.

Global Competitiveness: Poor

Overall Assessment: Good, cheap destination for nearshoring in Europe; supply of IT resource may be a problem, getting ready to become E.U.; costs are low but may rise, excellent infrastructure.

Major Players: In Bulgaria, there are nearly 1,100 companies operating in the sphere of high technologies, more of which are small.

Associations: Bulgarian Association of Software Companies (BASSCOM)

FUTURE

Similar to other EE/CE countries. Will continue to develop and be a player in the future due to lower costs and good infrastructure.

Belarus

Belarus is one of the most technologically advanced countries in Eastern Europe, and its competitive advantages make it an attractive outsourcing area. Three companies, EPAM, IBA and SAM, have well over 2,000 people currently employed in outsourcing. Belarus is involved with significant amount of outsourcing work, and in some cases more than other EE countries. Belarus was an "assembly plant" of the former Soviet Union, which resulted in a skilled and well-qualified labor force, along with a number of technical universities, schools, labs and scientific institutions. The Belarusian education system goes back to the time of the former USSR. There are many universities, institutes and colleges that train high-quality programmers, QA specialists, designers, etc. Every year, about 2,000 highly qualified IT specialists come to the market. One of the main advantages of outsourcing in Belarus is the low labor costs. Typically, the rates of Belarusian software houses are about seven times lower than those of the U.S. or Western Europe. Belarus is situated in Eastern Europe and close to European destinations. The Belarusian government actively supports IT outsourcing. An offshore-programming zone provides a legislative basis for offshore software development. There are also preferential taxation policies.

Thailand

Thailand is an emerging offshore location similar to other Southeast Asian countries. It is not as mature as India or China. According to experts, some good software outsourcing development providers are located here. If software localization services need to be performed in Thai, then having Thai-speaking people will be key.

Vietnam

Vietnam today has a stable and secure environment, and is quickly emerging as a viable destination in Southeast Asia. Vietnam has the fastest-growing economy in Southeast Asia and has fairly liberal foreign investment laws. Following the implementation of key reforms, the country now offers investors a stable business environment. It's a relatively young country with half the population under 30 years old. They are relatively energetic and intelligent. The Vietnamese IT market has grown 45 percent since 1998, with sectors such as software and telecoms set to grow at twice that rate. Programmers in Vietnam are paid $3,600 to $6,000 annually. Companies such as Anheuser-Busch, Bayer, Cisco, Harper Collins, McGraw Hill, Disney Interactive, IBM, NTT Nortel Networks and Sony are outsourcing software development projects to Vietnam. IBM is negotiating establishing its own development center there. In addition, the U.S. government has just signed its first deal to outsource software development to Vietnam. Quality human resources is key to Vietnam. The country's education system is excellent, with a focus on mathematics and logic that creates a ready supply of raw talent for the IT industry.

Professional skills are taught by Western training companies, which are training thousands of Vietnamese programmers in dedicated centers across Vietnam. The country has a vast pool of intellectual resources that remains largely untapped. The government set a goal of training 50,000 IT workers and reaching $500 million in software exports by 2005. Furthermore, the government charges zero tax for software exports and is fully supportive of IT outsourcing. The Communist party of Vietnam has emphasized that the software industry is a key area of national growth and in 2001 publicly recognized the importance of IT. Laws governing taxation, special zones, information and Internet use are now in place. Service levels are much higher for smaller projects in Vietnam than other in countries. Understanding of technical specifications is very high. Vietnam is showing good team collaboration and skilled management. On average, costs are half, sometimes even one-third or one-seventh, of those being charged by Indian software developers. The benefit to IT companies outsourcing in Vietnam is they retain key staff and keep project teams together for months at a time. It experiences low levels of attrition. Vietnam's most modern technopark, Quang Trang Software, can accommodate 10,000 developers. The Vietnamese IT force focuses on telecoms, GIS, CAD, finance, factory automation, health care and animation. Vietnam's expatriate IT community has been working and living in developed IT markets worldwide and is forming a crucial link between overseas customers and

Vietnam-based developers by helping to reduce cultural and language barriers. In terms of issues, English-language skills pose a significant challenge to companies outsourcing to Vietnam.

Most of the country is still focused on agriculture. Vietnam's IT infrastructure remains remarkably poor by Southeast Asian standards. Bandwidth is both limited and expensive, for example, as Internet access is owned and controlled by state-owned monopolies. International telephone lines are the most expensive in the world. The country has no low-cost, high-speed international data system yet. Telecommunications, power and buildings need improvement. There is also uncertainty about the region's stability and problems with intellectual property and copyrights laws. Illegal copying and selling of consumer and business software in Vietnam is rampant. The culture of piracy has existed there for years with little enforcement. Also, there is lack of project management and administrative skills. Infrastructure is the single biggest barrier to the growth of IT in Vietnam. No IT companies in Vietnam have completed ISO and CMM assessment certificate programs. English-language skills are improving due to various private language schools and corporate training program. The focus on project management and customer relationship management is also progressing, but at much slower pace. In the next few years, infrastructure will not be such a major issue. Vietnam has to position itself as a place with skilled resources and as a safe business environment. The key elements to do so are in place and further improvement will rank Vietnam as a very favorable destination. Moves are being made to improve connectivity and lower the exorbitant cost of leased lines and broadband services.

Moldova

With a population 4.4 million, the poorest country in Europe but with highly educated IT resources available for IT offshore outsourcing. The education in Moldova is at the highest level, and there are many excellent IT professionals located in the area. The labor costs are much lower than in other eastern European countries. In the future, it is considered to be of the emerging area for software development.

Pakistan

Pakistan has a large, low-cost pool of English-speaking workers. Operating costs are low and similar to other parts of Southeast Asia. The Pakistani government is offering a fifteen-year tax exemption on software exports, and has eliminated duties on technology imports and streamlined the investment process. Pakistan believes that if it is able to attract MNCs to outsource part of their services there, it could help its call centers and IT software houses. Pakistan also is expanding its call centers operations. About twenty to twenty-five call centers are operating commercially across the country. But overall, there is lack of democracy, regional instability and insurgency issues.

Kazakhstan

According to service providers, the market for computer services is estimated to mature in the near future, especially after taking into account the growing activity in the oil and gas sectors. The market for computer services, which is described as predictable, stable and developing, is estimated to grow at least 7 percent annually over the next two to three years. Kazakhstani companies are exploring business opportunities with foreign investors. An example of a recent project is an agreement to establish an Internet Data Center in Kazakhstan. Major vendors have set up authorized service centers and big clients prefer to use them. Training and local regulations remain major issues. There is a significant potential for the growth due to rising oil and gas business activity in the regions.

Ghana

Ghana's low cost of living, stable democratic government, and literate, English-speaking population make it well-suited as an outsourcing location. According to experts, call-center outsourcing here is 25 to 30 percent less than what it would cost in India. Ghana has attracted Affiliated Computer Services, a Dallas-based outsourcing company, which now employs 2,000 Ghanaians who process health forms for Aetna. Workers' English accents and the government's crackdown on corruption are attracting more companies.. Companies sometimes are able to circumvent the country's limited telephone infrastructure by relying on Voice over Internet Protocol. One of the major players is Rising Data Solutions.

Kyrgyz Republic

Kyrgyz Republic has good potential for computer programming offshore outsourcing. Some experts say a critical mass of qualified programmers in the country could be employed by foreign software companies. Given the salary levels of IT specialists in developed countries, programming services offered by local IT companies here are extremely price competitive. The long-term prospects for the IT sector will depend on the level of government support and the active participation of the private sector, as well as curbing the outflow of qualified computer specialists abroad. Kyrgyz universities continue to produce well-trained IT specialists. The cost of software development in the Kyrgyz Republic is significantly lower than in markets such as Israel, Ireland and India. The future of the IT industry of the Kyrgyz Republic looks encouraging. The industry's sales and the number of IT firms are growing steadily.

Nicaragua

Nicaragua is sending trade missions to outsourcing expos, subsidizing training and office parks and offering tax breaks. Nicaragua hosts three small telemarketing outfits and an employee support center for Latin American operations of Spanish telecom giant Telefonica. Hourly wages are about 75 higher than in India, but only half the cost in neighboring Panana and Costa Rica. A call center deal with big U.S. internet company will create 4,000 call center positions by 2009.

Country Example: Chile

CHILE: EMERGING LOCATION FOR OFFSHORING, OUTSOURCING AND BPO
By Carlos Alvarez, CIO and Vice-Minister of Economy, Chile

Chile has emerged as a leader in South America's business landscape, thanks to its political and economic stability, high level of education, and world-class telecom infrastructure. With a population of nearly 16 million people and a national workforce of 6.1 million, Chile is now a preferred location for offshoring, as confirmed by two prestigious rankings: A.T. Kearney (9th among 25 countries) and EIU (15th among 60 countries).

The country's IT industry includes over 2,000 companies, 17 percent of which are exporters. Total industry sales in 2004 exceeded US$3 billion, 12 percent of which were in software, 20 percent hardware, and 68 percent services. Comprising Chile's IT industry are approximately 70,000 permanent-staff IT positions and 10,000 temporary positions.

Chile's democratic framework and successful economy make it a regional favorite for outsourcing/BPO services. Additionally, there are several multinational companies with in-house offshoring projects in the areas of shared service centers, IT development, technical support, repair and assembly facilities, pharmaceuticals and biotechnology (Citigroup, Unilever, Santander Bank, Kodak, Nestlé, Air France, Delta Air Lines, Synapsis, Packard Bell, Cellstar, etc.)

Chile is a regional leader with vast experience and international recognition in the following industries: banking, finance, insurance, private pension, retail, logistics, international commerce, health administration, natural resources (mining, agriculture, and fishing), telecommunications, legal services and utilities. Such advanced sector development, combined with Chile's technological infrastructure, high-quality human resources, government support and low country risk, makes Chile a natural destination for the outsourcing/BPO industry.

The call center/technical support sector in Chile is evolving into a more value-added industry. Companies are developing a range of products and services, and the next step is the full internationalization of these offerings. There are currently 13,000 people in Chile working in the industry.

Several global companies provide outsourcing/BPO services from Chile, including IBM, EDS, Accenture, Telefónica, TATA-TCS and Softek, as well as several Chilean providers. Two examples of international BPO projects that have partnered with local firms are:

- Adexus - General Electric

Through the Chilean firm Adexus, General Electric's Aircraft Engine division runs a Center of Excellence in Chile, serving 100 countries. Among the center's functions is the preparation of electronic manuals for the maintenance of GE's aircraft engines.

- DTS - Hewlett Packard

Working together since 2003, DTS operates Hewlett Packard's technical support center in Chile for HP's home and home office customers and provides services to authorized distributors of its Image and Printing Group.

Sources: Fundación Chile (www.fundacionchile.cl), High Technology Investment Program-CORFO (www.hightechchile.com), National Association of IT Industry-ACTI (www.acti.cl), National Association of Software Companies-GECHS (www.gechs.cl), National Coalition of Call Centers (www.acccag.cl)

Country Example: Russia

THE RUSSIAN POLITICAL AND ECONOMIC CLIMATE
Excerpts from a Conversation with Russian Thought Leaders

Ambassador Frank Wisner, Vice Chairman of American International Group (AIG) and former ambassador to India, shared his perspective on U.S.-Russian business and political relations. While he thinks that U.S.-Russian relations have improved remarkably over the last decade, he noted there is a substantial degree of reassessment among policymakers in Washington, American businessmen, academics, and the press about where Russia is headed. According to Ambassador Wisner, Russian President Vladimir Putin's consolidation of power into the Kremlin has cast a cloud over Russia's nascent market economy and democracy. Russian reformers suffered major losses in the recent parliamentary and presidential elections, while regional leaders and state bureaucrats loyal to the Kremlin ("siloviki") are on the ascent. Ambassador Wisner said that for Western businesses this means their client is President Putin, which is both positive and negative.

The advantage is that Putin has brought stability to the country and enjoys overwhelming support of its citizens. This, in many ways, makes Western investment in Russia less volatile than it was in the 1990's when the threat of a

Communist resurgence was very real. Western companies know in no uncertain terms that if they want to do business with Russia now, they must first and foremost appeal to Putin.

The disadvantage is that Western businesses are accustomed to protections beyond just the will of the executive branch of government. Despite Ambassador Wisner's words of caution, he on the whole maintains an optimistic outlook and continues to help the American International Group explore and expand its insurance and mortgage businesses in Russia. "We are not shy about a market we see with strong economic conditions and new stability," he said.

Offshore Outsourcing to Russia

Tsvi Gal, Chief Information Officer of Warner Music Group, spoke about the great opportunities he sees for collaboration and innovation between American and Russian companies. Gal noted that Russia produces highly educated and motivated technology workers, whose creative approach to solving complex tasks differentiates them from other global talent. This flexibility, according to Gal, is one of the strong points of Russian companies that realize they work in a dynamic environment rather than a pre-dictated one.

Does it lead to unemployment of technology workers or provide cost savings to companies that might otherwise fail? Ambassador Wisner believes that the debate is monstrously ill-informed, and that the American economy's capacity to develop new jobs vastly outweighs those that are being lost. Global outsourcing is growing rapidly; the skills necessary for managing a global workforce are lagging behind.

OOBP.org Founder Eugene Goland said that the Russian economy is doing better than ever and that the Russian IT space is becoming an attractive target for U.S. solution providers. Russian employees have a strong sense of themselves as a team, always say "we" rather than "I" and take great pride in their work, all of which are qualities that Western companies require in a foreign partner. Russia is currently positioned like the second runner in the Olympics, and will be able to do in 2-3 years what it took India 10-15 years to achieve.

There is awareness of the deep level of development talent that exists in St. Petersburg and helped create partnerships among many of the participants. In the last seven years, over 1.3 million people have graduated from Russian universities and are working in the information technology industry. Loretta Prencipe, Board Member for DataArt and Editorial Director for Media First Public Relations, noted that the Russian university system produces what she calls "a different breed of computer science student" when compared to Western universities. The Russian education system places much more emphasis on basic and complex mathematics, science and computer science programs. "The complex engineering and computer science skills that were cultivated during the Soviet era have not been lost," Prencipe said, "and are now being applied to complex commercial development projects."

About the Authors and Contributors

Mark Minevich
Chief Strategy Officer, Enamics, Inc.
Co-Chair, BTM Institute

"Global Mark," as friends know him, could be described as a global change agent and visionary with one of the most influential international leadership networks. Mark is a Co-Chair of the BTM Institute - the Michael Nobel Harriet Fulbright Institute of BTM, and Chief Strategy Officer at Enamics, Inc. The Institute is the first international nonprofit organization of its kind that brings together cross-disciplinary global communities as a think tank to address the long-standing need to manage business and technology together. The BTM Global Leadership Council consists of a "who's who" of senior corporate executives, thought leaders, former government officials, and members of the investment community who specialize in Business Technology Management. In Enamics and the BTM Institute, Mark utilizes his domain expertise in the area of globalization and outsourcing strategy for research, publications, and strategic customer engagements. Mark is a sought-after public speaker, globally recognized technology visionary, leading analyst on globalization, and author of *The CTO Handbook: The Indispensable Technology Leadership Resource* (Aspatore Books). Mark is also a contributing author of *Winning 3-Legged Race: When Business and Technology Run Together* (Prentice Hall). Previously, he was an IBM executive, CTO and senior strategist of the IBM Next Generation Group, where, among his many accomplishments, he formulated the strategy for IBM's Venture Capital, Incubator Innovation and Going Global programs. Minevich is a former CTO of USWEB, and has advised the U.S. government on innovation as well as bilateral relationships with emerging economies such as Russia. Mark serves on various boards of directors and/or advisory boards across the world addressing issues related to globalization and outsourcing, as well as serving as a Chair for International Leadership Missions and Events with Chief Executives. Mark is a recipient of the prestigious Albert Einstein Award for outstanding achievement.

Frank-Jürgen Richter
President, Horasis
Former Director, World Economic Forum, Asian Affairs
Member, BTM Institute

Frank-Jürgen Richter is the president of Horasis: The Global Visions Community, a Geneva-based strategic advisory group focusing on long-term scenarios related to globalization and Asian business. Horasis delivers tailored advice, as well as access to a network of renowned experts. He has advised many of the past and present Fortune Top 500 companies throughout the world. Prior to founding Horasis, Richter was director of the World Economic Forum ('Davos') Asian Affairs. During this time he has developed extensive experience and knowledge of the world's economic, business and political scenes and its key players. As one of the leading analysts of Asian business and economies, he influences major business and governmental decisions with his public comments. An accomplished speaker who frequently keynotes public and private sector functions, Dr. Richter is well known for his contrarian approach on world issues. His writing has appeared in the financial and regional press, such as *The International Herald Tribune*, *The Wall Street Journal*, and *The South China Morning Post*. He has been interviewed by several publications and appeared on CNN, BBC, CNBC, CCTV (China Central Television), and the Voice of America. He is also an active scholar and has authored 26 books on international business. His most recent books include *Global Future* (Wiley) and *Asia's New Crisis* (Wiley).

Faisal Hoque
Chairman and CEO, Enamics, Inc.
Founder and Chair, BTM Institute

Faisal Hoque is Founder, Chairman and CEO of Enamics, Inc., Founder
and Chair of The BTM Institute - The Michael Nobel Harriet Fulbright
Institute of Business Technology Management, and author of *e-Enterprise*
(Cambridge University Press, 2000), *The Alignment Effect* (Financial
Times/Prentice Hall, 2002), and *Winning The 3-Legged Race* (BTM
Institute/Financial Times/Prentice Hall, 2005). A former senior executive at several multinationals, Mr. Hoque is an internationally known
visionary entrepreneur and award winning thought leader. He conceived
and developed Business Technology Management (BTM) to help organizations accelerate and maintain sustainable innovation by managing
business and technology together. An entrepreneur and innovator at
heart, Mr. Hoque built his first commercial business technology product
at the age of 19 while studying at the University of Minnesota. In 1994,
GE Capital recruited Mr. Hoque, then one of its youngest technology
executives, to launch one of the first B2B electronic commerce spin-offs.
Mr. Hoque has written numerous articles for such publications as
BusinessWeek, *The Economist* and *The Wall Street Journal* and is a sought-
after public speaker.

Mr. Hoque is passionately committed to raising awareness of social,
economic, and global cultural issues and actively works to promote non-
violence and economic development for the under-privileged. He serves
on several international boards of directors and/or advisory boards of
global organizations addressing these issues with Nobel Laureates,
accomplished business and industry leaders, leading academics, and
prominent government officials across the globe.

Contributing Authors

Carlos Alvarez
CIO, Vice Minister of Economy
Chile

Carlos Alvarez started his professional career as an industrial engineer (University of Chile), and received a master's degree in public administration from Harvard University. He has devoted his professional career to the public sector, where he has held positions mainly related to productivity promotion, investment attraction and innovation. He is currently leading the governmental ICT effort in Chile, and as part of that role he is also devoted to policy making in two main fields: widening the access to ICT services and improving Chile's capabilities for technological innovation. He is also President of the Biotechnology Regulations Committee; President of the Board of Innova Chile at the Chilean Economic Development Agency (CORFO); member of the Board of *Fundación Chile*; member of the Advisory Board of the Institute for the Connectivity of the Americas (ICA); and Professor of Public Sector Strategic Management at the University of Chile.

Simon Bell
Director
A.T. Kearney Global Business Policy Council
Arlington, Virginia

Simon Bell is Director of A.T. Kearney's Global Business Policy Council, a unique strategic service designed to help corporations and governments anticipate and capitalize on global geopolitical, socio-economic and technological change. He is principal author of the Global Services Location Index and has advised numerous clients on their global location decisions for IT, business processes, R&D and other functions. Over the last 15 years, he has worked with many of the world's leading corporations to develop market entry, manufacturing and sourcing strategies in India, China, Eastern Europe and Latin America. He has also worked with governments and industry groups in Asia, Africa, Europe, the Middle East and the Americas to enhance national and regional competitiveness and stimulate investment and exports in various industry sectors.

Marjan Bolmeijer
CEO
Change Leaders, Inc.
New York, New York

Marjan Bolmeijer is CEO of Change Leaders, Inc., an international consulting company specialized in board, CEO, and senior team development. The author thanks the participants of Change Leaders' exclusive Leadership Development for the C-Suite program for their input.

Augustine Chin
Consultant
A.T. Kearny
Alexandria, Virginia

Augustine Chin is a consultant with A.T. Kearney, (a global strategic management consulting firm). He has extensive experience developing offshore strategies for multinational organizations. He recently led a global team in a study of the China IT and business process offshoring landscape, and he co-authored a white paper on the China offshoring market. Prior to joining A.T. Kearney, he worked as director for a U.S.-based semiconductor company and an Asia-based investment management firm, helping to develop their China market entry strategies. He has a B.S. degree in electrical engineering from Ohio State University and an MBA degree from Cornell University.

Eugene Goland
President
DataArt
New York, New York

Eugene Goland is President of DataArt, a leading provider of high-end software outsourcing services for SMEs, specializing in enterprise application development, system integration and business automation tools, with industry-specific software expertise in the financial, telecom and media sectors. The company has been profitable every fiscal year and was voted the Best employer in the Russian IT sector in 2004. Goland is also a co-founder of Russia's premiere Web-based portal, Mail.ru, currently the second largest portal in Eastern Europe with 20 million users. Goland is Chairman of the Offshore Outsourcing Best Practices Association. As a recognized expert in IT outsourcing, he recently became Chairman of the SME Global Sourcing Chapter at the International Association of Outsourcing Professionals. Goland holds an Executive MBA from R.H. Smith and a B.S. degree in computer science from New York University.

Anupam Govil
CEO
Global Equations, LLC
Austin, Texas

Anupam Govil is a global business consultant who has advised leading corporations, outsourcing regions and service providers on optimizing offshore strategies and leveraging global delivery models. He is the Founder and CEO of Global Equations, an offshore advisory firm providing strategy, sourcing and cross-border M&A services to mid-market companies, private equity funds and service providers. He is a venture partner with Enhanced Capital Partners, an early stage venture capital firm focusing on the technology and services sectors. He is also a partner with Texas Global LLP, which is a business and investment advisory firm focusing on growth stage technology and services firms. He received a master's degree in computer science from J. N. University, New Delhi, and a B.S. degree in electronics engineering from Delhi University.

Stefan Inzelstein
President
Indiggo Associates, Inc.
Aventura, Florida

Stefan Inzelstein is a thought leader in holistic (or integrative) change. His career spans four decades as a Fortune 100 executive and an international management consultant. He spent 21 years with IBM, where he did pioneering work in complex project management, education, sales and general management. Inzelstein imagined, designed and implemented ISM, IBM's first and highly successful management consulting program for which he got an Outstanding Innovation Award. This led to the creation of IBM Global Services. After leaving IBM Stefan established consulting practices in Europe that focused on helping large organizations deal successfully with a changing world.

Ram Iyer
President and CEO
Argea
Princeton, New Jersey

Ram Iyer is the Founder and CEO of Argea, a Princeton, N.J., based out-sourcing consulting and implementation services firm. He is a seasoned executive and expert on outsourcing and has advised companies on the specialized aspects of outsourcing planning, implementation and gover-nance. He has worked at Boeing and Lucent, among other companies. He writes a monthly column for *Outsourcing Venture*, and has published articles in several other publications. He frequently conducts interna-tional webinars on outsourcing for The Conference Board. He graduated from the University of New Hampshire and the Massachusetts Institute of Technology's Sloan School of Management.

Dr. Michael Jackson
Founding Member and Chairman
Shaping Tomorrow
Sussex, United Kingdom

Michael Jackson is a Founder, Member and Chairman of ShapingTomorrow, a unique Web-based futures, strategy and change management portal for corporate innovation and risk management. His specific area of research is sustainable business futures. With over 30 years of experience in business management in the U.K., North America and Europe, he has significant exposure to corporate banking, consumer finance, and futur-ing. He was Chief Executive of Birmingham Midshires Building Society between 1990 and 1998, then the U.K.'s 4th largest. In that role he achieved a dramatic change for the better in the society's fortunes, mov-ing from near oblivion to a highly profitable, customer-led and award-winning business in just eight years.

Dr. Bruno Lanvin
Senior Advisor, E-Strategies
The World Bank
Geneva, Switzerland

Bruno Lanvin is the World Bank's lead advisor on e-strategies. From June 2001 to December 2003, he was manager of the Information for Development Program (*info*Dev). In 2000, he was appointed Executive Secretary of the G-8 DOT Force. Until then, he was Head of Electronic Commerce in the United Nations Conference on Trade and Development in Geneva and held various senior positions, including Chief of Cabinet of the Director General of the United Nations in New York, Head of Strategic Planning and later Chief of the SME Trade Competitiveness Unit of UNCTAD/SITE. He was the main drafter, team leader and editor of '*Building Confidence: Electronic Commerce and Development*, published in January 2000. In 2003 and 2004 he co-authored the *Global Information Technology Report*. He holds a B.A. degree in mathematics and physics from the University of Valenciennes (France), an MBA degree from Ecole des Hautes Etudes Commerciales (HEC) in Paris, and a Ph.D. degree in economics from the University of Paris I (La Sorbonne).

Dr. David Hee-Don Lee
Vice Chairman
World Trade Centers Association
Washington, D.C.

David Hee-Don Lee initiated the idea of World Trade Center University to provide world trade centers and their 750,000-plus affiliate corporate members an on-line university degree program in "e-world trade." Recognizing the need for better travel service, pricing and accommodations for the WTC membership, Dr. Lee also has coordinated a newly developed travel package, named WTC Business Tourism (BizTourism), which addresses the individual needs, logistical problems, scheduling and cost concerns of the more than 300 individual world trade centers. He is now working on the trade-specialized IPTV/Cable Networks worldwide.

Phyllis Michaelides
President
C-Level Associates, LLC
Providence, Rhode Island

Phyllis Michaelides has an international reputation as a leader in the area of Web, global enterprise, IT architecture, and emerging technologies. She has focused her attention on the potential of Web technology and scalable, secure architectural frameworks to deliver, maintain and integrate information and applications not only within a large enterprise but also extending to customers, suppliers and partners. In 2005 Ms. Michaelides retired from her position of CTO at Textron, Inc. Prior to that appointment, she held lead architectural strategy positions at Deere & Company and AlliedSignal (now Honeywell).

Janet Pau
Consultant
A.T. Kearney
Alexandria, Virginia

Janet Pau is a consultant with A.T. Kearney's Global Business Policy Council. She has worked extensively with governments on competitiveness and economic globalization issues and with global companies on offshore location strategies. She is one of the authors of A.T. Kearney's Offshore Location Attractiveness Index and also manages the annual Globalization Index™ published in *Foreign Policy* Magazine. Prior to joining A.T. Kearney, she worked with the United Nations, government entities in China and Hong Kong, and Watson Wyatt Worldwide. She received her master's degree in public policy from Harvard University and a B.A. degree from Yale University.

Umesh Ramakrishnan
Vice Chairman
Christian & Timbers
New York, New York

Umesh Ramakrishnan, the top ranking Indian American in the executive search industry, is considered to be one of the country's experts in the field of outsourcing and global leadership. Prior to entering the search industry, Mr. Ramakrishnan was the Chief Operating Officer of a global engineering firm that outsourced its design offerings. As Vice-

Chairman of Christian & Timbers, he advises CEOs and boards on global leadership, outsourcing and other leadership challenges.

Lee Swindall
Vice President, Market Research
Argea
Princeton, New Jersey

Lee Swindall is the Vice President of Market Research for Argea. He is a seasoned executive with experience in the financial services industry. He has worked in front office and back office roles at financial services firms in the United States, the UK and the Netherlands. He has spent the last three years researching and talking to companies that were considering or doing outsourcing, gaining a client-centric perspective. He is a graduate in economics and political science of the University of Illinois.

Randy Terbush
Vice President and CTO
ADP Employer Service
Roseland, New Jersey

Randy Terbush is a globally recognized leader in the Open Source Software community and co-founder of the Apache Software Foundation, one of the most successful Open Source Software projects. He currently leads the strategic enterprise architecture direction for a premiere Fortune 300 payroll, human resources and benefits service provider. Terbush is a key contributor in the evolution of information technology through his participation in executive roundtables, conference presentations and his writing. In 1996, to meet a growing demand for enterprise support services and commercial software enhancements for the open-source Apache Web server, Terbush founded Covalent and served as CEO and CTO.

V.N. "Tiger" Tyagarajan
Executive Vice President
Genpact
New York, New York

V.N. Tyagarajan (Tiger) began his career with the Unilever Group in Bombay, and later joined Citibank as Vice President and Auto Business

Director, Global Consumer Banking. He joined GE in 1994 as General Manager, Risk Management, at Countrywide and went on to become CEO at GE Capital's GCF and AFS operations in India. In 1999 he became CEO of Genpact, and was responsible for its exponential growth.

Huib Wursten
Managing Partner
ITIM International
Amsterdam, The Netherlands

Huib Wursten is one of the managing partners of ITIM International. He specializes in advising companies and supra-national organizations in how to manage global teams. His work has led him to delivering courses at the IMF in Washington and the European Central Bank. He has advised the Russian administration on the influence of culture on political and economic behavior. He has written an award-winning paper, "Mental Images: The Influence of Culture on Economic Policies," which was published for Nyfer, a research institute related to Nijenrode University.

Expert Voices

Dr. Jagdish Bhagwati
University Professor
Columbia University
Senior Fellow, Council on Foreign Relations
New York, New York

Jagdish Bhagwati is University Professor, Economics and Law, at Columbia University and Senior Fellow in International Economics at the Council on Foreign Relations. He was Economic Policy Adviser to the Director General, GATT, and also served as Special Adviser to the UN on Globalization, and External Adviser to the Director General, WTO. Currently, he is a member of UN Secretary General Kofi Annan's Advisory Group on the NEPAD process in Africa. Five volumes of his scientific writings and two of his public policy essays have been published by MIT Press. The recipient of six festschrifts in his honor, he has also received several prizes and honorary degrees. His latest book, In *Defense of Globalization*, was published by Oxford University Press in 2004.

Osvald Bjelland
Chairman
Xynteo LTD and the Performance Theater Foundation
Oslo, Norway

Osvald M. Bjelland is Chairman and Founder of The Performance Theatre Foundation, a non-profit entity which attracts the active participation of chairmen, CEOs and luminaries from politics, science, the arts, sports and academia. Osvald is also the Founder and Chairman of Xyntéo, a high level advisory firm and think tank serving business leaders challenged by the pressures of the global economy; advances in technology; more aware and demanding customers; greater availability of information, and mounting environmental issues. His interest and mission is to inspire breakthrough thinking, new technologies and business models in order to generate sustainable customer value in established and emerging markets.

Robert B. Carter
Executive Vice President & CIO
FedEx Corporation
Memphis, Tennessee

Robert B. (Rob) Carter is Executive Vice President and CIO at FedEx Corporation. In this role, Carter is responsible for the corporation's key applications and technology infrastructure. FedEx applications, advanced networks and data centers provide around-the-clock and around-the-globe support for the information intensive transportation, logistics and business related product offerings. Carter also serves as Chairman of the Board of FedEx Kinko's. Carter joined FedEx in 1993 and has more than 25 years of systems development and implementation experience utilizing a wide variety of technology. Carter earned his B.S. degree in computer and information sciences from the University of Florida and his MBA from the University of South Florida. He serves as a member of the Saks, Inc. board and the University of Florida Foundation Board of Trustees, as well as a member of several university and civic boards.

Dr. Vinton G. Cerf
Vice President and Chief Internet Evangelist
Google
Ashburn, Virginia

Vinton G. Cerf is Vice President and Chief Internet Evangelist at Google. He was formerly Senior Vice President of Technology Strategy for MCI, a global high-tech company. He also serves as Chairman of the Board of the Internet Corporation for Assigned Names and Numbers (ICANN). Widely known as one of the "Fathers of the Internet," Vinton G. Cerf is the co-designer of the TCP/IP protocols and the architecture of the Internet. In December 1997, President Clinton presented the U.S. National Medal of Technology to Cerf and his colleague, Robert E. Kahn, for founding and developing the Internet. In 2005, President Bush presented the U.S. Presidential Medal of Freedom to Cerf and Kahn for their work.

Jim Clifton
Chairman and Chief Executive Officer
Gallup Organization
Washington, D.C.

Jim Clifton is best known in the polling and survey research field for leading the acquisition of The Gallup Organization in 1988, at which time he became CEO of the organization founded by the renowned polling pioneer, Dr. George H. Gallup. Under Clifton's leadership, Gallup has enjoyed a tenfold increase in its billing volume and has expanded from a predominantly U.S.-based company to a global organization with more than 40 offices in 20 nations. Clifton is best known in the business world as the creator of The Gallup Path. This metric-based economic model establishes the linkages among human nature in the workplace, customer engagement, and business outcomes. The Gallup Path is integral to the performance management systems in more than 500 companies worldwide. His most recent innovation is designed to tell the 10 million people who lead, govern, and manage the world what the world's 6 billion citizens are thinking. This groundbreaking research project annually collects people's opinions in more than 100 countries to determine the general well-being or "soul" of a country, city, or culture. Clifton serves as Chairman of the Thurgood Marshall Scholarship Fund. He has received honorary degrees from a number of institutions.

Dr. Soumitra Dutta
Dean of Executive Education
INSEAD
Paris, France

Soumitra Dutta is the Roland Berger Professor of Business and Technology and Dean for Executive Education at INSEAD. Professor Dutta obtained his Ph.D. in computer science and his M.S. in business administration from the University of California at Berkeley. His research and consulting have focused on the inter-relationships between innovation, technology and organizational design.

John Furth
Executive Vice President
Discovery Communications
Washington, D.C.

John Furth received degrees from Harvard College and the Stern School of Business at New York University. After a brief stint as an investment banker at Deutsche Bank, he became head of the New York office of the European consulting firm, Roland Berger Strategy Consultants. In more recent years he has lead strategic planning divisions at Sony and Discovery Communications, specializing in international business development, organizational design and new media strategies.

Alan Ganek
Chief Technology Officer
Tivoli Software, IBM
Somers, New York

Alan Ganek is Chief Technology Officer, Tivoli Software, and Vice President, Autonomic Computing, IBM. As CTO of Tivoli, he is responsible for the technology, architecture, and strategy of IBM's Tivoli software brand, which enables on-demand computing environments by delivering products and services that help customers manage their information technology resources. He also leads IBM's corporate-wide initiative for autonomic technologies, which make computing systems and resources more self-managing and resilient, lowering the cost of ownership and removing obstacles to growth and flexibility. In 2005, Mr. Ganek received the Albert Einstein Innovation Award for his leadership in establishing the field of autonomic computing. Mr. Ganek received his M.S. degree in computer science from Rutgers University in 1981. He holds 16 patents.

Dr. Hubertus Hoffmann
Co-Founder
General Capital Group
Munich, Germany

Dr. Hubertus Hoffmann is a successful entrepreneur and investor, co-founder of the General Capital Group, a EURO 3.5bn-value investor fund for Germany, and Founder and President of the World Security Network Foundation, the world's largest elite network in foreign and defense affairs, based in New York. He is a former advisor in the European Parliament, the German Bundestag und U.S. Senate. He has been a foreign and defense affairs specialist for more than 25 years, and is a member of IISS and YPO.

Rustam Lalkaka
President
Business and Technology Development Strategies, LLC
New York, New York

Rustam Lalkaka is President of Business & Technology Development Strategies LLC, International Consultants. He has helped pioneer business incubation for empowering communities, attracting international business, and commercializing technology in some 40 countries. Earlier he was director of the UN Fund for Science and Technology for Development in UNDP, which managed a $100 million fund for strengthening technological capabilities. He was the head of industrial development operations at UNIDO, Turkey, and regional adviser on technology transfer at the UN Economic Commission for Asia, Bangkok. Before joining the United Nations, he helped establish a steel plant engineering company in India and headed its international operations in Germany. By training he is a metallurgical engineer from Stanford University, California. Lalkaka has lectured at conferences and as adjunct professor, published a hundred technical papers, been awarded honorary memberships in the Indian Institute of Metals, Polish Business & Innovation Centers Association, and other honors for work on venture creation and technology development.

Mitchel Lenson
Former Group CIO and Managing Director
Deutsche Bank
London, England

Mitchel Lenson recently retired as the Group CIO at Deutsche Bank with responsibility for IT and Operations for all operating divisions of the Deutsche Bank Group. He was a member of the Group Operating Committee and was on the Executive Committees of the Corporate & Investment Bank and the Private Clients & Asset Management divisions. He spent 25 years in the financial services industry, working for JP Morgan, UBS, and Warburg. He sat on the UBS Warburg Executive Committee. He has a business degree and an MBA from City University. He received the Einstein Award for Innovation and Transformation.

Harald Ludwig
Chairman
Macluan Capital Corp
Vancouver, Canada

Harald Ludwig is Founding Partner and Advisor to General Capital Group. He also is Chairman of Macluan Capital Corp., LBO pioneer in Canada. Ludwig has 20 years experience as principal investor in LBOs, mezzanine debt, CDOs, distressed debt, marketable securities, real estate, special situations and private equity funds. He is Chairman of Lions Gate Entertainment and serves as a board member of West Fraser Timber, Ltd.

Valerie Orsoni-Vauthey
CEO and Founder
MyPrivateCoach
San Carlos, California

Since 1992, Valerie Orsoni-Vauthey, master certified coach, has been providing life, business and weight-loss coaching to hundreds of successful clients. She is the CEO and Founder MyPrivateCoach. She is the author of numerous articles and e-books on several health-related topics and the author and co-author of three books. She is President of the Silicon Valley Coachville Chapter, a founding member of the International Association of Coaches, a member of the National Mental Health Association, and the E-Commerce Benchmarking Association.

Ramalinga Raju
Founder and Chairman
Satyam Computer Services Ltd.
Secunderabad, India

Ramalinga Raju is the Founder and Chairman of Satyam Computer Services Ltd., which is one of India's pre-eminent IT companies, servicing over 144 Fortune 500 and over 390 multinational corporations. It has more than 23,000 people working in 45 countries across five continents. He has an MBA from Ohio University and is an alumnus of the Harvard Business School. He has won several awards, including Ernst & Young Entrepreneur of the Year for Services in 1999, Dataquest IT Man of the Year in 2000, and CNBC's Asian Business Leader - Corporate Citizen of the Year Award in 2002. He is Vice Chairman of the National Association of Software and Service Companies, Chairman of IT Committee in Federation of Indian Chambers of Commerce and Industry (FICCI), and a member of the International Advisory Panel of Malaysia's Multimedia Super Corridor.

Atefeh Riazi
Worldwide CIO & Senior Partner
Ogilvy & Mather Worldwide
New York, New York

Atefeh (Atti) Riazi is Senior Partner and Worldwide CIO of Ogilvy & Mather Worldwide, a leading global marketing and communications agency with 497 offices in 125 countries supporting more than 2,300 clients. She oversees the global systems and infrastructure network supporting an integrated, cross-discipline organization providing marketing communications across all media. Under Atti's leadership Ogilvy & Mather has earned a place on *InformationWeek*'s 500 list of innovative IT organizations. She is an electrical engineering graduate with over 23 years experience managing large organizations in the manufacturing, engineering, advertising and transportation sectors. Most recently, she was Vice President and CIO of Technology for MTA New York City Transit.

Dato' Dr. Jannie Tay
Vice Chairman
The Hour Glass Limited
Singapore

Dr. Jannie Tay has led The Hour Glass' growth from a single retail oper-ation to a regional network of luxury watch boutiques across Australia, Hong Kong, Japan, Malaysia, Singapore and Thailand. In 2002, the company won the Singapore Brand Award, a national award recognizing Singapore-listed companies with the highest brand values. Her achieve-ments include being the first female president of both the Singapore Retailers' Association and the ASEAN Business Forum, founding presi-dent of the International Women's Forum in Singapore and current pres-ident of the Women's Business Connection. She was named as one of the 50 Leading Women Entrepreneurs of the World. She was awarded an honorary doctorate from Oxford Brookes University in 1999, the Louis Féraud les Honours Award in 1996 and in 2003 was conferred the Darjah Sultan Ahmad Shah Pahang (DSAP), which carries the title Dato'. Times Books International published her biography, *Time to Live - Jannie Tay's Journey*, in 2002. She is Chairman of Save The Planet Investments Pte Ltd, Singapore.

Dr. Shashi Tharoor
Under-Secretary-General
United Nations
New York, New York

Shashi Tharoor is currently Under-Secretary-General for Communications and Public Information at the United Nations, having previously served as Director of Communications and Special Projects in the Office of Secretary-General Kofi Annan. In the course of a 26-year UN career he has also served the United Nations High Commissioner for Refugees (including in South-East Asia at the peak of the "boat people" crisis) and led the headquarters team responsible for United Nations peacekeeping operations in the former Yugoslavia. A widely published writer and nov-elist, he is the author of nine books. He was named a "Global Leader of Tomorrow" in 1998 by the World Economic Forum in Davos.

Martin Wolf
Associate Editor and Chief Economics Commentator
Financial Times
London, England

Martin Wolf is Associate Editor and Chief Economics Commentator at the *Financial Times*. He was awarded the CBE (Commander of the British Empire) in 2000 for services to financial journalism. He is a visiting fellow of Nuffield College, Oxford University, and a special professor at the University of Nottingham. He has been a forum fellow at the annual meeting of the World Economic Forum since 1999. He was joint winner of the Wincott Foundation senior prize for excellence in financial journalism for 1989 and 1997. He won the RTZ David Watt memorial prize in 1994, granted annually to a writer judged to have made an outstanding contribution in the English language towards the clarification of national, international and political issues and the promotion of their greater understanding. He won the Accenture Decade of Excellence, the Business Journalist of the Year, and the Newspaper Feature of the Year awards in 2003. His most recent publication is *Why Globalization Works* (*Yale* University Press, 2004).

Editors

Terry Kirkpatrick
Editor-in-Chief
Enamics, Inc.
Stamford, Connecticut

Terry Kirkpatrick is Editor-in-Chief at Enamics, Inc. He has been a contributing editor of Booz Allen Hamilton's *strategy+business* and contributing and deputy editor of *CIO Insight* magazine. He has also written and edited for McKinsey & Co. and Gartner, Inc. He was editorial director at the Peppers and Rogers Group, where he launched *1 to1 Quarterly*, a thought leadership journal. At IBM, he launched the award-winning *Think Leadership* website for chief executive officers, as well as an internal site for the company's scientists and technologists. He had been a managing editor at *The Reader's Digest* and a business writer for The Associated Press.

Loretta W. Prencipe
Media First Public Relations
Washington, D.C.

Loretta W. Prencipe has experience as both an award-winning editor and attorney. She oversees the editorial direction of Media First Public Relations, which includes among its clients top technology, human resource, professional services and biotech companies. Prencipe also serves on the advisory board of DataArt, a provider of complex development services based in Saint Petersburg, Russia. Prior to joining Media First, she served as senior editor for *InfoWorld* magazine, developing its CTO coverage. Previously Prencipe was the editor in chief of *IT Recruiter* magazine and served as a radio correspondent. Prencipe is currently working on a multi-media project on the lives of women who immigrated to the United States. The accompanying book will be published in late 2006. Prencipe holds a B.A. in Russian studies and juris doctorate from George Mason University School of Law. She practiced law before embarking upon a career in communications.

Michelle Zelsman
President and CEO
Monsoon Communications
Alexandria, Virginia

Michelle Zelsman founded Monsoon Communications in 1997 to address the growing need for tailored, global communications strategies among the world's most influential organizations. She has consulted with such organizations as The World Bank, America Online, Georgetown University, Ernst & Young, United Way of America and the National Football League. An experienced journalist, Zelsman began her career covering military quality of life issues during Desert Storm. Later she covered technology for *InfoWorld*, illustrating how technology enhances the way corporate America communicates, improves business productivity and produces greater bottom line revenues. She is the former creative director for a technology-focused advertising agency.

Getting business and technology running together

AS the BTM Institute's first major publication, *Winning The 3-Legged Race - When Business and Technology Run Together*, shows that it is possible to subject business technology to a comprehensive set of management processes and standards. Using the Enamics BTM Framework™ as a foundation, this book proves that this is not just a technology issue. It is, instead, a business issue, one that will not see resolution until enterprises have a fundamentally better way to manage technology's contribution to the value chain.

Through Business Technology Management (BTM), enterprises manage technology in lockstep with the business and create environments in which technology helps *shape* (rather than simply enable) strategic choices. Leading enterprises are working to *synchronize* (rather than simply align) their business and technology decision making. And in the best-managed modern enterprises BTM will ensure that technology ultimately *converges* with the business. This book, therefore, explores what may well be the last opportunity for building and sustaining a competitive edge.

In a three-legged race, the perennial picnic game, two players run with the left leg of one tied to the right leg of the other. Those tied limbs become the "third leg." The teammates who coordinate best are sure winners. That's how executives have to think about managing business technology. If they don't, they run the risk that their competitors will.

Winning The 3-Legged Race examines the interplay of business technology with business strategy, governance, budgeting, organization, risk management, business processes, partnerships, and the marketplace – and offers the theory, real-world examples, and specific advice for executives on running, and winning, the race.

For information on this book please visit:
www.btminstitute.org/winningthe3leggedrace/

Faisal Hoque
Chairman and CEO, Enamics, Inc.
Founder and Chair, BTM Institute

Author of *e-Enterprise* (Cambridge University Press, 2000) and *The Alignment Effect* (Financial Times/Prentice Hall, 2002)

V. Sambamurthy
Eli Broad Professor of IT, Michigan State University
Eli Broad College of Business

Co-Chair, BTM Global Research Council, BTM Institute

Author of *Unleashing IT-Enabled Value Nets* (Society for Information Management, 2004)

Robert Zmud
Michael F. Price Chair in MIS, University of Oklahoma
Michael F. Price College of Business

Co-Chair, BTM Global Research Council, BTM Institute

Author of *Framing the Domains of IT Management* (Pinnaflex Educational Resources, 2000)

Tom Trainer
Senior Vice President and Global CIO
PepsiCo, Inc.

Co-Chair, BTM Global Leadership Council, BTM Institute

Carl Wilson
Executive Vice President and CIO
Marriott International, Inc.

Co-Chair, BTM Global Leadership Council, BTM Institute

Founded in 2003, the BTM Institute–the Michael Nobel Harriet Fulbright Institute of Business Technology Management (BTM) is the first international nonprofit organization of its kind that brings together a select group from the academic, corporate, government and thought leadership communities as a think tank to address the long-standing need to manage business and technology together. Today, it is the world's largest and most influential knowledge-based community solely focused on BTM, enabling the next generation of leaders to learn from one another. The Institute is chaired by Faisal Hoque, Founder of the BTM Institute and Enamics, Inc. and creator of BTM; Dr. Michael Nobel, the great grandnephew of Dr. Alfred Nobel and Chairman of the Nobel Family Society; and Ms. Harriet Mayor Fulbright, wife of the late Senator J. William Fulbright and Chairperson of the Fulbright Center.

BTM Institute
Michael Nobel Harriet Fulbright Institute of Business Technology Management

For more information visit: www.btminstitute.org

© 2005 BTM Institute   65 HighRidge Road | Suite 458 | Stamford, CT 06905 | t: 203-561-9746 | info@btminstitute.org | www.btminstitute.org

Winning *The 3-Legged Race* is organized into two main sections. Part I, "Preparing to Run," addresses BTM at the most strategic levels, where the board, the CEO, and the entire leadership team must be intensely involved if a company expects to be successful. Part II, "Leading the Pack," delves deeper into specific issues of actually getting business and technology to run together according to strategy. A distinguished group of contributing authors, including members of the BTM Institute's Global Research and Leadership Councils, along with BTM experts from Enamics, Inc., comprehensively addresses the critical concepts for BTM, and offers concrete executive agendas for progress.

Each chapter also includes the perspectives of noted executives and well-known academics around the world. Their contributions are labeled "Leadership Insights" and "Research Insights." If you were to add up the years these accomplished people, listed below, have devoted to studying, teaching, and practicing Business Technology Management, it would be many, many times greater than the 50 or so years we've had information technology itself.

Dr. Ritu Agarwal
University of Maryland
College Park, Maryland

William Allen
SVP, Human Resources and
Corporate Communications
Maersk
Madison, New Jersey

P.A.M. Berdowski
COO and CIO
Royal Boskalis Westminster
Papendrecht, The Netherlands

Dr. Anandhi Bharadwaj
Emory University
Atlanta, Georgia

Barbara Carlini
CIO
Diageo North America
Stamford, Connecticut

Lester Diamond
Assistant Director
United States Government
Accountability Office (GAO)
Washington, D.C.

Michael Fillios
Chief Product Officer
Enamics, Inc.
Stamford, Connecticut

Dr. Varun Grover
Clemson University
Atlanta, Georgia

Daniel Hartert
CIO
Royal Philips Electronics
Eindhoven, The Netherlands

Dr. John Henderson
Boston University
Boston, Massachusetts

Jean K. Holley
CIO
Tellabs, Inc.
Naperville, Illinois

Hideo Ito
Chairman and CEO
Toshiba America, Inc.
New York, New York

Kees Jans
CIO and General Manager
Schiphol Airport
Schiphol, The Netherlands

Dr. William Kettinger
University of South Carolina
Columbia, South Carolina

Terry Kirkpatrick
Editor in Chief
Enamics, Inc.
Stamford, Connecticut

Dr. Rajiv Kohli
College of William & Mary
Williamsburg, Virginia

James Lebinski
VP, Knowledge Products
Enamics, Inc.
Stamford, Connecticut

Dr. Jerry Luftman
Stevens Institute of
Technology
Hoboken, New Jersey

Victor Marty
Directeur General
Imnet
Paris, France

Steve Matheys
EVP, Sales and Marketing
Schneider National
Green Bay, Wisconsin

Dr. Lars Mathiassen
Georgia State University
Atlanta, Georgia

Alan Matula
CIO
Shell Oil Products
The Hague, The Netherlands

Dr. Warren McFarlan
Harvard Business School
Boston, Massachusetts

Mark Minevich
Chief Strategy Officer
Enamics, Inc.
Stamford, Connecticut

Frank Ovaitt
President and CEO
Institute for Public Relations
Fellow, Enamics, Inc.
Stamford, Connecticut

Honorio Padron
Chairman and CEO
The Padron Group, Inc.
Washington, D.C.

Dr. Krishna Palepu
Harvard Business School
Boston, Massachusetts

Alain Poussereau
CIO
Caisse Nationale
d'Assurance Viellesse (CNAV)
Paris, France

Dr. Arun Rai
Georgia State University
Atlanta, Georgia

Dr. Jack Rockart
Massachusetts Institute
of Technology
Cambridge, Massachusetts

Leon Schumacher
CIO
Mittal Steel
Rotterdam, The Netherlands

Steven Sheinheit
CIO
MetLife, Inc.
New York, New York

Rob Slagboom
VP, Information and
Communications Technology
Transavia Airlines
Schiphol, The Netherlands

Vincent Stabile
VP, People
JetBlue
Forest Hills, New York

Becky Wanta
Global CTO
PepsiCo, Inc.
Plano, Texas

Dr. Richard Welke
Georgia State University
Atlanta, Georgia

Mike Westcott
SVP, Human Resources
Diageo North America
Stamford, Connecticut

Dr. Leslie Willcocks
London School of Economics
London, England

Christopher Wrenn
Managing Director and COO
HVB Americas
New York, New York

© 2005 BTM Institute   65 HighRidge Road | Suite 458 | Stamford, CT 06905 | t: 203-561-9746 | info@btminstitute.org | www.btminstitute.org